TEDDY BEARS
AND HOW TO MAKE THEM

Margaret Hutchings

WITH ILLUSTRATIONS BY THE AUTHOR

DOVER PUBLICATIONS, INC., NEW YORK

MILLS & BOON LTD., LONDON

This reprint edition, first published in 1977, is
an unabridged and corrected republication of the
work first published in 1964 by Mills & Boon Ltd.,
under the title *The Book of the Teddy Bear*.

International Standard Book Number
American (Dover) Edition: 0-486-23487-8

Library of Congress Catalog Card Number
American (Dover) Edition: 77-70049

International Standard Book Number
U.K. (Mills & Boon) Edition: 0-263-06339-9

Manufactured in the United States of America
Dover Publications, Inc.
180 Varick Street
New York, N.Y. 10014

Mills & Boon Ltd.
17-19 Foley Street
London W1A 1DR

A Silver Wedding present to my husband with love.
I saved the bears for him because they are his favourites!

CONTENTS

ACKNOWLEDGEMENTS

The author remembers with pleasure the happy associations she had with so many people while preparing this book. She is most grateful for all the help she was given in so many ways, and in particular her thanks are due to:

The Bear Brand Hosiery Company, Mr. Peter Barker, Mr. John Betjeman, Messrs. Blackie and Sons, Mrs. Margaret Blake, The Trustees of the British Museum, The British Standards Institution, Mrs. Alfred Brockwell, Mrs. R. A. Butler, Mr. Donald Campbell, Mrs. N. de Clifford, The Coal Utilization Council, The Library of Congress, Mr. Harry Corbett, Mr. Barry Cork, Miss Mary Craig, Miss J. Crammond, The Doll Club of Great Britain, Messrs. E. P. Dutton and Co., Messrs. B. Feldman and Co., Mrs. P. H. Ford, The Great Ormond Street Hospital for Sick Children, Mrs. Jimmy Kennedy, Mrs. Evelyn Legg, Miss Freda Lingstrom, The London Express News and Feature Services, Merrythought Toys Ltd., Mr. Christopher Milne, Mrs. Daphne Milne, Mr. Benjamin F. Michtom, Dr. Desmond Morris, Mr. Archibald Roosevelt Senr., Mr. Archibald Roosevelt Jnr., The Theodore Roosevelt Association, Miss Sue Ryder, Frau Hilde Lefebvre-Steiff, The Members of Stondon Massey W.I., Mr. Stanley Unwin, Miss Gladys Whitred, The Zoological Society of London and all the doctors, teachers, parents and children who helped not only over the Teddy bear census but in many other ways.

The Sitting Thinking Bear in the frontispiece was originally designed for and has appeared in *The Farmer and Stockbreeder*.

Colour plates by Studio Swain, Glasgow.
Black and white plates by E. Nixon Payne, Chelmsford.
Line drawing of Archibald Ormsby-Gore by Mr. John Betjeman, of Pooh by E. H. Shepard, of Rupert by A. E. Bestall. Figs. 1, 2, 3 and 4 reproduce, as does Plate 2, cartoons by Clifford Berryman. The rest of the line drawings by the author.
In Plate 6, "Bobby" was kindly lent by Mrs. Miriam Harrison; "Teddy" by Mrs. Joan Galwey; "Sir Edward Bear Esq." belongs to the author.

LIST OF PLATES

FOREWORD

At the turn of the century, cartoons were an important part of the daily newspapers in the big cities of the United States. The cartoons were generally on the front page of the newspaper, and generally drawn by master craftsmen.

When my father was President, we children were naturally interested in reading the articles, but we always wanted to see and study the cartoons, and Mr. Berryman's cartoons were among our favourites.

In 1907, Mr. Berryman began to picture my father, Theodore Roosevelt, accompanied by two little bears. These bears delighted us, just as they have delighted children ever since that date. They were most alluring little animals and the magnificent skill of Mr. Berryman sky-rocketed them almost immediately into a worldwide popularity which they have maintained ever since.

Anyone should have known that eventually someone in England would realize that the world needed a biography of the "Teddy Bear".

Only in England are there people who understand that the familiar is not necessarily commonplace, and there are always people in England willing to study and write about the familiar and show that it is not commonplace.

For example, mankind has been very familiar with fishing. Certainly long before the caveman, primitive human beings were "tickling" trout and fishing was, as it is today, a sport and a business for a large part of the human race. It was not until Izaak Walton wrote *The Compleat Angler* that the fish took its true place in literature.

Margaret Hutchings has done exactly the same thing for the Teddy Bear and in my opinion it puts her along with good old Izaak.

Archibald B. Roosevelt
Cold Spring Harbor, New York

June 22nd, 1964

AUTHOR'S NOTE

I once stood talking to a party of schoolgirls who, as part of a handicraft outing, had been brought on a visit to my tiny workroom. Having "played" together for most of the afternoon with the toys piled high on the shelves, then demolished lemonade and sticky buns, we had reached the final question and answer stage. "How long do you think it will be before you run out of ideas?" asked a rosy-cheeked and pony-tailed moppet. "Never," I replied. "But you *must* one day, surely," she said—"you've made nearly everything I can think of and, after all, a Teddy bear is a Teddy bear and when you've made one you've made one!"

I hardly remember the children going, for already Elizabeth had given me a completely new idea. "When you've made one you've made one"—quite right, but you've only made ONE and the variations on every single animal in the toy world are endless.

So *The Book of the Teddy Bear* was born, and here is a third companion to *Modern Soft Toy Making* and *Dolls and How To Make Them*, containing all the Teddy bears for which you have asked. It would have had to be bigger—at least twice as big—to contain everything I should have liked, so in order to prune the pages to a practical number the choice of what should be included was made by some of the readers of the two companion volumes and I thank them all—they chose just what I should have done myself!

I have been so very much helped, by so many folk on both sides of the Atlantic, who could ill afford the time, but as is usually the case with busy people, they were always ready and willing to do all that they could in the cause of *The Book of the Teddy Bear*. I am so very grateful and hope that the results will give just a fraction of the pleasure to my readers, that the preparation of these pages has given me.

M. H.

INTRODUCTION

"The bear is a shaggy, slothful, wild beast, in all respects like a man and wishful to walk upright."

In writing these words, an ancient Greek alchemist touched exactly on the almost unfathomable appeal of the bear. Surely, never has a toy so caught the imagination of children as the Teddy bear. "Walking upright" as they do, yet not a human but a fluffy, lazy, lumbering, caricature of a well-loved animal, he somehow fills their every need.

Teddies go everywhere and do everything. There is not a corner of the globe that they have not penetrated, if not with children then with adults. Their appeal is universal and to all ages. They have gone into battle on guns, tanks and in haversacks; saved lives by intercepting bullets; flown all over the world in aeroplanes; been "drowned" in floods, burned in concentration camps and worshipped as Totems; are used extensively in advertising campaigns; collected by film stars, ballerinas and actresses; used as mascots and talismans; had endless books, songs and verses written about them; are taken to hospital, are indeed part of our everyday life—and all within the space of sixty years!

It is not always realized that a Teddy bear is not *just* a Teddy bear—the varieties are absolutely endless, one sort being more suited to a certain age group or type of owner than another.

After discussing his history and giving a glimpse into the exciting lives of twelve special bears, an attempt has been made on these pages to show at least some of the possibilities. Washable bears for the very young which lend themselves to the use of the pretty coloured nylon fur fabrics now on the market, some special bears in "attitudes" for lying on beds and suited to teenagers, glove bears for bedtime stories, and Goldilocks and the Three Bears (simply made "swing-legged" toys) are among the easiest. Tradition, in the form of jointed bears in many sizes, has not been forgotten, and opportunities occur for converting these into sort of first cousins of the traditional Teddy, by changing various parts of his anatomy. No apology is made for including koalas and pandas in a book on bears—this is toyland where realism has no place! The bears have their own toys in the form of miniature Teddies and pandas—and a chapter has been included specially for children, containing ideas for bears they can make themselves and one for bazaar fiends, in an effort to find really practical ways of turning Teddy bears into money-spinners. Short anecdotes have been added as "space fillers" at the end of chapters by special request of those who enjoyed them in *Dolls and How To Make Them*.

As some of the instructions are naturally duplicated and a certain amount of turning from one page to another is necessary, it is suggested that a set of bookmarks are made from folded paper. These can be slipped into the various pages mentioned in the text at the first reading of a set of instructions, and if labelled will help the worker to turn up a diagram or other reference quickly when she starts making her bear.

Do be sure you have chosen the right bear for the recipient you have in mind—no new baby will show interest in a 2-ft.-high jointed bear, neither will its mother appreciate a 2-in.-high miniature, which may well find its way into her offspring's mouth and choke him! The right bear for the right person, strong sewing and a sense of fun and enjoyment without which toy-making is an impossibility, will ensure success!

SOME BARE FACTS

WHY A **TEDDY** BEAR?

Why indeed? Why not for instance a Billy, Geoffrey or Freddy bear? The *Oxford Dictionary of Christian Names* tells us that "Teddy" is the American diminutive of Theodore, and "Ted" is the English diminutive of Edward.

There is no doubt whatever that the "Teddy" bear is named after the late President Theodore Roosevelt of the United States, who held office from 1901 to 1909. This member of the well-known family was fifth cousin of Franklin D. Roosevelt, who became so well known to the British nation during the Second World War, and an uncle of Eleanor Roosevelt, Franklin D's famous wife.

The fact that many Teddy bears are christened Edward (the author's included!) is a quite understandable misconception, Theodore being a name almost unknown to British children at least. From this misconception a tale grew up that the Teddy bear first had its prototype in the Australian koala, that one was seen and admired by Edward VII as Prince of Wales, at the London Zoo early in 1880, and from him and this visit grew the name of a bear toy.

Apart from the fact that the earliest Teddy bears did not remotely resemble a koala there seems absolutely nothing to substantiate this tale. Certainly, the London Zoo did have a koala in 1880, their first specimen being purchased on April 28th of that year, but there is no reference in the Zoo's Press cuttings, Annual reports, or Scherren's history of The Society, that the Prince of Wales visited the koala in 1880 and thus lent his name to the Teddy bear. He and other members of the Royal Family took a great interest in the collection at Regent's Park which they visited a number of times and to which they donated many animals, but the only records of his visits are to be found in Scherren's book and tell us that—

"... The Prince of Wales (now King Edward VII), accompanied by the Duke and Duchess of York (now Prince and Princess of Wales), visited the Gardens in May 1899 ... (he also came in June 1900)."

Having established therefore that the bear was named after Theodore Roosevelt (and the *Shorter Oxford English Dictionary* confirms this) it is interesting to see how such a thing came about.

War has been waged for many years for the "honour" of having made the first Teddy bears. Many people have joined in, the most notable contenders being the Steiff Company of Germany and The Ideal Toy Corporation of New York. The Theodore Roosevelt Association of New York wisely say:

"... the Teddy bear story and its origin is one story that we have felt we could take no side.

Personally we like the Steiff bears; we sell them in our souvenir shop. But all Teddy bears have made so many happy for so many years that the origin does not seem important . . ."

This is also the author's view! However, both the German and American tales are interesting.

Frau Hilde Lefebvre-Steiff, daughter of one of the six nephews of Margarete Steiff, founder of Margarete Steiff G.M.B.H., personally told the author their version of the tale when she visited the factory in Giengen. A reproduction of the portrait of Margarete, which hangs in the showroom of the Steiff factory, appears in plate 6.

"Margarete Steiff, a typical young German girl, had, at an early age, been stricken with Polio and severely crippled. Tied for the rest of her life to a wheelchair, she was never one to dwell on her ailments and like so many physically handicapped folk, thought only of the happiness of others. She never married and had a family of her own, yet was a great lover of children, so she particularly enjoyed their visits to her. One day she made a little felt elephant with which her small visitors could play. Such toys were a great rarity in those days and this plaything was much loved by the children. Soon their mothers began giving Margarete orders not only for copies of this but for other toy animals. So many orders arrived that so as to keep pace with them, she started to train other women of the locality to help her and eventually set up a small factory.

"By 1897 Margarete had absorbed, not only her brother Fritz but several nephews into her enterprise and toys were being exported all over the world. One nephew in particular was a great help to her, namely Richard. He proved a most competent designer and while studying art at Stuttgart, he spent many hours purposefully watching the bears at the Zoo. When, in 1902, he came to his Aunt with a model of a toy bear, complete with movable head and limbs, she was not particularly impressed. The toy was much larger than those she had previously made and instead of using felt, Richard had made his bear with fluffy mohair, which was expensive and difficult to get at the time.

"However, Aunt Margarete allowed the model to be sent to the United States in an attempt to find an agent for it, but she was not at all surprised when all the firms her nephews approached laughed and ridiculed at the shape and plumpness of the bear and no orders were received.

"The following year the bear went with the Steiff brothers to the Leipzig Fair but was kept very much in the background. When they were packing up their exhibit on the last day, they were approached by the representative of a leading New York import house. He told them that he was looking for something soft and cuddly—not the usual felt toys of the day. He had found the fair disappointing and unrewarding and wondered if something along the lines he had in mind could be specially created for him. Although by this time they were half ashamed to produce it, the brothers dived into a packing case and the much maligned bear was brought out. The American was delighted and almost before they realized what had happened had placed an order for 3,000, immediate delivery. The bear was now well and truly launched and before long an order for another 3,000 was received by the little factory in Giengen. Margarete was forced to agree that her nephew had designed what was probably a winner.

"During the early part of the bear's career in the States, preparations were in hand for the President's daughter's wedding. The bride was Alice, daughter of Theodore Roosevelt, better known, perhaps, as Teddy Roosevelt. A grand reception was planned and the caterer, anxious to have a unique and appropriate table decoration for this important occasion at the White House, was searching everywhere for inspiration. In desperation he went to New York, and the first thing he saw was a quaint little bear staring at him from a shop window. Knowing the President to be an ardent big game hunter, he bought a whole pile of bears and returned home to decorate the tables with them. Some he dressed as huntsmen, putting little rifles into their paws and erecting miniature tents among them, while others were dressed as fishermen and sat

2 An unpublished sketch of Theodore Roosevelt and the Teddy Bear, drawn by Clifton Berryman for his father (reproduced here by permission of the Library of Congress).

fishing out of gold-fish bowls, containing live fish. Not only the bride and her father but all the guests, were delighted with this unusual decoration—the President taking it as a great personal compliment. When the guests were approaching him to take their leave, one close friend of the family asked, 'Say, Teddy, you are an experienced huntsman, could you tell me to which species these bears belong?' 'Well, old friend,' replied Roosevelt, 'you really got me there so I think they must be a new species and are called "Teddy" bears!' Naturally the Press, who were present in great numbers, got hold of this tale and it was splashed all over the papers, thus the little bear became famous and thousands and thousands were ordered from all over the world."

Asked for proof as to the truth of this tale Frau Lefebvre-Steiff admits simply and honestly that she has none:

". . . I am really sorry that I cannot help you by giving you any material which proves that our Teddy story is authentic. All the Steiffs of the old generation are dead but already when a small girl I was told this story. At that time publicity had not yet made such progress and we did not need an invented story to make the Teddy popular. . . ."

On the other hand, there are many people still alive in America today who were at Alice Roosevelt's wedding, notably the bride herself, Mrs. Nicholas Longworth! The Theodore Roosevelt Association are quite firm in their statement that:

". . . there were no Teddy bears as decorations at Alice Roosevelt's wedding. That is a myth,"

and Mr. Archibald Roosevelt senior (brother of the bride and third son of Theodore Roosevelt) says:

"I cannot remember any feature of Teddy bears being at the wedding of my sister . . . certainly my father had nothing to do with the christening of it, i.e. naming it the Teddy bear. Either Mr. Berryman did that or it just grew up. . . ."

Leaving the pleasant little German tale we now turn to the equally interesting American one, as told in a letter to the author by Mr. Benjamin F. Michtom, son of the late Russian-born Morris Michtom, founder of The Ideal Toy Corporation of New York, who died in 1938 at the age of sixty-eight.

"The Teddy bear first appeared in 1903 as a result of a cartoon that appeared, by Clifford Berryman, in the *Washington Post*.

"My father saw this cartoon, and having always been an admirer of the President, wrote him a letter asking if it would be an impertinence for him to make a small bear cub and call it 'Teddy's Bear'. At that time there was a border dispute between Mississippi and Louisiana, and because the President was on a hunting trip in Mississippi and had refused to shoot a bear cub who crossed his line of fire, this cartoon appeared as a political cartoon, captioned: 'Drawing the line in Mississippi' (Fig. 1).

"As busy as the President of the U.S. was, he took the trouble to send my father a letter on White House stationery in longhand, saying in effect: 'I don't think my name is worth much to the toy bear cub business, but you're welcome to use it.' My mother, who was deft with the needle and helped make many of the samples my father used in his business, made a few samples of this bear. One he sent to the President, Theodore Roosevelt; one he took with the President's letter to Mr. Schoonmaker, then the buyer of Butler Brothers, a large wholesaler.

"In 1903, Butler Brothers took his entire output of these Teddy bears and guaranteed my father's credit with the mills, who supplied him with the plush. This was the beginning of the current Ideal Toy Corporation.

"He operated as an individual from 1903 to 1907, calling himself Ideal Novelty and Toy Company, and in 1907 he incorporated. In 1938, the name was simplified to Ideal Toy Corporation, but it has always been the same company.

"One of our original Teddy bears is on exhibit at Sagamore Hill, which is a museum commemorating the family residence of the Roosevelts in Oyster Bay.

"When my father died in 1938, newspapers all over the country wrote news stories and editorials about him, and Teddy Roosevelt's widow, Mrs. Edith Roosevelt, was kind enough to write us a letter consoling us on the passing of my father.

"The U.S. Government authorized our company to make Smokey the Bear the symbol of Forest Fire Prevention:

(a) because we are leaders in the toy industry;

(b) because Theodore Roosevelt was instrumental in organizing, as part of his conservation of natural resources programme, the Forest Fire Prevention Bureau; and

(c) because our company was the maker of the original Teddy bear, inspired by Theodore Roosevelt."

Asked for proof of this story in the form of the letter which President Roosevelt sent to his father, Mr. Michtom replied quite openly:

". . . The letter which my father received from President Roosevelt was in possession of my brother Dr. Joseph Michtom. When he died in 1951, we searched through his effects, not only for this but also for the charming letter of condolence which we had received from Mrs. Edith Roosevelt, the widow of Theodore Roosevelt, at the time of my father's death. Unfortunately, neither letter has ever been recovered. I, myself, was a child of two years at the time of the birth of the Teddy bear in 1902–3 and so my information is only for the early days of the making and selling of the toy. I was too young to recall the actual incidents which started it—they were related to me by my father."

In an article on The Ideal Toy Corporation, *The New York Times* of Sunday, December 7th, 1952, tells us that:

"The origin of the company is perhaps unique in American industry. It is probably the only company that ever grew directly out of a newspaper cartoon. It was the Berryman cartoon of Teddy Roosevelt refusing to shoot a bear cub which inspired Ben's father, Morris Michtom, to make a Teddy Bear. This took the elder Michtom out of a confectionery business and launched him in the toy business."

The Berryman cartoons and their reasons for being drawn are themselves of great interest.

Clifford Berryman was on the staff of the *Washington Post* at the time in which his first Teddy-bear cartoon appeared; becoming affiliated with that paper in the early 1890s. In January 1907, however, he joined the staff of the *Washington Star*. *Our Times*, by Mark Sullivan,[1] describes the event which was responsible for this cartoon "Drawing the line in Mississippi" (Fig. 1).

". . . On November 10 (1902) Roosevelt went on a bear hunt in Mississippi. . . .

"While he was in camp near Smedes, Miss., a newspaper dispatch described him as refusing to shoot a small bear that had been brought into camp for him to kill. The cartoonist of the *Washington Post*, Clifford K. Berryman, pictured the incident. For one reason or another,

---

[1] *Our Times*, by Mark Sullivan, published by Charles Scribner's Sons, New York.

Fig. 1. "*Drawing the Line In Mississippi*", *the political cartoon which inspired Morris Michtom's Teddy bear.*

25

Fig. 2. Extract from The Washington Post, *November 19th, 1902, (see opposite) and the Berryman cartoon "After a Twentieth Century Bear Hunt".*

whimsical or symbolic, the public saw in the bear episode a quality that it pleased to associate with Roosevelt's personality. The 'Teddy-bear', beginning with Berryman's original cartoon, was repeated thousands of times and printed literally thousands of millions of times; in countless variations, pictorial and verbal, prose and verse; on the stage and in political debate; in satire or in humorous friendliness. Toy-makers took advantage of its vogue; it became more common in the hands of children than the woolly lamb. For Republican conventions, and meetings associated with Roosevelt, the 'Teddy-bear' became the standard decoration, more in evidence than the eagle and only less usual than the Stars and Stripes."

Another Teddy bear cartoon (Fig. 2) marked the end of the President's unsuccessful hunt and appeared in the *Washington Post* of November 19th, 1902, with the accompanying article. There appears to be a slight discrepancy here, for after saying that no bears were killed we go on to read that—

". . . the bear killed yesterday will be taken to Washington on a special train"!

Berryman's "Teddy" bear continued to appear in all his many cartoons, becoming almost a second "symbol" or signature. One interesting example is "The President's Dream of a Successful Hunt" (Fig. 3), which appeared on October 11th, 1907. Published at the time Roosevelt was on a bear hunt in the canebrakes of Louisiana, this cartoon depicts Roosevelt the hunter, with one foot resting on a dead bear ("bad trusts"). Tied to his waist is a rope ("restraint"), at the end of which is another bear, alive but cowering ("good trusts"). In the background is Berryman's famed "Teddy bear", with a bagful of bears slung over his shoulder.

It was still being used in 1917, "On the Eve of War" (Fig. 4), and Plate 2 shows a charming drawing which the Library of Congress is quite sure was never published. Depicting the President with his arm round the Teddy bear, it was, according to a label pasted on to its back "given to my father John Paul Ernest", an indication that Mr. Berryman made the sketch specially for his father and not for publication.

·　·　·　·　·

EXTRACT FROM *The Washington Post*, WEDNESDAY, NOVEMBER 19th, 1902.

Smedes, Miss., Nov. 18— President Roosevelt's bear hunt in Mississippi is ended and he has not had even a shot at a bear. The last day of the chase was simply a repetition of the three preceding days, so far as his luck was concerned. Try as the hunters would, they could not get a bear within range of the President's rifle.

The dogs got a fresh trail this morning and the President and Holt Collier followed it half a dozen miles to the big Sunflower River. The bear crossed a mile below the ford; they went to this point, and believing he was making for the cane brake on the other side, they endeavoured to head him off. When they got into the brake however, they were disgusted to find that the bear had doubled back on his tracks and crossed the river still further down. It was then 1 o'clock, and as arrangements had been made to break camp at 2.30 o'clock the President was reluctantly compelled to abandon further pursuit of the elusive quarry.

Deer Hunters Had Luck

While the President was out after bear, Maj. Helm, Dr. Lung, and Secretary Cortelyou had a more successful deer drive on this side of the Great Sunflower River. They jumped up a buck and doe. Maj. Helm killed the latter from his horse at about forty yards.

Although the President had failed to kill a bear on this expedition he has enjoyed his outing, and speaks in high praise of the hospitality that has been accorded him. He philosophically attributed his ill-fortune to the traditional hunters' luck, and says the next time he goes after bear he will arrange to stay long enough for the luck to change.

The deer killed to-day and the bear killed yesterday will be taken to Washington on the special train. Old Remus, the greatest dog in the pack, whose last hunt was ahead of the President of the United States, was badly used up and with several of the wounded dogs was put in one of the wagons.

Fig. 3. "The President's Dream of a Successful Hunt", by Berryman.

28

ON THE EVE OF WAR

Fig. 4. "On the Eve of War" by Berryman.

29

Thus one thing leads to another—a bear hunt by an American President having the most extraordinary repercussions. It turned a small confectionery business into one of the biggest toy manufacturers in the world; made a chair-bound polio victim famous and established her family's fortune; as we shall see in "The Teddy Bears' Picnic" (page 48) brought an unknown song writer from one room in London to a beautiful home in Switzerland, and above all was the means of fulfilling the inner needs of childhood in the form of every child's very own bear!

Mark Sullivan's words that "for Republican conventions and meetings associated with Roosevelt, the Teddy bear became the standard decoration, more in evidence than the eagle and only less usual than the Stars and Stripes", leave one groping in mid-air and wondering if somewhere, somehow there might not be a link between the German and American tales, something that has become enlarged or altered by being handed down over the years, which would authenticate them *both*. Sad to say, however, such a link, at present, seems impossible to find.

A TEDDY BEAR CENSUS

A conversation which ended ". . . what DO children play with now that they no longer like Teddy bears?" and which the author overheard on a bus, sent cold shivers down the spine of one who was just embarking on a book on the subject! Thus the idea for a sort of "Teddy Bear Census" was born, to see what the situation (in the British Isles at least) really was in 1963—the results were interesting and reassuring, to say the least of it.

Three hundred and fifty children were asked to fill in a form like the one shown on page 32, which was completed by a little girl in Shropshire. Of these fifty were discarded because the children were too old, too young or had obviously been helped, prompted or their forms had been written by parents or teachers and were thus not true examples! In the 300 analysed all walks of life were represented. The children came from "London dormitory" districts, the seaside, river and creek, isolated country villages and those not so isolated, small and large towns, a New Town, the industrial slums of the north, coal-mining districts, various parts of large cities and London, University towns and wealthy residential districts. Counties covered included Hertfordshire, Huntingdonshire, Surrey, Essex, Shropshire, Glamorganshire, Middlesex, Devonshire, Cambridgeshire, Berkshire, Yorkshire, Nottinghamshire and Northumberland, as well as parts of Scotland and the Channel Islands.

All the children were of Primary School age, i.e. between about five and eleven years old, but the type of school they attended varied between County Primary Schools, Church Schools of various denominations, expensive private schools and preparatory boarding schools.

Of the 300 children questioned only 30 (i.e. 10%), had no Teddy bear; 18 of these were boys and 12 girls. Of these just over half came from a slum district where there is no home life in the accepted sense of the word, although the majority of families had T.V. This, it seemed, had to take the place of toys! In this district a great many of the children did not know what a Teddy bear was. (What a frightful situation in this modern day and age.) The other non-Teddy owners came mostly from a mining district, with the exception of two from a large town and two from the Channel Islands. These last four children added, however, that they had once had a Teddy but had given him away, and they were all in the upper age group. Every country child questioned had a Teddy bear!

Of the 270 children who possessed Teddy bears, 57 (20 girls and 37 boys) did not play with them, i.e. 20%.

Most of these children were in the upper age group of nine to eleven, when one would not expect a boy, at least, to be playing with a Teddy.

The younger boys and almost all the girls added that although they did not play with their bears they took them to bed every night, and many added also "bears are not to play with but to cuddle"!

Of the bear owners 7 children had two, 3 had three, 1 had four, 1 had five and 1 had eight Teddies. Therefore less than 5% had more than one.

Questioned about the colour of their bears, 92% of the bear-owning children had normal coloured Teddies, being variously described as brown, fawn, ginger, yellow, tan and grey. Many girls added rather indignantly ". . . of course", when giving this information, as though it were unthinkable that he could be any other shade! Of the remaining minority most were white, or black and white (obviously pandas), with a smattering of other colours, mostly pink. It was interesting to note that nearly all the coloured bears were owned by town children.

The sizes, big, medium and small, were distributed almost equally, only one child adding that her bear was not big but ENORMOUS!

Forty-five per cent of the children had called their bear "Teddy", ". . . because he *is* a Teddy", and once more, many had added ". . . of course" as though this were the *only* name. Five per cent favoured diminutives of the word and Tedkin, Big Ted, Little Ted or plain Ted were much in evidence. One lady bear rejoiced in the name of Tedwina, ". . . because he's a she not a him"!

In the other 50%, there were a large group of obvious Teddy bear names such as Pooh, Brumas, Sooty, Rupert, Yogi and Panda, and "because he looks so sweet" Honey, Honeybunch, Sugar, Candy, Treacle, Syrup and Toffee cropped up in all parts of the country. Ordinary boys' names such as Johnny, Tim, Bert, Christopher, Albert and George appeared seldom and when they did, the bear had usually been named after a favourite uncle, school-friend or the father who had presented him. Edward was rare. Girls' names such as Sylvia, Flora and Judy were rare and when they did occur, the reason given was usually ". . . because he's a girl bear and wears a dress". Descriptive names, such as Cuddles, Tubby, Growly, Woolly, Brownie, Sandy, Snowy, Pinky, Ginger, Fluffy, Curly and Happy were very common and had been bestowed for obvious reasons. Of the very few unusual names that Teddy bears had been given, every one had been chosen by Daddy! These included such masterpieces as POLYPHEMUS because he only has one eye, FREDERICK because when he grows up he will be Fred Bare, PYTHAGORAS because my sister hates geometry, THEODORE (for obvious and very correct reasons) and GLADLY because he's cross-eyed and we sing about him in a hymn, "Gladly my cross-eyed bear"! Some of these names appeared in various parts of the country and more than once, which showed that Daddy may have been reading magazines or watching T.V. and that his masterpiece was perhaps not so original as it at first appeared!

Most children classed their Teddies as unusual because they only had one eye, one ear, one leg or the stuffing was coming out. However, as the majority of bears seemed to be invalids of some sort, this turned out to be the rule rather than the exception and was not

WHAT IS YOUR NAME?

Natalie Price

HOW OLD ARE YOU?

8 Year's old

HAVE YOU GOT A TEDDY BEAR?

yes

IF SO, DO YOU OFTEN PLAY WITH HIM?

not very often but sometimes

WHAT COLOUR IS HE?

light ~~tieth~~ brown

IS HE BIG, MEDIUM SIZE OR SMALL?

He is big

WHAT IS HIS NAME?

Growly

WHY DID YOU CALL HIM THAT?

Because every time you turn him over he growls

DID YOU THINK OF THIS NAME YOURSELF?

Yes

IS THERE ANYTHING SPECIAL OR UNUSUAL ABOUT YOUR BEAR? Yes when
L had him he fell off the line
when father chistmas pegged him on

OUT OF ALL THE TOYS YOU HAVE EVER HAD, WHAT WAS YOUR FAVOURITE?
I like growley best

P.TO

32

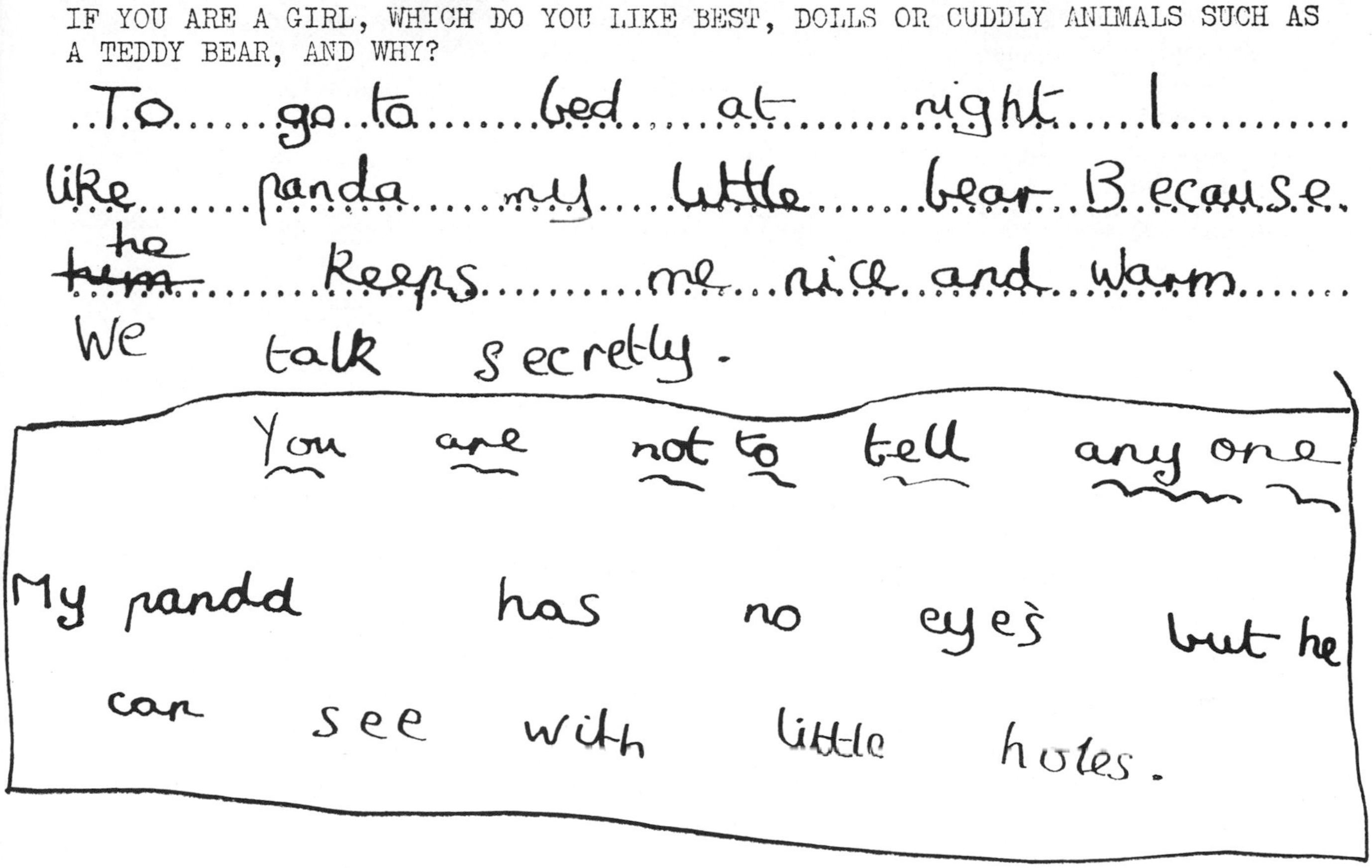

IF YOU ARE A GIRL, WHICH DO YOU LIKE BEST, DOLLS OR CUDDLY ANIMALS SUCH AS
A TEDDY BEAR, AND WHY?

To go to bed at night I like panda my little bear. Because ~~tim~~ the keeps me nice and warm. We talk secretly.

You are not to tell any one

My pandd has no eyes but he can see with little holes.

Fig. 5. A Teddy bear census form, filled up by a Shropshire child. (Natalie has kindly given me permission to quote the last sentence after all.)

as "unusual" as their young owners thought. It was indeed unusual to find a bear which was still whole and in one piece. The only truly unusual Teddies emerging were one 2 ins. high, one forty years old and one obtained on a free gift scheme some thirty years ago.

By an extraordinary coincidence, exactly half of the children said that out of all the toys they had ever possessed their Teddy bear was their favourite. Most of the other half were children of about eight to ten years old, by which time many of the girls had turned to dolls and dolls' prams and houses and the boys to tricycles, lorries, trains, tanks, guns and Meccano and similar construction toys.

The girls answered a further question, "Which do you like best, dolls or cuddly animals and why?" Sixty-one per cent preferred cuddly animals and in almost every case this was because ". . . they are lovely and warm to take to bed and cuddle". Thirty-seven per cent chose dolls because they could be dressed and undressed and they could do more with them. This group were mostly older girls, although some of the ten- to eleven-year-olds admitted that they used to like dolls but now that they were bigger preferred Teddies and cuddly toys ". . . because I can have them sitting on my bed and keep them for ever but dolls are babyish". One nine-year-old lady said that dolls' faces were often ugly and got on her nerves! The remaining 2% had no preference and said that they loved all dolls and cuddly toys alike.

Of the 300 children questioned, only one said that although she had a Teddy bear, she did not play with him, he had no name, she had no favourite toys and liked neither dolls nor cuddly animals, in fact, she added, "I don't like anything much." Poor, unhappy little girl, without doubt a problem teenager in the making!

Did you know that Mrs. R. A. Butler (wife of our distinguished statesman) still has her childhood Teddy bear? Almost fifty years old, he is called "Buffs" after the Regiment in which her late father served during the First World War, when Mrs. Butler was a child.

"Buffs" is a very big bear, about 2 ft. 6 ins. high and is one of the few to wear clothes, including always "a pair of sand shoes", because they were the only sort which could be bought to fit him. Although her bear was her constant companion and went everywhere with Mrs. Butler, he was never a favourite with her children, indeed they discarded him completely on account of his size. Perhaps being a large bear has its disadvantages!

Did you know that a Teddy bear had appeared on a German postmark?

Used by the Giengen post office for franking letters during the Jubilee celebrations of the Steiff factory, it appears below, by the courtesy of the German postal authorities, who sanctioned its re-use for one occasion during 1963, so that readers of The Book of The Teddy Bear *could see it!*

THE TEDDY BEAR'S GOSSIP COLUMN

Teddy bears are personalities, each one having his own characteristics, and although our own bear is quite naturally the most precious, we meet others in all walks of life, often taking them for granted and never giving a thought to the stories behind them.

In this Gossip Column various Teddy owners have kindly supplied interesting titbits about their bears. Many of them you will know from meeting them on Television, in books or in advertisements, but two of them are so far unknown—Miš who represents the sad Teddy bears of the world, and Budkey Walla who represents an ordinary bear belonging to an ordinary little girl.

ANDY PANDY'S TEDDY

Andy Pandy the little clown, with his friends, the lovable Teddy bear and rag doll Looby Loo, have become one of the safe, familiar patterns in the lives of pre-school age children. Without doubt they are among the most popular characters in the "Watch with Mother" series because, as with the others, the under fives (and many older children) can identify themselves and their daily lives in the things these characters do.

Andy first appeared on B.B.C. television in 1950. He was not devised as a model of good behaviour, "But," says Freda Lingstrom the producer, "it soon became clear that parents were using Andy as an example for their young—'Andy Pandy wouldn't do that,'—'Andy *never* cries or loses his temper,' and the character was in danger of becoming a little prig. He couldn't do anything adventurous or silly such as stand on his head, slide down the banisters or drink the cat's milk." Therefore in 1951 a mischievous foil was introduced to play with Andy, in the form of a Teddy bear.

This charming addition worked, "For," says the producer, "Andy Pandy's Teddy is only a baby. He tries to do what Andy does with not much success and it provides the very young viewers with great amusement, which at the same time makes them feel pleasantly superior. The children laugh at Teddy when he does silly or naughty things and they love him, but it is Andy Pandy whom they copy." Another amusing addition was the idea of Looby Loo. To Andy Pandy and his Teddy she is just an ordinary rag doll, they do not know that when they are not looking or are asleep, she comes to life and, being a very kind person, often makes good damage created by them or clears up after them. She is a secret between Maria Bird who tells the story and the watching children, a secret of their very own which again gives them a pleasant feeling of importance.

Made of fluffy golden fur fabric and about ten inches high, Teddy is, of course, a string puppet and a very good one, no hint of dangling strings ever spoils the fun! He was kindly made by Chad Valley as a gift. The voices of Maria Bird who writes the music and tells the story and Gladys Whitred who sings the songs are almost as familiar to Andy's fans as those of their own mothers, and seem to strike just the right note for the age group concerned. Miss Whitred herself says, "Although I was performing in opera at the time of making the films, I always toned my voice right down, imagining as I sang, that I had my own small son listening."

At the time of going to press, this feature has run consistently for fourteen years and much credit is due to those concerned when it is realized that only thirty films exist, which are shown over and over again, not only in this country but in Sweden, New Zealand and Australia. Obviously, children grow up and go to school so that they can no longer watch the programme, but in the holidays they return to it with undiminished pleasure. A sure proof, if any were needed, that children love repetition and that a Teddy bear is such a fluffy, cuddly and altogether adorable person that they can forgive him anything, loving him all the more when he can't manage to do all the things they can do.

ARCHIBALD ORMSBY-GORE

John Betjeman himself made the charming sketch of the much loved Teddy bear of his childhood which is shown above, and of him he says, "Archie is still with me. He has been with me as long as I can remember, so he must be well over fifty as I am fifty-seven. He is about a foot high when he is sitting down and is very patched. His eyes are wool, his ears and nose are of some sort of cloth. Originally he was of golden fur but this only survives on his back and behind. He is very protestant looking."

Not only does Mr. Betjeman still own Archie, but he does so openly, with pride and with no apology. What a breath of fresh air in our modern, sophisticated world! In his vivid autobiography *Summoned By Bells*,[1] he delights us with a nostalgic description of the feeling of safety and security his bear gave him as a child and of the emptiness and desolation felt without its presence.

> ". . . Safe were those evenings of the pre-war world
> When firelight shone on green linoleum;
> I heard the church bells hollowing out the sky,
> Deep beyond deep, like never-ending stars,
> And turned to Archibald, my safe old bear,
> Whose woollen eyes looked sad or glad at me,
> Whose ample forehead I could wet with tears,
> Whose half-moon ears received my confidence,
> Who made me laugh, who never let me down.
> I used to wait for hours to see him move,
> Convinced that he could breathe. One dreadful day
> They hid him from me as a punishment:
> Sometimes the desolation of that loss
> Comes back to me and I must go upstairs
> To see him in the sawdust so to speak,
> Safe and returned to his idolator . . ."

Here is the very essence of Teddy bear worship as experienced by most of us at some time during our lives, but it takes a John Betjeman to put it into words!

Devotees of this great and very human poet will know that he is exactly the sort of person one would expect to own a Teddy bear rejoicing in the glorious name of Archibald Ormsby-Gore.

[1] *Summoned By Bells*, by John Betjeman, published by John Murray, London, and Houghton Mifflin Company, Boston, U.S.A.

BIG TEDDY AND LITTLE TEDDY

Josephine and her large family of dolls and Teddy bears were part of the everyday life of most little girls in the 1920s and no nursery bookshelf was complete without at least some of the twelve entrancing books[1] containing their adventures.

Big Teddy with his gruff voice, who constantly seemed to be in trouble, and Little Teddy, one-armed and one-legged, were two of the many lovable characters. Big Teddy is shown above as the clergyman "Mr. Mandeville", dressed in a handkerchief surplice all ready to officiate at what must surely be the classic doll's wedding.

"Now Mr. Charles Esq., here is a very nice lady who has choosed you as her bridegroom. I hope you would have choosed *her* if I had let you choose."

Then he turned to Dora and said: "Miss Dora, Madam, here is a very nice gentleman for your husband. I think you will like him better than Mr. Quacky-Jack Esq."

At this moment someone began humming a tune. Of course, it was Quacky! He was pretending he didn't care.

"*Silence!*" said Mr. Mandeville and Quacky was quiet.

Then Mr. Mandeville said to Charlie: "Will you be a good gentleman always?" and Charlie said, "Yes, I will."

Then he asked Dora, "And will you?" and she said, "Yes." Of course he didn't mean she was to be a good *gentleman*—he meant lady—but we wanted to have the service finished, and to get to the wedding breakfast, so he was rather hurried at the last.

Needless to say, as Big Teddy was the clergyman Little Teddy was given the job of proposing the health of the bride and groom which he did in his own inimitable style! "Ladies and gentlemen, may you all live happy ever after, especially Dora and Charlie."

Unfortunately, neither Mrs. H. C. Cradock who wrote the stories nor Honor C. Appleton who illustrated them are still alive, and no one is left in the firm of Blackie and Son, who published them between 1915 and 1939, who can remember whether Josephine and her dolls were real or imaginary characters. It is good to see, however, that Blackie have re-issued six of the books in a smaller size so that these enchanting creatures can be enjoyed by yet another generation.

[1] See bibliography, page 281.

BUDKEY WALLA

Budkey Walla was a German bear. Not only was he German but he was without doubt the most beautiful bear in the world, or so thought Evelyn, his young owner, when her father brought him back from this mysterious land across the sea, way back in 1910. He had above all, a distinguished face—not the blunt features that today's children prefer, so when she clasped him in her arms and examined his shapely nose it was inevitable that she said at once, "Budkey Walla"! Exactly what that meant, history does not relate, it may even have been something rather rude, but in that era anything especially lovely, entering that particular household, was a budkey walla.

When Evelyn was eight years old, it became necessary to cycle to school each day, three miles there and three miles back again, which is quite an adventure for a little girl. It was then the thing to do to take one's best toy to school, not once but every day, and needless to say Budkey Walla had to go. To take him on a bicycle was something of a problem, but nothing daunted and so that all the world might see her treasure, Evelyn strapped him pillion-wise to the carrier and cycled happily through the country lanes, carrying on long conversations with her bear. This seemed a good idea to the rest of the class and within a few days, almost every child was arriving at school with a doll or toy strapped to the carriers of their bikes. Budkey Walla's "mother" decided that this would never do and that she must go one better still—after all her bear was a *very* clever bear and she was a very clever rider, so in future he would ride to school unstrapped, clinging to her with his paws. In spite of dire warnings from the rest of the family all went well for several days, but in the end the inevitable happened and one evening on arriving home, the carrier was empty and the beautiful Teddy bear missing! Frantic retracing and careful searching of the three miles back to school yielded no results. Evelyn went to bed distressed and in disgrace. She was completely undone, her world at an end and all she received from her elders was a chorus of "I told you so's."

There were no telephones in the village but her parents, although seemingly unconcerned, were not idle during the next few days and, determined to turn the mishap into a lesson to their daughter, made many secret and discreet enquiries. A few days later a policeman arrived at the house and demanded to see "Miss Evelyn." "Are you the owner of a Teddy bear? Yes? Then he is in prison, guilty of riding unstrapped on the back of a bicycle and he must remain there all night."

The next day the poor child could hardly get through her lessons because of the awful thought of visiting the police station and retrieving her beloved. After school, white-faced and swallowing hard, Evelyn timidly knocked on the door of the police station and was admitted by the sergeant, tall and imposing in his blue uniform. Taking down a huge bunch of keys, he led the way through seemingly endless passages, each one more gloomy than the last, until finally, through the bars of a cell, Budkey Walla became visible, sitting on a wooden bench all alone and with a glass of water and a plate of stale, half eaten bread beside him! "Let this learn you, young lady, and in future try not to be so cocky," said the sergeant as he unlocked the awful door, and Evelyn scooped up her dearest friend, weeping bitterly while she covered him with kisses.

To this day Budkey Walla's "mother" cannot pass a policeman in the street without wondering guiltily what she has done wrong—which is probably why it takes her so long to park her car!

This dapper Teddy bear, complete with top hat, is the well-known trade-mark of Bear Brand Ltd., the hosiery manufacturers. He originated from the first trade-mark of the parent company, Bear Brand Hosiery Co. of Chicago, and started life as a grizzly bear. This was thought to be too unattractive for promoting feminine merchandise and was changed to a lovable type of Teddy bear.

Mrs. P. H. Ford, wife of one of the firm's directors, visited the Chad Valley toy factory and examined hundreds of Teddies before she made her final choice and called her perfect specimen by the obvious name of "Chad".

Mrs. Ford is so fond of Teddy bears that she has built up an enormous personal collection of them, gathered from all over the world. One of them is an interesting Russian bear which appears to be made from wood and covered with black material. She always has two bears seated together as she feels they may be lonely and says that she has resigned herself to the fact that they will always be fat—due to lack of exercise! Her husband is also a bear lover and has an even larger collection than his wife.

Chad was once drawn by Saroux of France with the idea of animating him for television. However, this idea proved to be too expensive and was shelved for the time being.

COSY

A cuddly, yellow, nylon bear just 14 ins. high, "Cosy" was adopted as a symbol by the Coal Utilization Council some years ago. On the advice of their advertising agents they accepted the suggestion that a Teddy bear symbolized the word "cosy" and could be related to solid-fuel house warming.

The bears are specially manufactured for the Council, who supply them to coal merchants all over the country for use in their window displays and for showing on their counters.

Cosy's picture appears in many magazine and newspaper advertisements and on posters and he has become a well-known character among children—a fact which always makes for success in the world of advertising. He was also featured in the lyric of a jingle which was issued by the Decca Company and recorded by the Carson Twins for the Council's use on Mobile Exhibitions and from Radio Luxembourg.

In addition to the stuffed bear the Coal Utilization Council each year uses a live bear cub, also called Cosy, which takes part in many solid fuel exhibitions, show houses and other displays and from which they receive a great deal of Press publicity.

MIŚ

(Told by Sue Ryder and Mary Craig
of the Forgotten Allies Trust)

The sound of the last departing convoy had long since died away. The silence was oppressive, as was the sudden emptiness of the vast stores which had so recently been brimful of treasure.

In a corner, spread-eagled on the floor and covered with dust and snow, lay a Teddy bear, ignored in the haste of the convoy's departure. An old Teddy bear he appeared to be, with one leg missing, his fur torn and mildewed, straw trailing from his burst seams and his squeak long ago reduced to silence. For four years he had lain at the bottom of a huge pile of toys—thousands and thousands of toys from all over Europe. For these were no ordinary stores. This was Auschwitz, evil-smelling and pestilential. The year was 1944.

Miś was not really so very old at all, although it seemed to him that more than a hundred years had passed since his world had come to an end. Before that, he had been a proud and happy bear; he had known a white house, and sunlight, picnics on the grass, the laughter of children, the joy of sleeping in cool white sheets with Stani.

Stani . . . Miś felt the need for tears when he thought of his young master, the little boy with the tousled head and wide grin, who had whispered secrets to him in the dark, and had hugged him tight, calling him "darling bear", and vowing never to be parted from him. It had been Stani's fourth birthday, he remembered, when the soldiers came. The honey cake had been left uneaten and the presents were still in their gay wrappings, for there had been no time to open them. Stani, not understanding, had run for his bear and held him close as the family had been herded into the street. With hundreds of others they had been marched to the station. Miś had thought it was a game at first, though Stani had held him clutched close to his heart. But at the station it was a game no longer. They had been forced into trucks as though they were cattle, and Hell had begun. No air, no water, no light, no hope. He could still hear the cries of the children, the despairing curses of the men. A few had died there, others had gone mad. How could one ever forget the appalling fetid stench, and the fear, the terrible fear?

43

How long the journey had lasted Miś did not know—it seemed to be several weeks—because this had become but a part of the greater nightmare. He didn't know whether it was night or day when they arrived at the station and, bewildered and terrified, were lined up on a ramp alongside. He remembered the doll a soldier had snatched from a child and stamped on the ground. Then had come the parting. Stani's father had been dragged away with the other men, and Stani and his mother, clinging together, had been stripped of their possessions. How Stani had screamed and fought to keep him, but it was no use, even though Miś had lost a leg in the struggle. He had watched them both disappear through a door marked "Decontamination" and had heard the hiss of escaping gas, the agonizing cries, and even though he had waited and waited in conditions too terrible to describe, he had never seen either of them again. Now, having heard the curses and awful talk of the guards, he knew that the only way out of Auschwitz was through the furnaces whose chimneys smoked day and night.

Miś now found himself in the store-house in an indescribable scene. There were thousands of toys, dragged like himself from their sorrowing owners; but there were stranger things besides . . . piles of clothes, shoes, spectacles, human hair, photograph albums, even gold teeth and artificial limbs.

Was it really only four short years ago? The soldiers had cleared most of the store-houses now, and sent their loot to Germany. With their going, Miś sensed obscurely that the long night was passing, but he felt too tired and too old to care. Thoughts and memories so crowded in on him that he only gradually became aware of a new sensation. Smoke was filling the store and tongues of flame were already licking greedily at the walls. Miś's eyes were stinging, and as the swirling fire roared nearer, the past and present became a confused blur in his mind. This was how it had to end: he felt almost happy now. As the flames scorched his fur, his last thoughts were with Stani, the cool sheets and the white house, a world ago when life had been sweet.

Epilogue

Some of Miś's companions who survived today lie in huge piles in glass cases together with babies' bottles, booties and dolls. They are there as a part of the museum at Auschwitz for those people who never suffered in the concentration camps to come and see. The world forgets that Stani was only one of 20 million who died in Auschwitz and other camps.

RUPERT

A well-known character in his red jersey and checked trousers, Rupert has been a favourite with children for over forty years.

In the summer of 1920 the *Daily Express* used some of Mary Tourtel's illustrated stories for children, and later that year she suggested creating a central character to run through each of them. A bear was chosen and named "Rupert". Thus on November 8th, 1920, the first story "The Adventures Of A Little Lost Bear" began, the captions being written in verse by Mary Tourtel's husband, a sub-editor on the Express.

The feature became so popular that the Rupert League was started, and Stanley Marshall who became its "Uncle Bill" was brought from Newcastle to run it. However, it became so unwieldy through its great success that in 1935 it had to be brought to an end. In the same year Mary Tourtel's sight failed and she had to resign when Rupert had appeared without a break for fifteen years. An experiment was then tried and a contract given to an outside firm to do the story photographically. This only ran for two weeks. Since then A. E. Bestall has been the Rupert artist and his drawings have appeared in the *Daily Express* with only two breaks in 28½ years. Once the feature was crowded out by one of Sir Winston Churchill's wartime speeches, and later all features were omitted from the paper on the death of Pope John. With such a record it is no wonder that Rupert and his relations are so well known. Most youngsters know their Rupert Annuals off by heart within a few days of receiving them and will hastily correct any misguided adult who dares to make the slightest mistake when reading the words aloud!

SOOTY

Sooty must surely be THE star puppet of television, but as the majority of children only meet him through this medium they are often quite unaware that he is not, in fact, made of white fur fabric. Seeing a Sooty puppet or Teddy bear in a shop or his picture in colour in a book can be something of a shock, albeit a pleasant one!

Harry Corbett, Sooty's manipulator and script writer, bought his first Teddy bear puppet in a little novelty shop on the North Pier at Blackpool in 1948. In his own words "The only idea in my mind being to amuse my three-year-old son David." Four years later, however, the bear made his television debut and achieved such overwhelming success that Eric Fawcett, producer of the show, decided that it needed to be given some originality, and a name of its own to turn it into a personality, "For," he said, "this bear is going places."

Enquiries were made as to the bear's maker, who was eventually found to have been an elderly lady, making just a few puppets in her spare time for sale at the shop on the pier but who had since died. After much experiment, a Teddy bear puppet of a golden-yellow colour with small black ears was evolved and the manufacture taken over by Chad Valley, one particular worker always making those supplied to Harry Corbett. It was the black ears and little smudge of a nose that suggested the name "Sooty" and the puppet was no longer an "IT" but a "HE" with great character. With such a name it had to follow that his doggy friend and fellow mischief-maker should be called "Sweep"!

Twelve years later Sooty is still going strong, and has become almost an institution in most homes possessing both a television set and small children. The thing that seems to intrigue his audience most is his magic powder and Sooty gets many letters about this, also many requests to borrow his magic wand. According to his correspondents ". . . it would be useful for ever so many things", or ". . . I could use it to magic Mummy's wrinkles away!" Lucky Mummy!

It says much for the ingenuity of the G.P.O. and for the fame of the bear that envelopes, bearing one hardly decipherable word in a childish scrawl—"Sooty"—are safely delivered to the Corbett house near Leeds, not only from this country but from as far away as Australia and New Zealand where through the medium of film many new friends have been made.

In Guiseley Sooty is accepted by the local children as part of the Corbett household, and young visitors from farther down the road often ring the bell and ask in all sincerity, "Is Sooty in and can he come out to play?" So as not to disappoint them Harry has to think quickly for the right answer. He tells an amusing story of how one day when he was particularly busy, on being asked this question he replied that Sooty had a grass snake and had gone out to collect worms for it. The small visitors left and Harry settled down to work, but in an hour or so the children were back, to know if Sooty had in fact found some worms. Seeing that it was useless to hedge further, Sooty was brought to the door with a real live grass snake wound round his neck (borrowed from Peter, the youngest Corbett of all!) A host of little eyes gazed like organ stops at the snake and a blissful five minutes was spent playing with their favourite bear. The youngsters eventually left, issuing invitations to Sooty to bring the snake to get worms from their garden the next day.

Obviously interruptions like this must constitute a hindrance to such a busy person, but it is a great tribute to his showmanship that Harry Corbett tries to find time to please and not to disillusion Sooty's young fans, by becoming one of them. After all, on their reactions Sooty's success, and therefore his own, depends.

THE TEDDY BEARS' PICNIC

Since the inception of the Teddy bear a great many songs and jingles have been written about him, but only one has really withstood the test of time—"The Teddy Bears' Picnic".

From the time the lyric was written in 1932, records of the song and sheet music have sold consistently. The beginnings of the piece are interesting, for the tune is almost as old as the Teddy bear himself.

Following the appearance of the Berryman cartoons in the U.S.A. (discussed in Section 1) and the naming of the toy "Teddy", John W. Bratton, being greatly amused at the craze of the moment, composed a little instrumental piece as a take off of the time when *Teddy* Roosevelt went on a *bear*-hunting *picnic*. Appearing in 1907 and carefully timed no doubt to coincide with the campaign then warming up in preparation for the Presidential elections of 1908, when Roosevelt was seeking re-election, it was published by Witmarks in New York and later by Feldman's in London. At first the tune was played quite a lot by light orchestras and instruments like the "G" banjo, but eventually lapsed into the realm of background music for such animal acts as performing elephants and was also frequently used as "entrance" music for the giant in pantomime and sometimes for the clown. One cannot say that it enjoyed any really marked success.

Just before Christmas, 1930, the late Bert Feldman approached Jimmy Kennedy (lyric writer of such successes as "The Isle of Capri"), and asked him to try his hand at writing some words to the old tune. Being a newcomer to Tin Pan Alley, Jimmy was, of course, most anxious to please and went home (to his one room!) to write the lyrics which were to be used by a troupe in Manchester, for pantomime. They *were* used but still nothing much happened to the song.

However, there was not much longer to wait, for in 1932 Henry Hall, who had just taken over at the B.B.C. from Jack Payne, was looking for items for children. He had to compete with Children's Hour which was put out at the same time as his programme but on the other wavelength. His manager got hold of "The Teddy Bears' Picnic", it was orchestrated and immediately put on the air, sung by Val Rosing. The reaction was amazing —letters, telegrams, phone calls and requests of all types poured into the B.B.C. for information about sheet music and recordings of the song. Feldmans were flabbergasted and quite unprepared for such a deluge.

Henry Hall and the B.B.C. Dance Orchestra rushed out a recording on Columbia and this disc is still a best seller, although now over thirty years old, being in its third million. This, of course, is only one of many recordings, for most leading singers of England and America have recorded the song in one form or another, so the total number of discs sold must be astronomical, as they are obtainable all over the world.

Children are notoriously curious and as soon as they know the words of "The Teddy Bears' Picnic", want to have the "gaps" filled in! "How many Teddies were at the picnic?" they ask. "What were their names?" "What wood was it in?" "What did they have to eat?" "Did they only have ONE picnic?" and so on. Jimmy Kennedy felt that in order to help harassed parents, these questions simply had to be answered, so as a sequel to the song he wrote a charming little booklet *The Story Of The Teddy Bears Picnic*,[1] illustrated by Roy Lance. This booklet answers all the questions and perhaps the most appealing of the many characters portrayed is "Me Too", the greedy baby bear!

Mr. Kennedy was able to tell this little story from his home in delightful Lausanne, instead of from where he wrote the song, in his "one room". There is no doubt that the fact that an American President once went bear hunting, helped to contribute to this happy ending and of such are the extraordinary twists of fate!

[1] See bibliography page 281.

WINNIE-THE-POOH

"Wherever I am, there's always Pooh,
There's always Pooh and Me.
Whatever I do, he wants to do,
'Where are you going today?' says Pooh:
'Well that's very odd 'cos I was too.
Let's go together,' says Pooh." [1]

Incredibly few people seem aware of the fact that Winnie-the-Pooh and his friend Christopher Robin really did and still do exist!

Mr. Christopher Milne, the only son of A. A. Milne (who brought the small boy, his Teddy bear and the rest of the now famous toys to life in his books), and who now appropriately enough is the proprietor of a bookshop, says of Pooh:

". . . he was about two feet tall, light fawn, silky fur (about half-an-inch long); got darker and balder with age; once or twice went to the cleaners; frequently lost his eyes; was vocal only for a short period but thereafter dumb; never wore any clothes; was my fairly constant companion on both real and imaginary journeyings. When I went to school he and the others retired inside a glass case in what was always known as 'the nursery' and remained there until the war. After that I lost touch with them. They all went to America to help sell the books, toured around a bit and finally settled down with their American publishers. . . ."

In 1955 Messrs. E. P. Dutton and Co. issued a leaflet announcing the arrival of the toys in the United States, at the top of which appears the picture shown in Plate 5. It is something of a shock to discover that Eeyore is so large and Piglet so small! The leaflet, only one copy of which now remains in the hands of the publishers and which was kindly lent to the author, gives vivid descriptions of the toys.

WINNIE-THE-POOH AND FRIENDS VISIT AMERICA

"A world famous group of distinguished visitors from England is making an extended tour of the United States. They are finding a warm welcome wherever they go for they are Mr.

[1] From the book *Now We Are Six*, by A. A. Milne. Copyright, 1927, by E. P. Dutton & Co. Inc. Renewal, 1955, by A. A. Milne. Reprinted by permission of the publishers; also by permission of Methuen of London (first publication 1927). Figure of Pooh from the book *Winnie-the-Pooh*, by A. A. Milne. Copyright, 1926, by E. P. Dutton & Co. Inc. Renewal, 1954, by A. A. Milne. Reproduced by permission of the publishers; also by permission of Methuen of London (first publication 1926).

Edward T. Bear, better and more affectionately known as Winnie-the-Pooh and his inseparable companions, Kanga, Piglet, Eeyore and Tigger. Their visit was arranged by Mr. Elliott B. Macrae, President of E. P. Dutton and Co., who succeeded in persuading them to make the journey when he visited them in Sussex, England, at the home of Mr. and Mrs. A. A. Milne and Christopher Robin with whom they have been residing all their lives.

"As might be expected, Winnie-the-Pooh, the most famous member of the party, is the natural leader of the group. Eeyore is as shy as ever and his admirers will be relieved to hear that he is equipped with the famous tail which caused considerable anguish when it was lost in one of the more memorable chapters of WINNIE-THE-POOH. Tigger is without question the most alert and handsome of the lot; his brilliant green eyes contribute to this impression and his stripes are of the approved jungle variety. Kanga appears to wear a kind of hopeful expression in spite of the fact that Roo is lost in Sussex. Piglet is only 3½ inches tall and there is an air of indomitable excitement about him which should be part of the equipment of any traveller making his first visit to a strange land. As a matter of fact all of them are enjoying this new adventure with unconcealed pleasure, a feeling which is certainly shared by their countless friends who are having an opportunity to meet them as they make their public appearances in major cities throughout the country. The inhabitants of The House at Pooh Corner are accompanied by a birth certificate in the handwriting of A. A. Milne which establishes their validity without question.

"This birth certificate reads as follows:

BIRTH CERTIFICATE

When the first stories of Winnie-the-Pooh were written there were three animals in the nursery, stuffed animals to the visitor but to the resident very much alive. They were Pooh, Piglet and Eeyore. Pooh had been the first birthday present, Eeyore was the Christmas present of a few months later. Piglet was an undated arrival at the hands of a stranger, who had often noticed a little boy walking in the street with his nurse and sometimes stopped and talked with them.

With these three friends and an imaginary Owl and Rabbit, the stories began and as they went on additions to the family were made in the persons of Kanga (with Roo in her pouch) and Tigger. It must be confessed that the newcomers were carefully chosen, with the idea of not only giving pleasure to the reader but also fresh inspiration to the chronicler of their adventures."

Pooh must surely be one of the world's only Teddy bears to possess a birth certificate! Mrs. Daphne Milne, Christopher Robin's mother, remembers that:

". . . Pooh came from Harrods and was given to Christopher Robin on his first birthday. (They were almost the same size!) He was adored and they were completely inseparable and was made to talk in a growly Poohish voice—I think by me! 'Alice' was our Nannie. She was only called 'Alice' once because it made a convenient rhyme with 'palace'. After leaving Nannie to go to school I expect Christopher was a little teased but we had him taught boxing and he had a very useful 'straight left' which soon put a stop to teasing. . . ."

To the casual reader of the Pooh books, it is something of a mystery that first we meet "Edward Bear" then "Pooh" and one wonders when and why the transition took place. The changeover appears to be connected with a lovable fuzzy bear called "Winnie", who lived on the Mappin Terrace at the London Zoo among the Polar bears and who was, according to her keepers, an American Black Bear, so tame that children were allowed to play with her. As is obvious to all his readers A. A. Milne was exactly the sort of father for whom keepers opened secret doors and cages, and Christopher Robin often played with Winnie on the many Zoo expeditions father and son had together. Thus when Edward Bear said one day in the nursery, that he would like a very special name all to himself, one not quite so commonly used as "Edward", his young owner at once thought of his favourite Zoo bear, then of a swan he once knew who was called Pooh and christened him "Winnie-the-Pooh" on the spot, in spite of the fact that he was a HE bear!

Philip Street in his book *The London Zoo*,[1] mentions Winnie and tells us that among other things she used to love "Winnie's Cocktail", a mixture of condensed milk and syrup, which was brought to her by the children who came to play. No doubt Christopher Robin with his father or "Alice" often brought such an offering on days when they did not go to the palace! It is interesting to learn from Mr. J. Crammond, information officer at the Zoo, that for obvious reasons this bear's name was later extended from "Winnie" to "Winnie-the-Pooh".

Pooh and his friends, having travelled all over the United States, appearing on television, in libraries and bookshops, are now earning a well-earned rest and are temporarily retired for restoration by a suitable museum, after which a special enclosed case is to be built for them in the reception room of their American publishers. Here future generations will be able to visit them and make their acquaintance.

In spite of his obvious contentment and his happiness in his new life, Pooh must often think with nostalgia of the days when he played with Christopher Robin in their tree in a Sussex garden (see Plate 4), during those safe, happy days of "Alice", between the wars.

---

[1] *The London Zoo*, by Philip Street, published by Odhams.

3 Donald Campbell with Mr. Woppit in the cockpit of "Blue-bird", July 1960 (by permission of the British Petroleum Co. Ltd.).

4 Christopher Robin, aged about six, in his tree with Pooh and Piglet (kindly supplied by Mrs. Daphne Milne).

5 The original Eeyore, Pooh, Piglet, Tigger and Kanga as they are today (reproduced from a leaflet by kind permission of Messrs. E. P. Dutton & Co.).

MR. WOPPIT

As he is owned by Donald Campbell, it is safe to say that Mr. Woppit is undoubtedly the fastest Teddy bear on earth!

The two first met in 1957 when Peter Barker, Donald Campbell's manager, placed the bear in the cockpit of the jet-propelled Bluebird Hydroplane just prior to a world's water-speed record attempt. In fact, Mr. Woppit now has three world's water-speed records to his credit and is the current holder at 260·3 miles per hour, a record achieved at Coniston Water in May 1959.

His bear was also with Mr. Campbell in the Proteus Bluebird car on the Bonneville Salt Flats in Utah, 1960. In September of that year he survived the fastest automobile crash in history, here described by the driver himself.

"The Bluebird was travelling at some 365 miles per hour when the vehicle encountered a patch of wet salt. The car went out of control and was airborne for more than a thousand feet during which time it was performing the most extraordinary aerobatic manoeuvres and finally ended up a total wreck some three quarters of a mile from where it left the course. I survived with a fractured skull and lying in hospital some four hours later, realized with horror that Mr. Woppit was still in the cockpit. An urgent radio message was despatched and Mr. Woppit accorded a police escort from the flats to the hospital. He was examined on arrival but was found to have survived with nothing worse than a nose out of joint!"

Of a slightly foxy appearance but sometimes described as a cross between a koala and a baby bear, Mr. Woppit is some 8 ins. high and made of light-brown fur fabric. He has green shoes and ear linings and a scarlet jacket which appears to be rather too small for him and from which he is literally bursting. He represents a character which first appeared in the very first edition of the children's comic *Robin*, on March 28th, 1953, when he fell out of a baby's pram and met Mokey the donkey coming down the road. The two have been adventuring together ever since, being joined later by Tip Top the scarecrow. The fact that this last character at first rejoiced in only a single leg seriously curtailed his movements and caused endless problems for script writers and artists alike, accordingly Tip Top was nudged into doing a good deed and his reward was that he should have a second leg, which was a great relief to all concerned!

The Woppit toy bear which is Mr. Campbell's mascot is manufactured by Merrythought Ltd., and at the time of his appearance in *Robin* Peter Barker was the paper's deputy editor, so it is not surprising that when he became Donald Campbell's manager he chose this toy as a talisman for the distinguished breaker of speed records. The two are pictured together in Plate 3. Although Woppit still appears in *Robin*, the character is somewhat changed and would not be recognized as being even remotely related to Mr. Campbell's friend. Today's version more closely resembles a piglet and is slightly bizarre, although still a great favourite. The change in character appears to have coincided with a change of artist and a new policy under which the plots of *Robin* stories became slightly more ambitious.

"Woppit" is just the sort of name which one might expect to have a reason behind it and a delicious piece of folklore exists in this connection. Apparently the original idea for the character was conceived when one of the editorial staff decided to make a cuddly toy for her own small child. This project was not perhaps as successful as it might have been, because when the creature was finished the recipient gave his mother's offering one startled look and cried "Woppit", being the nearest thing he could say to "What is it?" The *Robin* staff decided that this was altogether too good a name to let go and thus when Woppit fell out of the pram on that "very dusty road" he was intended to personify the battered and much loved soft toy owned by almost every child and was not necessarily a cross between a koala and a baby bear at all!

Donald Campbell's own model climbed rather higher in the social scale, being given the prefix of "Mr.", and Messrs. Campbell and Woppit still go everywhere together. Their latest achievement has been to set up a new world land speed record, reaching an almost unimaginable 403 m.p.h. To be fastest on both land *and* water is a distinction so far held only by Sir Malcolm Campbell, Donald Campbell and—Mr. Woppit.

Did you know that possibly the earliest English advertisement for a Teddy Bear appeared in 1909? Morrells of Oxford Street offered "Old Mistress Teddy that lived in a shoe. Morrells Unique Christmas Novelty consisting of one large and twelve Baby Bears, sledge, ladder, bottles, bowls, etc., contained in a large Crimson shoe 15 ins. in length. Price complete 21s"—a lot of money in those days but what fun and what a good idea!

GENERAL INSTRUCTIONS FOR MAKING A TEDDY BEAR

Read these through very carefully before starting on any of the bears. Then read section IV and having decided which Teddy to make, read right through the instructions given for that particular bear. This will give you a clear plan, an overall picture of what is involved and will help you to avoid mistakes.

THE TOOLS YOU WILL NEED (Fig. 6)

Most of the "tools" needed for making a Teddy bear can be found in the average home. You will need some **stuffing sticks** in various sizes—large ones such as an old wooden knitting needle (Fig. 6 (1)), piece of dowelling (Fig. 6 (2)) or even the handle of a wooden spoon are needed to persuade the stuffing into the biggest bears, smaller sizes such as wooden meat skewers (Fig. 6 (3)) are useful for many jobs, and a bundle of cocktail sticks (Fig. 6 (4)) or orange sticks (much stronger) are needed for stuffing such tiny parts as eyes, noses and the Teddy bears for the Teddy bears in Section X. You may find it useful to have a V-shaped notch sawn in the end, to help grip the filling.

For jointing, a pair of **round** or **snipe nosed pliers** (Fig. 6 (6)) for turning the cotter pins are needed—with *narrow* points, and a pair of **cutting nippers** (Fig. 6 (5)) is a must for cutting wires behind eyes. Both of these are almost certain to be in the family tool chest.

A **toymaker's needle** or **long packing needle** (Fig. 6 (7)) is the only sort that will go right through the head of the largest bears if inserting glass eyes (an address for obtaining this is given on page 68).

Scissors should be *small* and *very sharp*.

A **wire brush** (Fig. 6 (8)) is used to give the bears a final brush up. A new suède shoe-brush will do well for this if you do not possess the correct thing.

PREPARING THE PATTERNS (Fig. 7)

Patterns need to be accurately prepared or quite different results from those aimed at will be the consequence. Paper patterns are not successful on bulky materials like the fur fabrics used for Teddy bears, so it is worth while preparing a set of cardboard templates.

Trace the pattern concerned from the back of the book on to thin cardboard, such as cereal boxes or the pieces found inside a new shirt, and cut out a complete set of patterns for the bear you have chosen to make. Be sure to cut smooth, accurate outlines. Mark in any arrows, letters, openings or other directions, and label each piece, e.g. "Leg (2 pairs F.F.)". Punch a hole in each piece and string them together with a pipe cleaner.

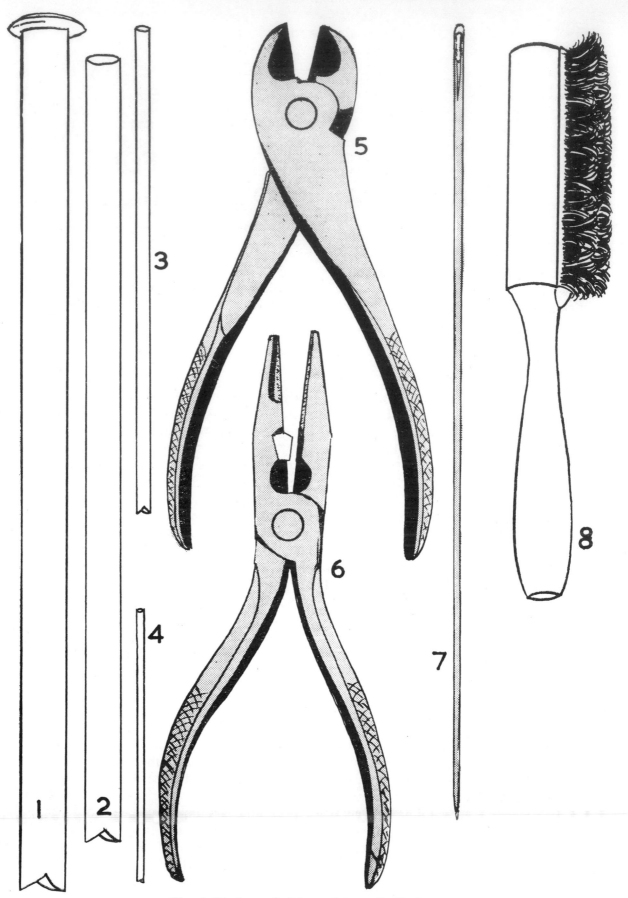

Fig. 6. Tools needed for making a Teddy bear.

Finally, label each set of patterns by writing on the main body-piece the name of the bear, e.g. "*Miniature Jointed Bear*", so that another time you will be able to find immediately exactly what you want and will not be confronted with a puzzling pile of unrecognizable patterns. Keep the sets in a special box so that they are always ready for use.

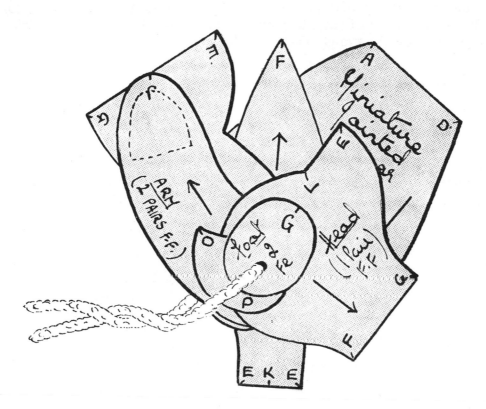

Fig. 7. A pattern, prepared and ready for use.

Note. On the patterns in this book:

Fur fabric pieces are labelled F.F.—e.g. "Body (1 pair F.F." means "Body, cut 1 pair in fur fabric".

Felt is labelled Fe.—e.g. "Paw (2 Fe.)" means "Paw, cut 2 in felt".

In a book of this type many of the pattern pieces are naturally used for several of the bears. In order to check that you have cut out all the necessary pieces, the number needed for each bear is given after the directions for cutting them out, e.g. See page 91 under "METHOD" (6 pieces in all). Always check this point carefully before starting to sew.

ENLARGING OR REDUCING A PATTERN (Fig. 8)

There is absolutely no need for any complicated processes if you wish to enlarge or reduce a pattern. All that is necessary is to draw round the pattern concerned on a piece of squared paper, with for instance, 1 in. squares as in Fig. 8 A. Then draw exactly the same number of squares each one correspondingly larger (e.g. 2 ins.) or smaller (e.g. $\frac{1}{2}$ in. as in Fig. 8 B) and copy each pattern piece on to this paper, making sure that each curve crosses a line in just the same place as it does on the first paper. A series of "dots" placed where the curves will cross the straight lines sometimes helps.

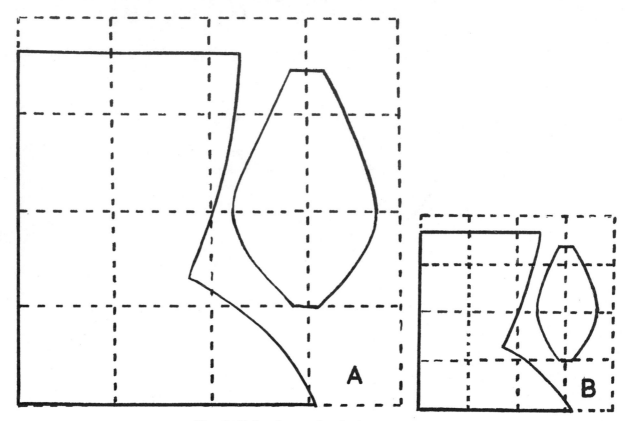

Fig. 8. Enlarging and reducing a pattern.

CHOOSING MATERIALS

Fur fabrics

Fur fabric has made great strides in the last few years, new shades and textures appearing often and new basic materials such as rayon and nylon being used in their manufacture.

These materials are usually 48 ins. wide and all the quantities given in the sections on making bears are based on this assumption, as are the layout plans, but occasionally an even wider material is found in the shops.

Nylon is wonderful material for washing, it does not mat or "ball up" and resists dirt well. It comes in either long or short pile, and in every imaginable colour. Pastel shades in the shorter pile are very suitable for the Babies' Washable Bears and the longer piles are to be preferred for the deep, cuddly effect required on larger designs. Always reject a nylon fabric with a tough "rubberized" backing. This is extremely difficult to sew and is so stiff and unresisting that it is impossible to model your bear into a "cuddly" shape.

Wool fur fabric is also useful and comes in long and short piles. It does, however, pick up the dirt more easily than man-made fibres, although it has the advantage of being a little cheaper.

Mohair has a silky appearance and a long straggly pile. It is usually one of the cheapest of the fur fabrics and if great care is not taken over the choice of colour, quickly makes the most handsome Teddy look cheap. We are most of us familiar with the commercially made bears in a poor quality mohair of the most vivid yellow colour, which flooded the shops a decade or so ago. It is as well to keep these in mind when choosing mohair in order to avoid the same effect.

Mohair was used for the bear with a bee on his nose in the Frontispiece, and in this pleasant colour is attractive.

Mixtures. A certain amount of mixing of fibres does wonders for a basic material and there are now some useful ones on the market. A nylon, rayon and mohair mixture was used for the medium-sized jointed bear on Plate 9, with pleasing results, and a wool and rayon mixture is an excellent and attractively fluffy material when obtainable (see the two Thinking Bears in the Frontispiece).

Colour names are as fascinating as those used in ladies' fashions and include such lovely "Bearish" names as "Honey", "Chestnut" and "Copper".

Where to buy

It is not usually possible to find much variety of fur fabrics in the average shop and some useful postal addresses are given on page 67. The best plan is to write for prices and a small pattern, giving a description of what you want; if you mention this book, the firm concerned will know more easily just what it is you are seeking.

Bundles of fents or remnants are sometimes useful and two addresses are given for obtaining these by post. One does, however, have to take the rough with the smooth, and remember that what you get is all in the luck of the draw, some parcels being far better than others.

Market stalls and sales sometimes yield up very useful size pieces, which even if soiled are worth buying. Fur fabrics wash beautifully and when dry look like new.

Two hints on choosing materials

1. The name of the material used for the original model is given at the beginning of the instructions for making each bear. A glance at this, then at the illustration of the bear concerned, will help to give you an idea of the effect that particular material gives.

2. It is useless to make up a bear in mohair and expect it to look anything at all like the same bear made, for instance, in short-pile nylon or vice versa—they will look entirely different! A glance at Plate 8 will help to illustrate this point. One bear alone was made of wool fabric and the rest of nylon—it is not difficult to pick out the odd one!

Felt and leather

Felt is obtainable in almost any shade from drapers, handicraft shops, dry-goods and large stores. Small pieces are needed for paws, footpads and, sometimes, noses of the bears. In some cases leather may be substituted, although it would be extravagant to buy it specially. Many needlewomen have useful scraps of kid and suède in their piece drawers (good parts of old gloves perhaps) and there can be no doubt that a Teddy bear made in a beautiful long pile nylon of a soft beige or fawn colour, with leather "accessories", is indeed an aristocrat among bears, looking "worth a million"!

CUTTING OUT

Fur fabric

As you work through the book you will see that minimum quantities of materials have been given for each bear, and where it is only just possible to squeeze a particular bear out of a certain length of material a layout plan has been included to help you. Where more material has to be bought than is needed for the bear in question, a suggestion has been given in each case for using up the surplus. Fur fabric is not cheap and none of us want to waste it.

The run of the pile varies on various fabrics, some running lengthwise and some across the material from selvedge to selvedge. An examination of the fabrics in a warehouse revealed that when one thought a "rule" had been found an "exception" always cropped up! Therefore examine your own length carefully, stroking it to see which way the pile runs; then turn the material over and with a soft pencil or tailor's chalk mark a large arrow following the direction of the pile. In this way you can work easily on the *back* of the material without constantly turning to check if you are placing your pattern correctly.

All the pattern pieces to be cut in fur fabric have an arrow marked on them indicating the way they should be placed when cutting out. Each arrow shows the way the fur would stroke on a real animal, i.e. downwards on head, body and limbs, upwards on ears. Therefore if you place the pattern pieces with their arrows pointing the same way as the arrow you have just drawn on the back of your fur fabric, your Teddy bear will stroke correctly. A glance at one of the layout plans (Fig. 27) should help you to understand this. It does not take much imagination to realize how strange a Teddy bear would look if his fur all "grew" upwards!

Place the pattern pieces in the most advantageous position on the back of the material and draw all round each one with a soft pencil or tailor's chalk (which is easier to use if bought in pencil form). *Do not use a ball-point pen*—these smudge and stain the material.

Remember when placing pieces which need a "pair", that this is a different matter from merely cutting "two". One piece in each case should be reversed, still keeping the arrows pointing the same way, or you will have two right arms, two left legs or both sides of the head facing the same way. Look at the head pieces, then at the body and limbs on the layout plan for the jointed bear (Fig. 46). This will help you to understand how important this is. Much material can be wasted by a mistake in cutting out.

After drawing out your pattern cut out the pieces, always using *small* and *very sharp* scissors. Embroidery or nail scissors are ideal; large or blunt ones useless. Cut only the backing of the material, never the pile, by sliding the points of your scissors along *under* the pile and taking small snips (Fig. 9 A). Never take large, slashing cuts which *include* the pile as in Fig. 9 B. The longer the pile on your material the more important this is, so that the "fur" is left to cover and partially hide and soften the seams, instead of being cut away to give them an exaggerated and sharply defined appearance.

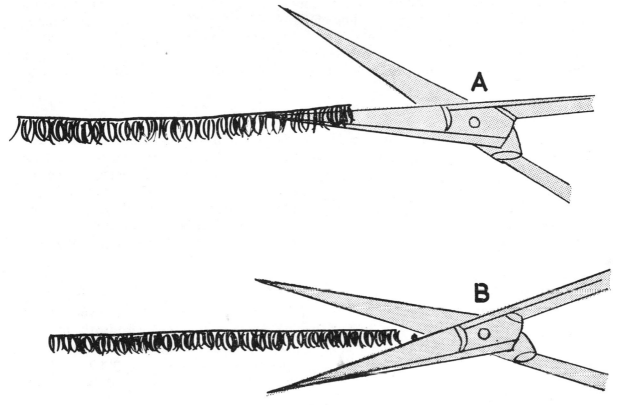

Fig. 9. Cutting fur fabric.

Felt is of course more simple to cut. There being no pile or right and wrong side the pattern may be fitted on to it this way and that like a jig-saw puzzle and the pieces cut out quickly.

All turnings are allowed throughout the book

Folds on pattern pieces

The size of the page of a book is limited and in some cases it has been found necessary to print only half a pattern. In this case the fold going down the centre of the pattern piece has been clearly marked, and after one half has been drawn the cardboard template should be turned over while the other half is drawn. Alternatively, the half pattern can be traced twice on to the cardboard when making the template, so that a complete pattern is cut and used normally. A glance at the pattern for the Bedtime Teddy on page 202 will help you to understand this.

Piecing a section on to a pattern

For the same reason it has been found necessary to "piece on" certain parts of the anatomy of some of the bears. A glance at the pattern for the Bear with Bee on page 216 will show that his "seat" and tail were just too large to go on the page. They have there-fore been, as it were, torn off and need piecing on again when tracing the pattern. First trace the main part of the body, including the broken line 1–2, then move the tracing paper so that this broken line rests on the one on the tail and seat piece, and so that the two 1s and the two 2s match and draw the seat so that it correctly joins the body. When you transfer your tracing to the cardboard it will be all in one complete piece—ignore the broken line.

Two hints on cutting out

1. Difficulty is sometimes experienced in drawing circles for eyes neatly and accurately. Try collecting some drawing-pins (thumb-tacks to the U.S. reader) with various-sized heads. Select the size you need, place the felt on a drawing or pastry board. Push the drawing-pin through the felt so that it is just secure. Draw round it—then cut out.

2. When drawing round your pattern pieces place the material face downwards on a pillow-case to keep it clean. After cutting out, the work can be kept in the pillow-case and carried about in it, which can again be used as a table or lap cover each time you sew.

STITCHING

No fine needlework is needed in Teddy bear making—just strong, plain sewing on the wrong side of the material, using Sylko (or other good quality machine thread) or pure silk double. The pieces should preferably be **pinned** together first even if in only one or two places. For instance, when joining a head gusset to a side of a head, put at least one pin at each end and one in the centre. Long slim pins are best and they get in the way less if placed at right angles with the seam (Fig. 21 (1)).

After pinning **tack**. It is easier to tack fur fabric by using a large oversewing stitch, pushing the pile inwards towards the right side of the work, as you sew (Fig. 21 (1)). This tacking need not be removed, but can remain permanently where it is, to add extra strength and in the case of the Glove Bears to neaten the inside seams, which receive constant friction from the hand.

Final **stitching** can be done on the sewing machine or back-stitched tightly by hand according to the size and shape of the piece on which you are working and which method you prefer (Fig. 21 (2)).

It is quite pointless in this modern day and age to plod away at a lot of hard sewing which could just as well be done on the machine; on the other hand machining needs to be done *very* accurately and only after careful tacking or the shape and character of the bear will be lost.

There are also some parts of a Teddy bear which are easier to hand sew, e.g. inserting footpads.

The ideal way to work is to have a sewing machine set up and near at hand, while making your bear, sitting in a comfortable chair by the fire or in the garden and just going to the machine for a few moments as and when necessary.

It is strongly recommended that you start by making one of the washable bears in Section V. The instructions for these have been set out so as to give the quickest and most pleasant way to work, i.e. several seams are first tacked, then taken to the machine to be stitched. More parts are then added to this first lot by tacking, then taken to be machined, and finally the bear is fully assembled first by tacking, then on the sewing machine. Making one of these bears will show you in what order the various seams are most easily tackled and *in all the sections which follow it is assumed that the word "stitch" always means first pin, then tack, then stitch.* This has been done merely to avoid useless repetition.

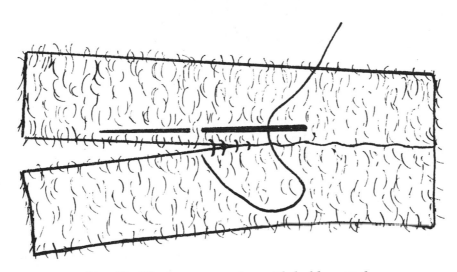

Fig. 10. Closing an opening with ladder stitch.

Ladder stitch (Fig. 10) is always used to close openings and sew on such parts as ears and in some cases arms. This is quite simply a small running stitch taken first on one side of an opening, then on the other, not too near the edge. The raw edges then turn themselves neatly inside and are invisible. *Never oversew an opening,* it will make an ugly ridge, the stitches will show and your bear be spoiled. When ladder stitching an ear in place, pin it first, then take a stitch first on the bear's head, then on the ear, working along the front and then down the back (Fig. 17 (7)). The stitches will not show at all.

Easing one piece to fit another

One seam accidentally made slightly wider than another can sometimes mean that a little easing is necessary—e.g. fitting an arm into an armhole, the head of a glove toy on to its body or one side of a head gusset to a side of the head. Don't worry about this, the pile of fur fabric hides a multitude of sins—just ease one to fit the other with the aid of a few pins before tacking and stitching.

Stab stitch (Fig. 11) on the right side is used for The Teddy Bears for the Teddy Bears in Section X, because the parts are too small to turn after sewing. This stitch is virtually like a very small running stitch, but because felt is too thick a material to "run" in the accepted sense of the word, the needle is stabbed through backwards and forwards. Use matching silk or Sylko for this—a single strand only and a very fine needle (an 11 is ideal). The stitches sink into the felt so as to become almost invisible.

Fig. 11. Stab stitch.

Some hints concerned with stitching

1. When pinning ears in place, try map or "berry" pins with round, coloured heads (Fig. 17 (7)). These will not get "lost" in the pile and are more easily removable.

2. If pinning seams becomes tedious, try using the tiny coloured clothes pegs about ¾ in. long (sold for taking on holiday for pegging up nylons, etc., to dry in your bedroom). This is a quick and effective method of making sure the pieces fit properly.

3. When machining a seam, it adds strength if you turn without breaking off the cotton and return again a little outside the first row of stitching—you can then tie off all the cottons together as they will all be at one end and a nasty but important job is halved.

4. After stitching, when turning parts the right way out, the wrong end of your stuffing stick or the handle of a wooden spoon is sometimes useful as a "pusher".

5. It is inevitable that a certain amount of "pile" will be caught in the stitching, so when your bear is finished go over the seams with the eye end of a large darning needle, pulling out this pile. Finally, brush up the whole thing with a wire brush.

STUFFINGS AND HOW TO USE THEM

Stuffing with foam rubber (small coloured pieces of foam rubber obtainable from Woolworths and most stores).

No one could possibly pretend that this is pleasant material with which to work. It has a habit of going just where you don't want it and of sticking to the inside of the toy. However it is cheap, easily obtainable and most hygienic. It is used in Section V for filling the Bouncy Bears, which are completely washable.

6 Margarete Steiff, 1847–1909.

7 Three "geriatrics", family treasures who are almost next door neighbours. "Teddy", *c*. 1913; "Sir Edward Bear Esq.", *c*. 1921; and "Bobby", *c*. 1904. The two small bears are German—made by Steiff.

8 Fourteen "Bouncy Bears", all washable, are curious about a pile of parcels! (Bears made by Stondon Massey W.I.).

"Filling" is a better word than "stuffing" in this instance, because that is just what you do with foam rubber.

It is a good plan to work wearing a plastic apron or with a sheet of paper on your lap, so that any pieces that bounce out are caught and can be tipped back in the bag and used again.

Take small handfuls at a time and start with the farthest away parts, i.e. head (fill nose well), neck, arms, legs and body in that order. Never "*stuff*" just "fill", so that the completed bear is pliable and bouncy. Discard any hard lumps and cut any large ones in half with old scissors. Never use this filling for jointed bears, any type which should be firm or any that need "modelling". Use a strong stuffing stick to help the pieces into the head and neck, but if you can get your thumb into the arms and legs you will find this the best tool for persuading them into place.

Stuffing with kapok (a natural material which envelops the seeds of a tropical tree). Obtainable from Woolworths and drapers (dry goods stores).

If the toy is not to be made washable there is no doubt that this good old "stand-by" takes a great deal of beating. It can be separated into the tiniest wisps and used most successfully for stuffing even such small parts as the limbs of the tiny bears in Section X.

Always take a small "ball" at a time, rolling it in your hand and pushing into place with an appropriate-sized stuffing stick.

Do not just "fill" when using kapok but "stuff" firmly and model your bear at the same time, taking care to fill his snout right to the tip and to push out his cheeks sideways to make his face broad and fat. Kapok is fairly weighty and would make a very big bear much too heavy; wood wool is therefore used in conjunction with it in all large bears, in order to keep the weight down. If you are at all asthmatical or suffer from catarrh, it is a good idea to tie a "mask" round your nose before working with this material, as it can have quite a nasty effect. Tiny specks float round the room and have an infuriating habit of rising with the heat and collecting in an almost uncanny fashion along edges of pelmets and round lamp-shades! The kitchen therefore is the best place to work when you first start using kapok—wearing an apron and a mask—or better still and in good weather, in the garden. After a while you become so used to handling it that you are able to work cleanly, without getting any on you, the outside of the bear or the lampshades!

Stuffing with wood wool (very fine, soft wood shavings such as china and fruit are packed in; many shops will gladly give it to you, or it can be bought from the address on page 68).

This material is only necessary for filling up the main cavities of very large bears which would otherwise be too heavy for their small owners. Fill snouts and all odd corners with kapok, then continue stuffing with very small "balls" of wood wool. It will give an excellent and very firm effect. When you think you have finished, feel carefully to see if there are any empty "dimples" and if so fill them with kapok, using a long stuffing stick. Wood wool is often used for jointed bears, for these need to be very firm indeed, but never heavy —it is ideal material for the job.

Stuffing with sheep's wool

Country women can often collect this material off hedges and barbed wire fences. Carefully washed it makes a wonderful toy filling.

A postal address for obtaining it *in minimum quantities of ½ lb.* is given on page 68, and it comes in two qualities—"Sofwool" which is of a superior type, with a wonderful resilience and elasticity, making it an ideal, if luxurious filling for small, cuddly Teddies, and "Toy Filling" which is also 100% pure wool but being in shorter lengths is naturally less resilient and not so expensive.

Both are, of course, absolutely washable, and the bears need only light filling.

Stuffing with man-made fibres

These very modern fillings are in the luxury class, but are so clean, and such a joy and delight to use, that they must be mentioned.

A postal address is given for obtaining them on page 68, the minimum quantity obtainable being 1 lb.

When ordering it should be mentioned that the loose "opened" form for toy filling is required, or the wrong sort (for quilting) may be sent.

Terylene (Dacron) (loose, "opened")—really a luxury filling, soft and very resilient and delightful to handle and use.

Polyester (loose, "opened")—very similar to Terylene, but as it has rather less "crimp" a little more is needed to get the same result. A little cheaper.

Q. C. Special (loose, "opened") is very much cheaper than the other two fillings, though still of a high standard of purity. It is a blended selection of good quality man-made fibres which has been introduced to meet a special demand and can be thoroughly recommended.

As suggested on p. 67, U.S. readers will find inspiration in their "yellow pages" when seeking for comparable supplies.

If the bears are very tightly filled with any of these materials so that the stuffing is not floating about loosely inside, they should wash quite successfully. The fibres in all these materials are unbreakable, there is therefore no problem of loose pieces floating in the atmosphere!

Chopped-up rags

Never use these for stuffing—they will make your bear heavy, lumpy and "unloving". Having bought a nice piece of material for the outside, it is worth while and equally important to use something *really* suitable for the inside.

Do, however, save the tiny pieces of fur fabric when cutting out. Those that are really too small for using in a better way may be popped into the tummy of your bear. Check first, though, to make quite sure the pieces are not large enough to make a miniature jointed bear, for only such very small pieces are needed (see page 242).

Two hints concerning stuffing

1. Oversew round all openings before stuffing to prevent the material fraying.

2. For very special work bind the opening by tacking a soft piece of silk all round it, to protect it, keep it clean and prevent any stray stuffing from clinging to the outside of the toy. After filling, remove binding and close opening.

SOME USEFUL ADDRESSES

Considerable difficulty is sometimes experienced by people living in country areas in finding shops who sell such things as fur fabrics, joint sets and glass eyes. A list of addresses of firms who accept postal orders is given below. Most of them are quite used to sending goods all over the world, so it is hoped this will be a help not only to readers in Great Britain but also to those from overseas. Readers in the U.S.A. will find their best resource in consulting their invaluable "yellow pages", but I have included on page 69 a few specific addresses which I hope will be of help to them.

FUR FABRICS BY THE YARD ($\frac{1}{4}$ yard minimum):

> Dryad, Ltd.,
> Northgates,
> Leicester LE1 9BU

FUR FABRIC REMNANTS (sold per lb.):

> Fred. Pollard, Ltd.,
> Factory Lane,
> Padiham,
> Burnley,
> Lancashire.

BROWN GLASS EYES:

> Northern Handicrafts, Ltd.,
> Belle Vue Mill,
> Westgate,
> Burnley,
> Lancashire,
>   and
> Dryad, Ltd.,

LOCK-IN WASHER-FITTED SAFETY EYES AND THE TOOLS FOR INSERTING THEM (not less than 30 pairs of any one size or type):

> The Margrave Manufacturing Co., Ltd.,
> Margrave Works,
> Heathmans Road
> (by Parsons Green Station)
> London SW6 4TJ
>   and
> Dryad, Ltd.

HARDBOARD JOINT SETS:

> The Margrave Manufacturing Co., Ltd.
>   and
> Northern Handicrafts, Ltd.

PLASTIC JOINT SETS:

> Dryad, Ltd.

TOY MAKER'S NEEDLES, SQUEAKERS AND PLYWOOD "BASES":

> Northern Handicrafts, Ltd.
>   and
> Dryad, Ltd.

"MAN-MADE FIBRE" FILLINGS:

> Messrs. John Hudson & Co.,
> North Beck Mills,
> Keighley,
> Yorkshire.

FLESH PINK STOCKINETTE:

> Dryad, Ltd.

CRÊPE HAIR:

> Ellisdons Bros., Ltd.,
> Denbigh Road,
> Bletchley,
> Bucks.

MUSICAL BOXES:

> Swisscross, Ltd.,
> 202 Tulse Hill,
> London, S.W.2.

TINKLERS (not less than 10 doz.):

> The Margrave Manufacturing Co., Ltd.

GROWLERS:

The Margrave Manufacturing Co., Ltd.
and
Swisscross, Ltd.

EYES WITH A DIFFERENCE:

An extensive range of glass and plastic eyes on wires and ranging in size from 6 mm. to 1 in. may be obtained in many colours and varieties from The Margrave Manufacturing Co. Ltd. (address above), but only in quantities of not less than 3 dozen pairs of any one size or type.

MOST OF THE NECESSITIES FOR TEDDY BEAR MAKING can of course be obtained from:

"The Needlewoman Shop",
146-148 Regent Street,
London, W1R 6BA

either by making a personal visit or by post.

Some U.S.A. suppliers:

Readers are urged to first contact their local fabric and/or hobby and craft shops or departments. Many shops now stock most of the materials needed to make the Teddy Bears described in this book. If you are having difficulty locating materials locally, the following mail-order companies will be happy to send you their catalogs:

Dollspart Supply Company
5-06 51st Avenue
Long Island City, New York 11101

Standard Doll Company
23-83 31st Street
Long Island City, New York 11105

The following wholesale suppliers will be happy to refer you to local retail outlets:

A. & S. Atterman, Inc.
357 Wilson Avenue
Newark, New Jersey 07105
Fiber Fillings

Lorraine Textile Specialties, Inc.
1750 Plaza Avenue
New Hyde Park, New York 11040
Fiber Fillings

Commonwealth Felt Company
211 Congress Street
Boston, Massachusetts 02110
Fabric and Eyes

Schoepfers
138 W. 31st Street
New York, New York 10001
Eyes

Essex Fibre Mills, Inc.
P. O. Box #95
Lyndhurst, New Jersey 07071
Fiber Fillings

Shigoto Industries, Ltd.
350 Fifth Avenue
New York, New York 10001
Eyes and Needles

THE ANATOMY OF A TEDDY BEAR

Just as every doctor has to study the anatomy of the human body, it is essential that we who hope to make him, should take time to study the anatomy of a Teddy bear. Because one shape or method is suggested for a particular bear in the pages that follow, it does not mean that something else cannot readily be adapted. You will have read the previous section on tools, materials, fillings, etc., and will probably have made your choice as to these. Now read carefully through this section, turning up each figure or illustration as and when it is mentioned so that you will have a clear picture of how a Teddy bear goes together and what small details will make or mar your efforts. All this will save time in the end!

New techniques can be difficult to master and we all get on better if we know *why* we are aiming at certain results. If you find you cannot achieve these results in the same way as shown by the diagrams, you can often reach the same end by a different and perhaps better method—who knows, you may invent something new to pass on to others, which is always exciting!

NOSES AND MOUTHS

Noses can easily spoil a bear, especially if they are too large and "spread out". The secret of what is so often called by teenagers a "twee" Teddy bear (and what a good word it is), is a perky little upturned nose. The majority of the bears within these covers have their head gussets designed so as to give a tip-tilted snout, and all that remains is to see that this important little part is very fully and firmly stuffed and to place the right-sized nose in the best position!

Embroidered noses (Fig. 12)

These are more or less traditional on a Teddy bear and are quick and easy to do. Work with all six strands of black or *dark* brown embroidery cotton (light brown makes the bear look insipid). Thread a long piece of the cotton into a long, slim darning needle and make a small knot at the end. Clip the fur away from the tip of the bear's snout, tapering it gradually back to the normal length at about an inch from the tip. This will make the work easier as you will be able to see what you are doing and there will be no stray wisps of fur fabric to pop up through your stitches later (Fig. 12).

1. Start by having the knot at the very "tip" of the snout, where it will afterwards be covered, and bring your needle out a little below the snout, where you wish the base of the nose to be. Take a stitch to one side, right *over* the tip of snout, on to the head gusset.

2. Take another stitch in the other direction. The nose, which will be fan shaped, is now outlined. If you think it is too big or too small, pull out your stitches and start again. Keep on until you get it just right. It's worth it!

70

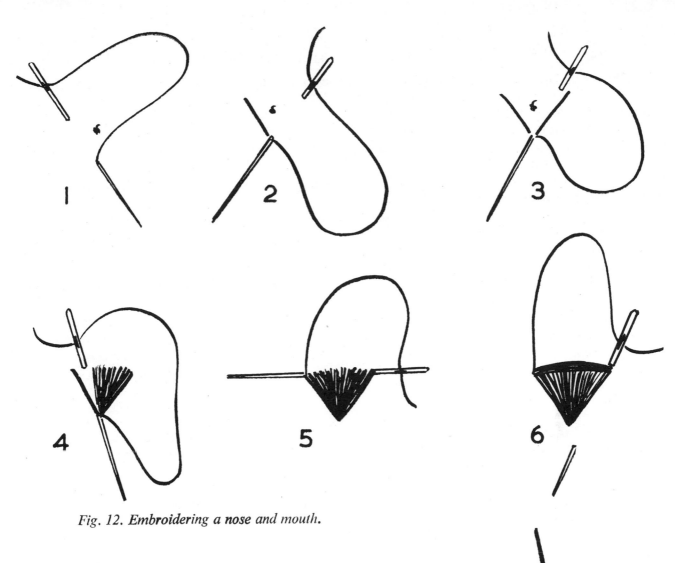

Fig. 12. *Embroidering a **nose** and mouth.*

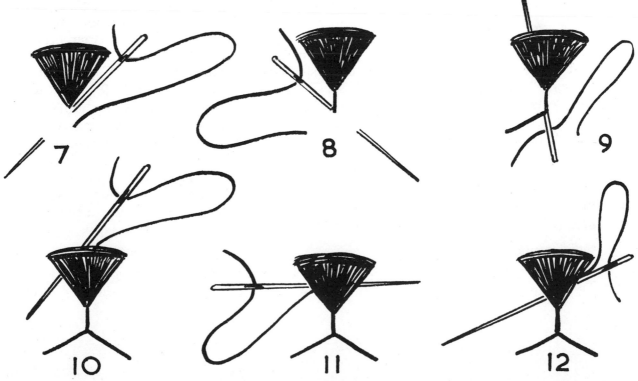

3 and 4. Fill in this fan shape with a series of closely placed stitches, radiating from the lower centre point. Make it thick and solid.

5. Bring out the needle on top of the nose and take a few stitches *across* the top to neaten it and cover any "ragged" edges.

6. Bring the needle out a little way below the lowest part of nose so as to be ready for working the mouth.

7. Take a stitch upwards to the base of nose, bringing out your needle again, lower down and to one side.

8. Take a stitch up to meet base of first mouth stitch, bringing out your needle again, lower down and on the other side.

9. Take a stitch up to meet the other two, bringing out your needle on top of nose. Study the bear carefully and make quite sure you like his expression. If not satisfied, undo the last three stitches and try again. The mouth may make him look sad if it droops too much, on the other hand if it turns up he may look slightly inane, with a blank sort of grin! A glance through the illustrations in the book will show some of the varied expressions which can be achieved. When you are satisfied with both the nose and mouth, fasten off the cotton securely by—

10, 11 and 12, taking several stitches backwards and forwards behind the nose. Cut off cotton.

Two hints concerning embroidered noses

A. If embroidering a nose on a foam rubber stuffed bear, do not dig the needle too far into the snout, as this type of stuffing is so difficult to pull a needle through—keep the stitching fairly shallow.

B. If having difficulty in unpicking a completely embroidered nose, slide some pointed scissors along behind the stitches and cut right through the centre of them. Then pull each strand out separately, using your pliers. This makes the job quick and easy.

Felt noses

Some people find felt noses easier to make and they can be very saucy if carefully made and placed, although they are, of course, no use for a washable bear. There are two main shapes used, but both give virtually the same results. The pattern given for Bruin bear on page 262 is a semi-circle with two "pleats" or "folds" taken out, one on each side, while that given for the Thinking Bear on page 208 has darts to join up instead of pleats, and the "corners" have been cut off at the base. Both these patterns form a little "cap", with the pleats or darts as nostrils, and this may be sewn at a jaunty angle to the top of the tip of the snout and stuffed so that it "sticks up", as illustrated in Fig. 49 B, or sewn right over the end of snout, with no stuffing in it, as in Fig. 49 A, to give a more sombre version suitable for the rather more sedate Polar Bear.

A similar tip-tilted effect to that shown in Fig. 49 B can be achieved by cutting a circle of felt, gathering it all round the edge, stuffing it and pulling up the gathers to form a "knob". This may be done with cotton material if a washable bear is wanted and you prefer not to have an embroidered nose.

Open mouths

These are fiddling to do, but give a very professional appearance and a good finish to a Teddy. A felt mouth lining is folded in half and inserted into a slit cut in the head of the bear, like a small gusset. The process is described on page 98 for the Thinking Bear, and shown in diagrammatic form by Fig. 29.

Note. A koala's nose and mouth are completely different from those of a bear and are separately dealt with in the appropriate places (Sections VII and IX).

EYES AND EYELIDS

It is no exaggeration to say that the eyes are the focal point of a Teddy bear. If they are not in exactly the right position, nothing can make the bear attractive. The most common fault is that they are placed too high, too close together or crooked. All young things have the appearance of possessing long foreheads and their features seem to be very low down on the face—therefore place the eyes wide apart and low down for a frank, youthful and appealing Teddy. Eyes too close together will make him look mean, and if too high he will look surprised and in pain! It is well worth spending a lot of time experimenting in order to get these important organs *just right*. Above all be sure not to make him cross-eyed!

Felt eyes

Eyes of this type, without doubt, are those which give a Teddy bear most charm. All that is needed are three flat circles, strategically placed, and full instructions for making and attaching them are given on page 99 and Fig. 30. It is very important to raise the eyes with a little stuffing (Fig. 30 E) or they are inclined to have rather a "staring" effect. It is also important to soften the edges by pulling out the fur fabric caught in the stitches while the felt is being sewn to the face (Fig. 30 F), so that the edge of the eye is embedded in the fur in a natural way and there is no harsh outline.

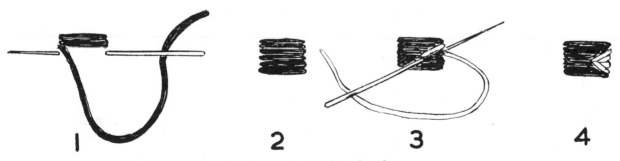

Fig. 13. A simple embroidered eye.

Embroidered eyes

For a washable bear the most satisfactory type of eye is a simple embroidered one, simple being the operative word! A glance at Plate 8 will show that these little bears have all that is required in the way of expression and their eyes merely consist of a small black or brown rectangle embroidered with three strands of cotton, a small white highlight being added afterwards. Fig. 13 shows how these are worked in simple satin stitch and the size shown is very suitable for the Babies' Bouncy Bears and Pram Teddies in Section V. Where a different size is more suitable, a sketch is given actual size with the patterns for the toy concerned, e.g. the Bedtime Teddy on page 202, which has been made slightly more square to suit the shape of the bear. After embroidering, always go round the edge of the eye with the eye end of a large darning needle, pulling out any pile which has been caught in the stitches. This softens the edges and is why the bears on Plate 8 do not appear to have *rectangular* eyes!

Should you really want to make a more elaborate eye, or to make several bears with different expressions, try using the idea given in Fig. 14—a brown rectangle, with a black pupil added and the position of the highlight changed.

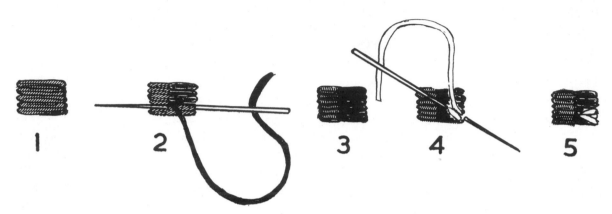

Fig. 14. Another idea for an embroidered eye.

Note. 1. Always make sure both highlights are on the same side of an eye, i.e. either both on the left or both on the right and that they are placed at the same angle, otherwise your bear will develop all sorts of squints!

2. Always embroider one colour on top of another as shown in Figs. 13 and 14. This builds up several layers and gives the eye a certain roundness and depth.

Raised washable eyes (Fig. 15)

Sometimes a washable eye, similar to the felt eyes on the Honey Bears, is needed—for instance, if any of the bears in Section VI were made to be washable, felt would not be suitable. In this case a trouser button is used to raise and mould the shape, and cotton material and embroidery cotton gives the colour. Work as follows (Fig. 15):

1. Take two trouser buttons the size you wish the finished eyes to be and placing each one on a piece of white cotton material, domed side upwards, draw all round the outside edge.

2. Draw lines to indicate the iris, pupil and highlight. Embroider these parts in brown, black and white stranded cotton, using two strands and satin stitch or closely placed rows of stem stitch, filling in very solidly.

3. Cut out a circle about twice as large as each button, having the embroidered eye in the centre, and run a gathering thread all round the outside edge.

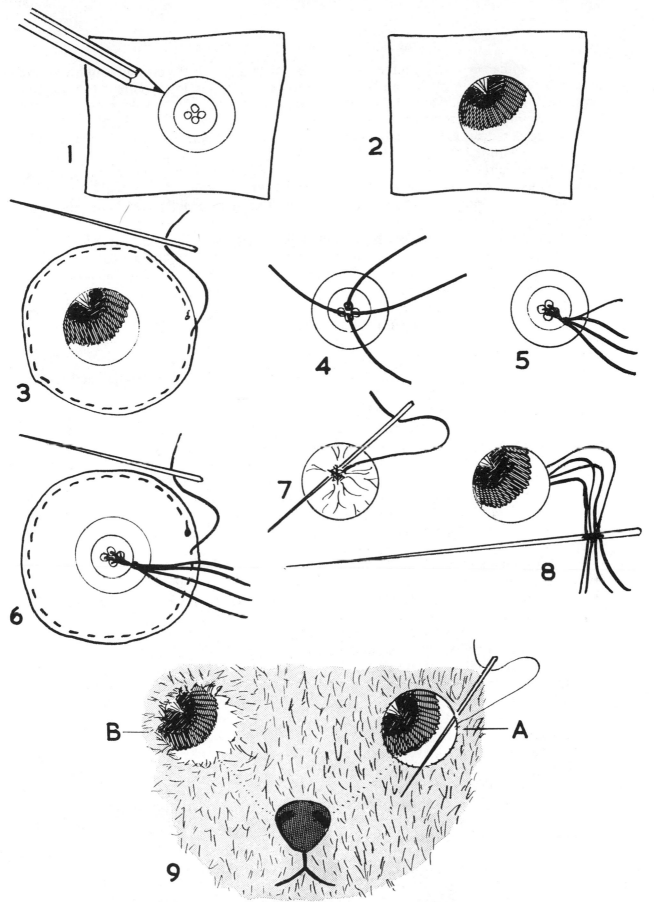

Fig. 15. The construction of raised, washable eyes.

4. Take some very strong thread which will not break with the strongest tug, or substitute fine string or fishing line and cut four pieces about 10 ins. long. Thread two lengths on to each button, emerging on the concave side.

5. Knot these ends together.

6. Place a button on the centre back of each circle of cotton material, domed side downwards, with the strings coming from the back.

7. Pull up gathers tightly and fasten off securely at back of button, stitching across several times.

8. Thread the strings into a large needle and insert the eyes, exactly as given for the glass eyes on page 77 and Fig. 17.

9. Twist the eyes to a cheeky, thoughtful angle making sure that the highlights are on the same side and at the same angle, and if the bear is for a very young child, for added strength and safety work round the outside edge of each one with a long, fine needle and white Sylko, hemming the cotton covered eye to the fur fabric of the head (A). Go round the edge with the eye end of a large darning needle to pull out any pile which has got caught in the stitching and soften the outline (B).

Glass and plastic eyes

This type of eye is used in Section VIII for the traditional Teddy bears—merely because they *are* traditional. No one could pretend, however, that they do nearly as much for a Teddy bear as the felt eyes on the Honey Bears in Section VI.

They are, of course, a potential source of danger to the *very* young, because even if properly inserted they can break from their shanks and could be swallowed. It is a comforting fact, however, that extensive enquiries revealed that few youngsters *do* actually swallow these eyes in spite of their parents' fears! When approached on the subject, The Hospital for Sick Children in Great Ormond Street said, "Accidents do happen to children because of bad workmanship in toy making, and of course there have been several cases of children swallowing glass eyes from Teddy bears over the years, but we are happy to say this has never reached alarming proportions!"

This is indeed a good omen and is possibly because more and more "home" toy makers are learning how to insert them safely (or substituting felt eyes), and more and more manufacturers are using safety "screw in" or washer type eyes (discussed on page 81). It is interesting to note that of several "family" doctors questioned, none had ever had to deal with a case of a glass eye being swallowed, but three had had to cope with a similar object being pushed up a child's nose and one with an eye in a child's ear!

Glass eyes are available from most handicraft shops, but plastic are more difficult to find (addresses for both, pp. 67–9). They come in most colours and sizes, brown being the most suitable for the average Teddy bear, and the size being chosen to suit the size of the bear. Sizes are measured in millimetres and vary from shop to shop. For instance, where one firm runs a range of 5, 9 and 13 mm., another's sizes are slightly different—7, 10, 12 and 14 mm. When buying eyes get the nearest to the measurement given in the materials list for the bear you are making but err on the large side, as small eyes make a Teddy look mean. Occasionally the colour is a little "anaemic" and this is easily improved by adding a felt "backing" before inserting. Merely cut a circle of brown felt the same size or slightly larger than the eye (if you want a light-brown eye to appear a deeper shade) and thread it on to the eye wire before making the shank.

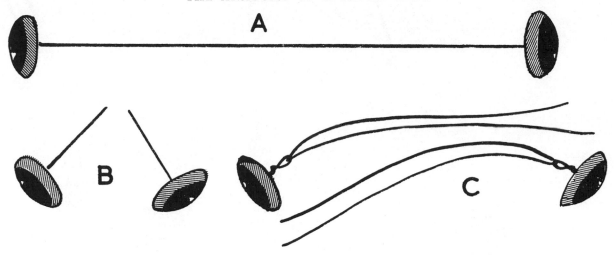

Fig. 16. Preparing glass eyes.

Preparing glass eyes (Fig. 16)

Eyes are usually sold in pairs, one each end of a wire (Fig. 16 A). Cut the wire in half, then shorten each end, leaving about $\frac{3}{4}$ in. behind each eye (Fig. 16 B). Using small round-nose pliers, twist each wire into a shank, so that the eye looks like a boot button. Keep the shank as slim as possible so that it slips easily into the bear's head, and make sure there are no gaps through which the string can slip.

Use something very strong for inserting the eyes—button thread, fine string or fishing line are all suitable, but whatever you choose make quite sure it will withstand the strongest tug without breaking.

Inserting glass eyes in a stuffed Teddy bear (Fig. 17)

1. Tie the eye to a long length of thread, so that the shank is in the centre, and thread this double into a long needle (for very large bears, a toy maker's needle is ideal, address on page 68). Push needle into head at the position where the eye is to be (keep it low down!)—

2. and bring out on top of head, in a position which will eventually be covered by the ears. Remove needle.

3. Thread *one* string into needle and pushing this back into the original hole bring it out about $\frac{1}{2}$ in. away from the other string.

4. This is so that there is some material between the two strings to stop the knot from pulling through.

5. Tie off securely, using several knots and pulling the eye right back into the head, so that the shank goes into the hole which was made by the needle and the eye forms a socket because it is so tightly pulled in. It is a help if someone puts a thumb on the eye and pushes it for you, while you are tying the knots.

6. Cut off strings.

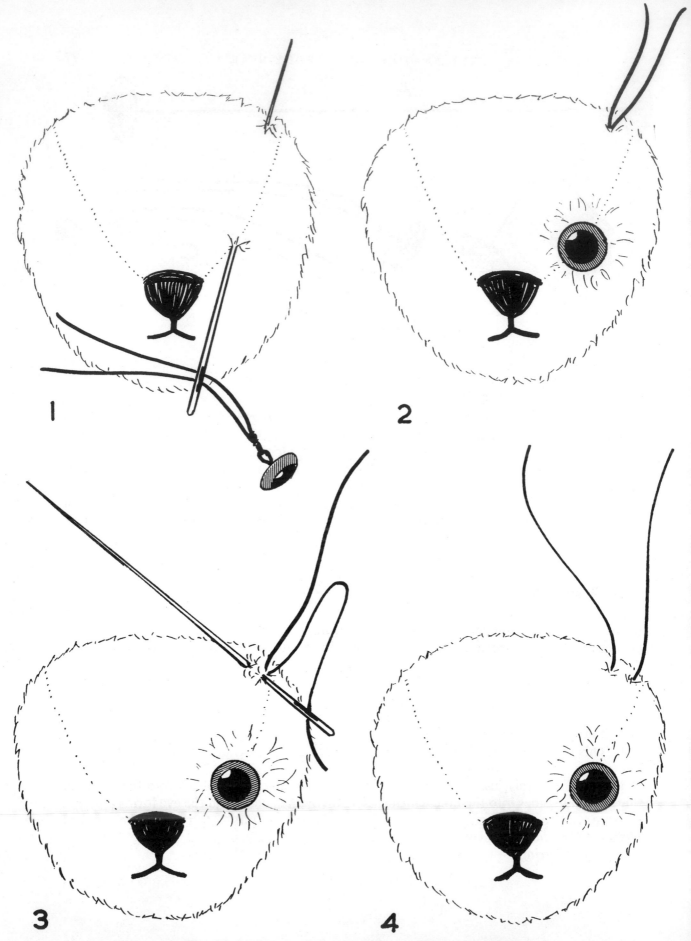

Fig. 17. Inserting glass eyes after stuffing the head.

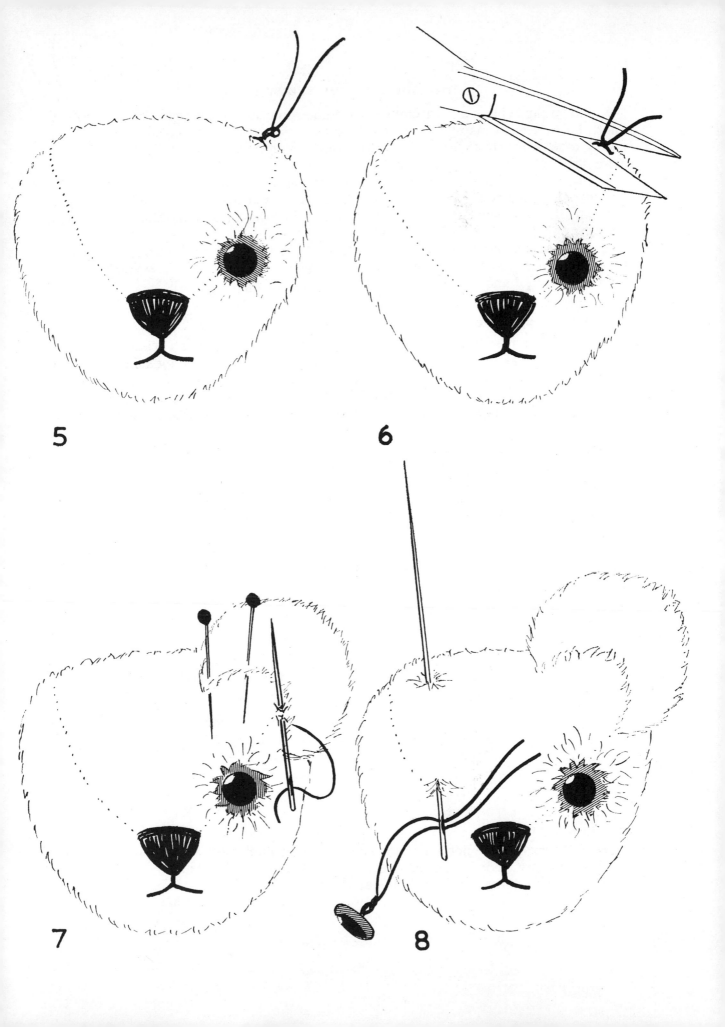

5

6

7

8

7. Pin an ear in place in an attractive curved position, so that the centre of it covers the knot. Large-headed map pins are useful for this as they will not become "lost" in the pile. Ladder stitch ear to head, using strong thread and working first along the front, then along the back, for absolute security.

8. Insert the second eye and sew on the ear in the same way.

If inserting glass eyes in a Teddy on which the ears have been previously attached, work in exactly the same way but tie the knots close in behind the ear or in the front curve of the ear, where they can be "lost" in the pile.

It completely spoils a bear to tie the eye knots in the nape of the neck, for if done tightly and therefore safely, they will form two ugly dimples in a place where they will show a great deal and give an amateurish finish to your work.

Inserting glass eyes before stuffing

On rare occasions the need arises to insert glass eyes *before* stuffing a bear. This would be necessary if making a very softly stuffed Teddy, where the head is not sufficiently firm to tie in a glass eye securely, and sometimes in the case of a Glove Bear, where the finger tube in the head and the soft stuffing make the normal method difficult or impossible. Felt or embroidered eyes can usually be substituted, but if it is essential to use glass ones, work as follows (Fig. 18).

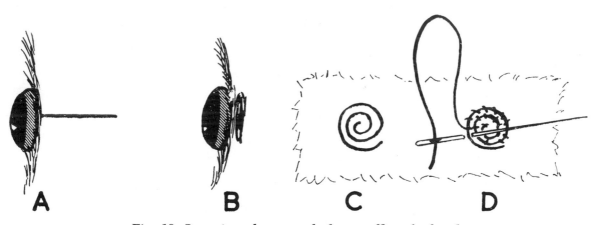

Fig. 18. Inserting glass eyes before stuffing the head.

A. Push wire through material, having made quite sure you have chosen the best position. (This is extremely difficult to decide until the head is shaped by stuffing and is why the method is only recommended as a last resort!)

B and C. Twist wire into a spiral, flat against back of material.

D. Secure wire with a few stitches.

Modern safety eyes

Screw-in type eyes are not at present available to the public in Great Britain. They are expensive and are made by one manufacturer by whom they are patented. It seems a pity that a firm should make such an issue out of safety, then patent that safety out of reach!

9 The four sizes in Traditional Jointed Teddy Bears are playing with their own miniature bears.

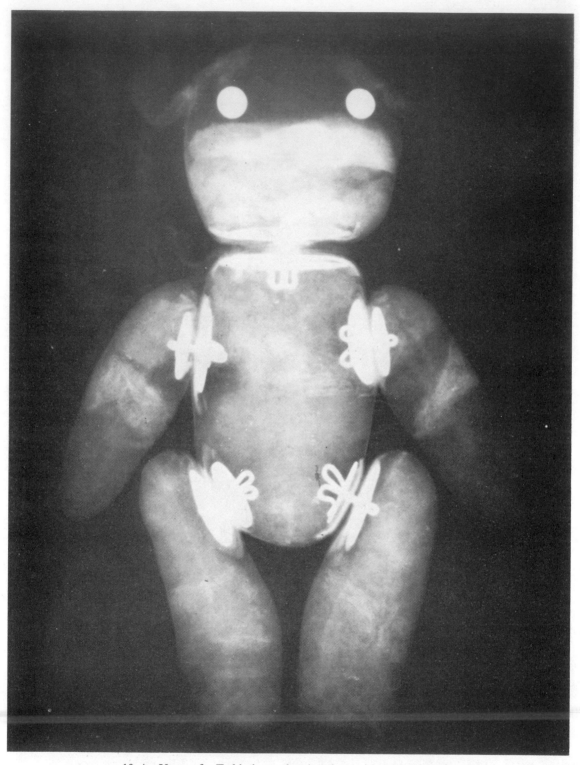

10 An X-ray of a Teddy bear, showing the position of the joints.

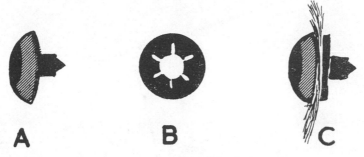

Fig. 19. Washer-fitted lock-in eyes.

Washer-fitted lock-in eyes (Fig. 19). Most of the largest manufacturers in the country use these and they are available to the public, but unfortunately, in no smaller quantities than three dozen pairs of any one size or type. This, and the fact that a small hand tool is needed for inserting them, puts them out of the range of individual workers. However, because they may be useful to schools, colleges, hospitals or other groups an address for obtaining them is given on page 67.

These eyes, which must be inserted *before* stuffing the bear, are plastic and are in two parts (Fig. 19):

A. the eye with a "stud" behind it, which is pushed through a small hole in the material, and—

B. the washer which is pushed on to the back of the eye (C) with a small hand tool.

This type of eye complies with B.S.I. specifications (described below), and withstands the pull of over 60 lbs., the manufacturers claiming that once the washer is in place it is impossible to remove it. The author tried hard to remove several washers, but certainly had no success!

The British Standard Code of Safety requirements for playthings in respect of eyes in stuffed toys.

Although, of course, the code of the British Standards Institution is intended primarily for the guidance of commercial manufacturers it is necessarily of interest to those of us who make toys at home, even if only because it shows up our shortcomings!

"Eyes shall be attached in such a manner that they cannot be gripped by human finger nails or teeth as simulated by the test detailed in Appendix B or, if they can be so gripped, the method of securing them to the toy shall be such as to withstand removal by a weight of 50 lb. applied in the manner specified in Appendix B. . . ."

The test in question—vividly described in the aforesaid Appendix B—consists virtually of hanging the toy up by the eye, suspended on a special apparatus. A 50-lb. weight is then attached to the toy, left freely suspended for five minutes, and the eye must not pull out!

It is a matter of speculation as to how many of our home-made Teddy bears would stand up to this test and is a great argument (if one were needed), on the side of using harmless felt or embroidered eyes, instead of glass ones!

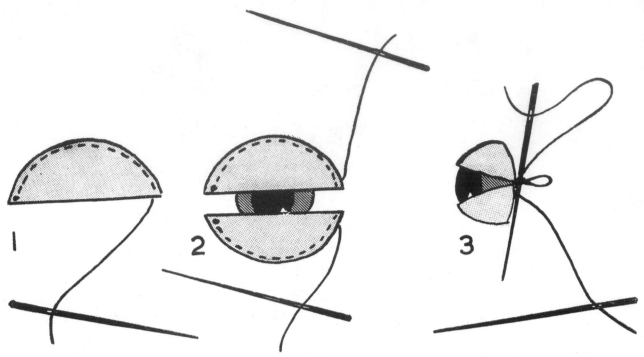

Fig. 20. The construction of eyelids.

Eyelids

On a felt eye these are usually hemmed in place as described for the Sleepy Bear on page 105, but for a slippery glass eye the process is rather different (Fig. 20).

1. Cut one or two felt lids for each eye, according to what toy you are making, e.g. a koala needs two lids in order to achieve its characteristic "slit-eyed" appearance. Run a gathering thread round outer, curved edges.

2. Place two lids over each eye, leaving a gap in the middle and gluing them firmly in place. Leave overnight to set thoroughly.

3. Pull up the gathers and fasten off round the shank at back of eye. It is then ready to be inserted in the usual way.

Note. For a toy needing only one lid on each eye—work in just the same way.

EARS

A Teddy bear's ears are a simple crescent shape, four being cut for each bear. These are placed together in pairs (Fig. 21) and—

1. first pinned then tacked,
2. then backstitched or machined all round the long curved edge;
3. they are then turned the right way out and the opening either
4. ladder stitched invisibly or
5. oversewn, depending on which way the ears are to be attached to the bear.

For absolute safety ears are inserted *into* a slit and the head gusset of the bear, in which

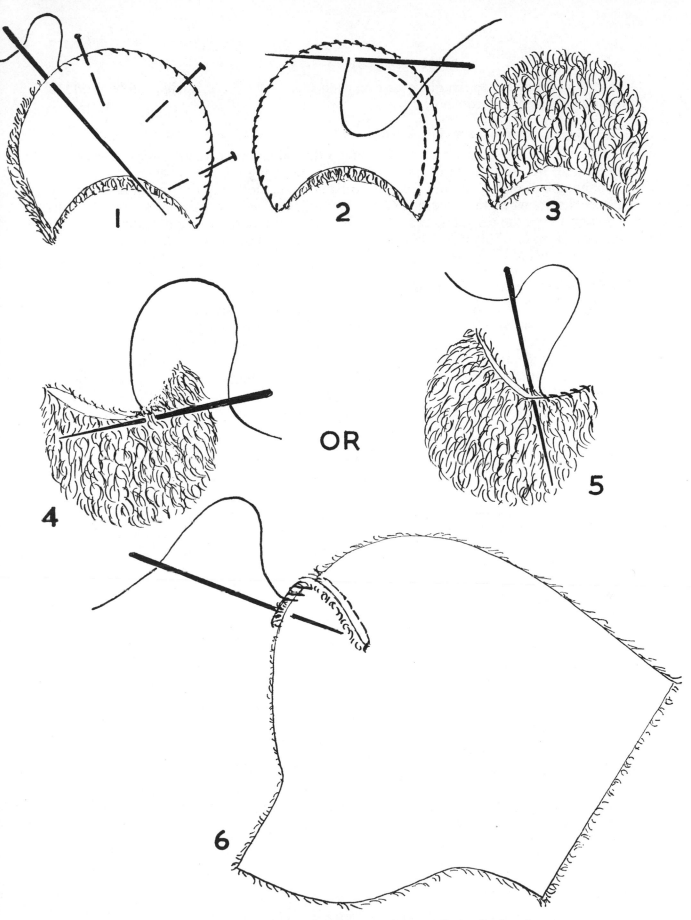

Fig. 21. Making an ear and inserting it into a slit in the head.

case the base of the ear can be oversewn as in Fig. 21 (5), for this edge will be inside the bear's head and will not show.

Inserting an ear into a slit (Fig. 21 (6))

Cut a slit in the head piece as indicated on the pattern concerned. Insert half the base of ear into this and oversew firmly in place on the wrong side, then backstitch. Curl the remaining half of the ear forwards, towards the nose, along top of head, and oversew in place. Later, when the head gusset is attached, there will be four thicknesses to stitch through where the ear joins, and when the head is turned right way out, the ears will be already in place. This method is used for the Honey Bears, Glove Bears and the Three Bears, and could easily be used for any of the others if preferred.

Sewing an ear on after stuffing the head

This method is used for the washable bears because it seemed a simpler way for beginners to work, and for the traditional jointed bears so as to cover the knots formed by the threads tying in their glass eyes (although these *can* be hidden in the folds of or behind an ear inserted into a slit). For this method the base of the ear needs closing invisibly with ladder stitch (Fig. 21 (4)), as this edge will be on the outside of the head and will show. The method of attaching these is described on page 77 (under "Inserting Glass Eyes in a Teddy bear") and illustrated in Fig. 17 (7) and (8).

PAWS, FOOTPADS AND CLAWS

A little thought is needed when choosing material for paws and footpads, as these can easily add "sparkle" to an otherwise dull bear. For an ordinary Teddy, felt is almost traditional, but may be replaced by suède, kid or other soft leather, and this often makes a bear look "expensive". The Babies' Washable Bears and Bedtime Teddy Bears have no such refinements as paws and their footpads are simply made of the same fur fabric as their bodies. The Pram Teddies, while still washable, do have contrasting footpads and the addition of paws. For washability the fur fabric reversed can be used and looks most effective, or chamois leather is very suitable.

Embroidering claws on stuffed feet and paws

These present no problems, being simply four straight strokes representing the four "divisions" between the bear's five claws, worked in the full thickness of black or dark-brown stranded cotton. Most people, however, have difficulty in deciding how to begin and finish off, a knot being useless because it would show and be a target for small, experimenting fingers.

Thread a long piece of the cotton into a long, slim, darning needle (Fig. 22).

1. Push the needle through the fur fabric part of limb.
2. Pull the thread through
3. until the end disappears into the limb and does not show. Push the needle back into the same hole from which the cotton emerged, but bring it out at a different point on the limb.

4, 5 and 6. Do this several times, until when you pull the thread very sharply it is quite firmly "anchored". Bring the needle out on top of the "hand" or foot.

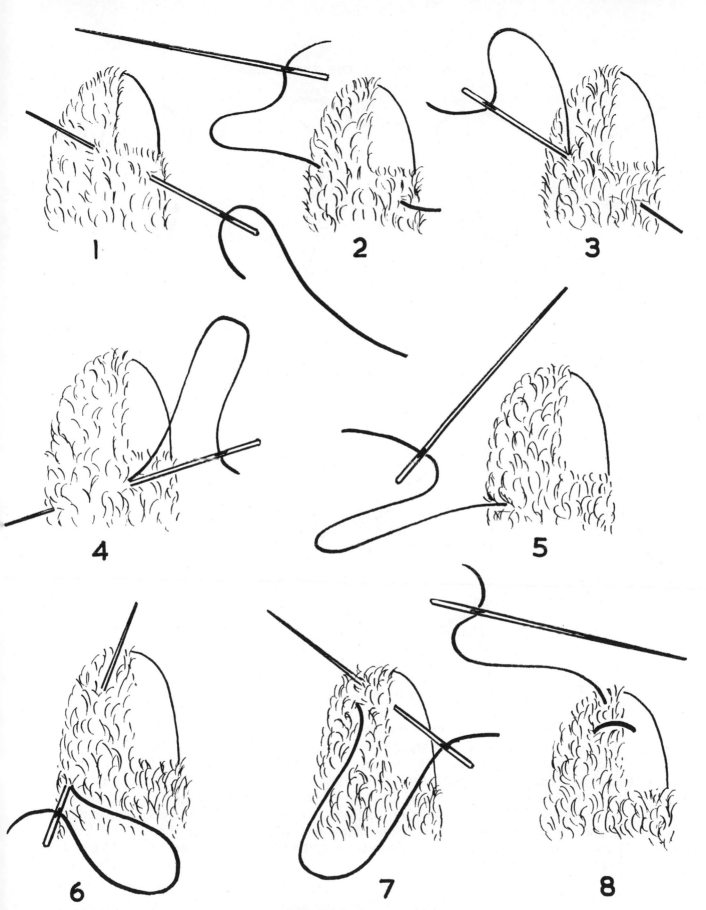

Fig. 22. Embroidering claws on a Teddy bear's paw.

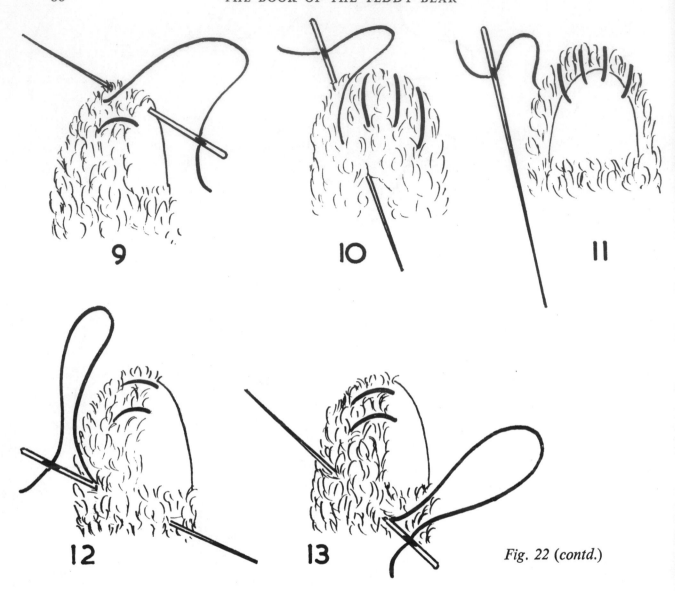

Fig. 22 (contd.)

7 and 8. Take a long stitch over tip of limb—just on to the felt pad or paw (if there is one).

9, 10 and 11. Work three more similar stitches.

12 and 13. Finish off as you began, by taking the thread through the fur fabric part of the limb, at various points—always putting the needle back into the hole from which the thread has just emerged, so that no stitches show on the outside—and keeping on until you are quite sure it is well finished off. Cut off the cotton close to the limb. These long stitches are easily caught up in play, so they do need to be absolutely secure or there will soon be lengths of stranded cotton dangling from the ends of the Teddy's limbs. "Hands" and feet are both done in the same way, the stitches on the feet being placed two on each side of centre front seam.

Embroidering claws on the "hand" of a glove bear

The hand of a Glove Bear, being hollow, needs slightly different treatment, because it is impossible to start and finish in the same way. Start with a substantial knot, sliding the needle up inside the hollow arm and bringing it out at the correct place for starting the first claw. Embroider four claws in the usual way (Fig. 22 (7, 8, 9, 10 and 11)). Finish off by taking a series of stitches backwards and forwards through the fur fabric part of limb, leaving just a *tiny* stitch each time, which will not show when the fur fabric is pulled over it.

Realistic claws and pads

For a more realistic bear instead of a traditional "Teddy", stiffened claws and stuffed, raised pads are not difficult to make. They are used for the Polar Bear Cub and Bruin Bear (Plate 11). The technique is described on page 147 and illustrated in Fig. 48.

Because of the pipe cleaners used for stiffening, these are, of course, not suitable for a baby's bear, otherwise the idea could be adapted to fit almost any of the other designs.

A "VOICE" FOR YOUR BEAR?

Whether or not you give your bear a "voice" is, of course, a matter of personal choice. Various types of noises are on the market, some suitable for one type of bear and some another. Four of them are discussed here and it should be remembered that no bear is washable if he has either a growler, squeaker, tinkler or musical box inside him, although he could always be dry cleaned. If you do this at home, French chalk or a dog's dry shampoo are very useful!

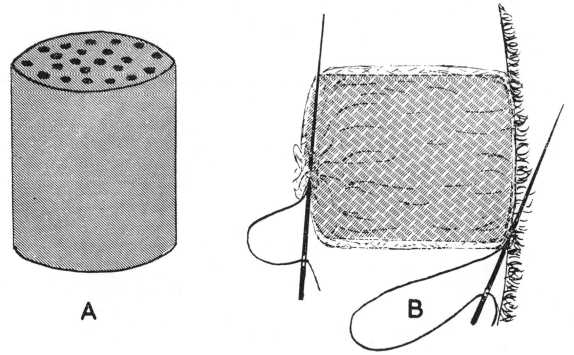

Fig. 23. Inserting a growler.

Growlers (Fig. 23)

A growler consists of a cylindrical cardboard container with "pepper pot" holes at one end (Fig. 23 A). Inside is a weight which when tipped presses on a small bellows and forces air through a "reed". These are most suited to a large bear with a wood wool filling, like the larger jointed bears in Section VIII. Care should be taken when choosing a growler, as a great many of them sound more like a cow's "moo" than a bear's growl!

To fix them in the bear, wrap the cylinder in a piece of *strong*, lightweight material such as curtain net and gather this up at the plain end as in Fig. 23 B. Place the end with the holes (through which comes the noise) inside the body of bear after stuffing the top half only and flat against the centre of back. With a long slim needle and strong thread stitch the net surrounding end of growler to the fur fabric back of bear, working from inside to outside, and making the stitches invisible on the outside. Pack wood wool firmly round the growler so that it remains securely in place and finish off the bear in the normal way. The Teddy bear will growl when tipped backwards and forwards! (Address for obtaining growlers on page 69.)

Squeakers (Fig. 24)

A squeaker consists of a small bellows, which when pressed forces air through a high-pitched reed (Fig. 24 A). These are suitable for small, softly stuffed bears such as those in Section V, and should be wrapped in net and inserted just as given for the growler above—reed to the outside (Fig. 24 B). Check, when stuffing, that the bear is slim enough for the hand to be able to press front and back of his body so that the squeak works, and remember that with this inside, your bear cannot be washable so you might just as well fill him with kapok! (Address for obtaining squeakers on page 68.)

Fig. 24. Inserting a squeaker.

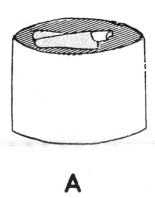

A

B

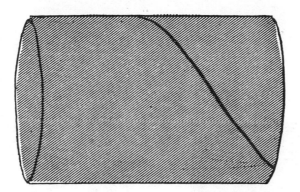

Fig. 25. A tinkler.

Tinklers (Fig. 25)

A tinkler consists of a cardboard cylinder inside which are steel "pins" of various lengths. Suspended from one end is a weight, and when the cylinder is rotated, this hits the pins and makes a pleasant tinkling sound. These are, of course, primarily intended for rolling toys, but add interest to a Teddy bear as they tinkle when he is shaken. The bear should be large and firmly stuffed, therefore the larger jointed bears in Sections VIII and IX are very suitable. The sound will be louder if a wood wool filling is used. All that is necessary is to place the tinkler right in the centre of body when stuffing, making sure that the packing is firm enough to keep it securely in place. (Address for obtaining tinklers on page 68.)

Musical boxes (Fig. 26)

Musical boxes fall into the luxury class, for they are naturally more expensive than other forms of "voice". What a lovely present, however, is a beautifully made Teddy with a "wind up" tune in his back! Dozens of tunes are available, the most suitable perhaps being "The Teddy Bears' Picnic" and "Happy Birthday to You".

The movement of a musical box for a soft toy must, of course, be protected from the stuffing, which would otherwise clog and put the whole thing out of action. It is, therefore, encased in a small tin and supplied with a key (Fig. 26 A), which fits on to a protruding screw.

The tin should be encased in a piece of material, thick cotton would be suitable or fine wool, as the movement is fairly heavy, and a hole made at the base for the screw to protrude (Fig. 26 B). This is then stitched to the inside of centre back of bear in the same way as a growler or squeaker, and a hole made in the fur fabric to allow the key to be screwed on to the screw protruding from tin. The bear needs firm filling with wood wool, which should be carefully packed round the musical box so that it is rigidly in place. Only large bears are suitable, and once more the larger sizes in Sections VIII and IX will be found the best recipients! (Address for obtaining musical boxes is given on page 68.)

Note. For the techniques of jointing see Section VIII, page 124.

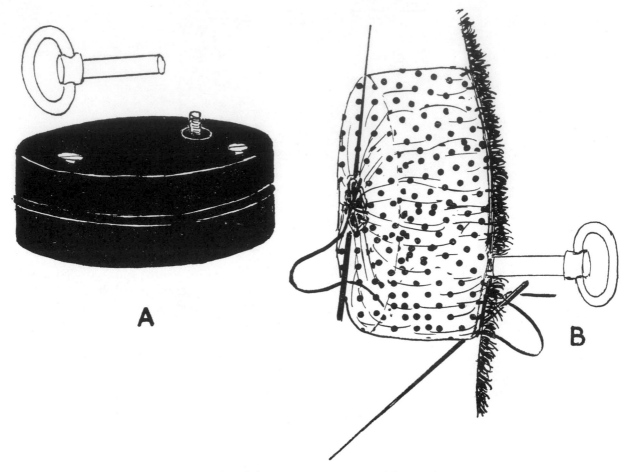

Fig. 26. Inserting a musical box.

Did you know that some years ago, before modern methods of inducing anaesthesia were perfected, the toy-making firm of Merrythought Ltd. were asked by a Manchester surgeon to make him a special Teddy bear for the purpose? Finding that in some cases he was unable to give a child an anaesthetic in the normal way, he had the bear made with a rubber tube connected to its mouth and gave it to the child to hug. The anaesthetic was then passed through the tube and the child lost consciousness without experiencing all the frightening, suffocating sensations of having chloroform or ether dripped on to a mask over his face.

WASHABLE BEARS FOR THE VERY YOUNG

SIMPLE BEDTIME TEDDY

For any small child's bedtime all that is required is quite literally "something to cuddle"! Washability is, however, a very important factor, especially during winter months when Teddies are clasped to chests which have been well rubbed with all sorts of medicaments!

This pattern is very simple indeed to make up and extremely quick. It has no odd corners to make foam rubber filling difficult and is eminently suitable for a beginner. The nose and eyes are simply embroidered with stranded cotton.

Height: sitting, 9 ins. Pattern page 202. *Weight:* approx. 3 ozs.

Materials

¼ yard long-pile nylon fur fabric 48 ins. wide. This will not be enough for two Teddies, but there will be sufficient material over to cut out the "bear from 2 flat pieces" on page 279.

1½ ozs. foam rubber.

Brown and white stranded cotton for embroidering nose and eyes.

Method

Cut out the pieces as given (noting carefully the "folds". See page 61) and a circle 3 ins. diameter for the "snout" (6 pieces in all).

Back

Place the back of body and back of legs together right sides facing (i.e. legs upwards over the body). Tack, then stitch B–A–B. This is the back of "seat".

Front

On the wrong side fold across the top of each arm C–D and stitch across, following the curve shown by broken lines. This "tuck" will make the arms extend forwards. In the same way stitch across the top of each leg E–B to bring the legs forward.

Assembling

Place the front and back together and tack, then stitch, all round G–B–D–H–C–I–J–J–I–C–H–D–B–G. Tack, then stitch K–E–K. Open out bottom of leg, insert limb base and, matching letters, tack, then stitch K–L–G–L–K. Cut a neat slit in centre back M–L. Oversew edges to prevent fraying and turn the bear right side out through this slit.

Ears

Using matching Sylko, stab stitch across the base of each ear as shown by broken lines J–I, to prevent stuffing going into them.

Stuffing

Fill the bear lightly with foam rubber, pushing out the seat well and making sure the neck is firm. Close back opening neatly.

Finishing off

Gather all round the outside edge of snout circle. Pull up gathers and stuff circle to form a knob about the size of that shown on pattern. Fasten off gathers. Ladder stitch snout very firmly to front of face, working round two or three times for absolute safety. Using brown stranded cotton embroider nose and mouth (Fig. 12) and eyes (Fig. 13). Add a tiny white highlight to each eye. The nose needs to be at the top of the snout and the eyes about 1½ ins. apart level with the top of snout. Suggested shapes are given actual size with the pattern on page 202.

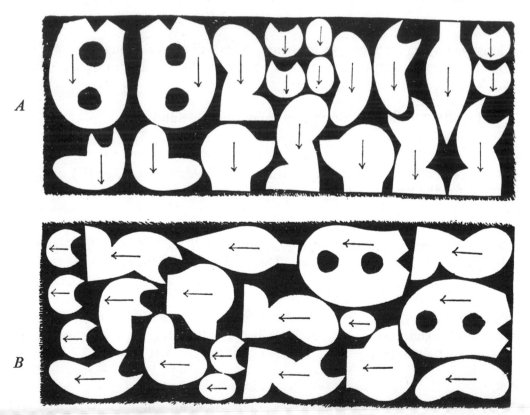

Fig. 27. Layout plan for cutting one Bouncy Bear from a piece of material 9 ins. × 24 ins. (i.e. ¼ yard 48 in. material cut in half widthwise). A. With the pile running DOWN *the material. B. With the pile running* ACROSS *the material.*

BABIES' "BOUNCY" BEARS
Illustration Plate 8

Taking the worker one stage farther because they have inset arms and legs, these little bears are very soft and "bouncy". They are intended for the *very* young—a first cuddly toy, so the pattern has been specially designed with a slim neck on top of sloping shoulders and legs which "stick out" well; these all form a convenient handle for a tiny hand to grasp and hold. The hand that picks up a toy for the very first time *is* tiny and quite incapable of holding anything large or heavy. These bears weigh approximately 3 ozs. There are no refinements such as paws or "pads" and no decorations of any sort.

Two shapes are given for the arms, so that by using both the same or one of each and varying the angle at which they and the legs are inserted, an inexhaustible number of variations can be made in the attitude and position of the bears.

Try making two alike—it's virtually impossible! The fourteen bears in Plate 8 were made up by fourteen different people—all members of one Women's Institute. They all made them together sitting in one room, but no two turned out alike in any way at all—even the size varied owing to depth of seams and turnings taken. This is as it should be and shows what a joy the individuality of your own Teddy bear can be.

Height: standing, about 12 ins.; sitting, about 7 ins. Pattern pages 204–6. *Weight:* approx. 3 ozs.

Materials

¼ yard short-pile nylon fur fabric 48 ins. wide. (Pastel shades are attractive.) *Note.* If cut carefully this will make two bears (layout plan, Fig. 27), but ⅛ yard is not sufficient for one bear.

1½ ozs. foam rubber for filling (see page 64).

Brown, black and white stranded cotton for embroidering claws, nose and eyes.

Method

Cut out the pieces as given, using whichever arm pattern you prefer, or one of each (see page 60 on cutting out). Do not cut out the holes on body pieces for arms and legs yet. (*Note.*—On the layout plan, Fig. 27, one arm of each shape is used.) (19 pieces in all.)

Body

Tack shoulder darts A–B–A. Oversew edges of openings C–D (see page 66).

Legs

Place each inner leg on an outer leg and tack front seams E–F and back seams G–H.

Arms

Place each inner arm on the appropriate outer piece and tack all round I–J–K.

Ears

Place the pieces together in pairs and tack all round L–M–N.

Head

Tack head gusset to the top of one side of head N–O.

Now machine all these tacked seams and tie off ends.

Tack, then machine other side of head to the gusset N–O–P. Tack, then machine front seam R–N–Q (see Fig. 45 for folding end of head gusset).

Footpads

Matching letters, tack each footpad into the base of a leg, then backstitch them firmly in place, working all round twice. Turn the completed legs right way out.

Assembling

Cut out the holes for the legs on each body piece. Now hold one body piece in the position it will be on finished bear (i.e. opening at base, dart at shoulder), and try the appropriate leg against it to decide in what position you want it. It could be straight down (as standing bear in Plate 8) or extending forwards so that the bear sits. The bear could lean back (as some do in Plate 8) or sit upright (like others on Plate 8). The position needed for sitting upright is rather deceptive and the legs should be stitched at the angle shown in Fig. 28 A. If you stitch them at the angle shown on Fig. 28 B, the bear will lean backwards. Tack each leg into its hole and backstitch all round twice, very firmly.

Turn arms the right way out and try them against the body to see in what position you want them. Even if you are using the same pattern for both arms you can vary the position, having one up and one down. Cut out the armholes in both body pieces, tack each arm in place, then backstitch all round twice very firmly.

Place the two body sides together; tack from S–C and T–D, marking the front with a piece of coloured cotton, so that you are not confused when putting on the head later. Stitch these two seams (the legs will protrude through the opening at base). Turn the head right way out and slip it upside down inside the neck end of body. Adjust the position so that Q on the head matches T on the body (which you have marked with coloured cotton) and P on the head matches S on the body. Tack, then backstitch twice all round T–A–S–A–T. In this way the head will face straight forward. Should you want your bear to have his head turned to one side adjust the position accordingly and tack it as you want it. Turn the bear the right way out.

Turn ears the right way out; turn in and ladder stitch lower end L–N (Fig. 21 (4)).

Bind opening C–D on body (see page 66).

Finishing off

Fill carefully with foam rubber (see page 64) first the head, then neck, arms, legs and body. The bear should be soft, light and "bouncy"! Remove binding and close opening C–D.

Look at Plate 8 and sew on ears very firmly at an attractive curved angle (see page 84 and Fig. 17 (7 and 8)).

Using brown stranded cotton make claw markings on paws and feet (see page 84 and Fig. 22).

Embroider nose and mouth using the same colour (see page 70 and Fig. 12).

Embroider the eyes, taking your ideas from page 73 and Fig. 13.

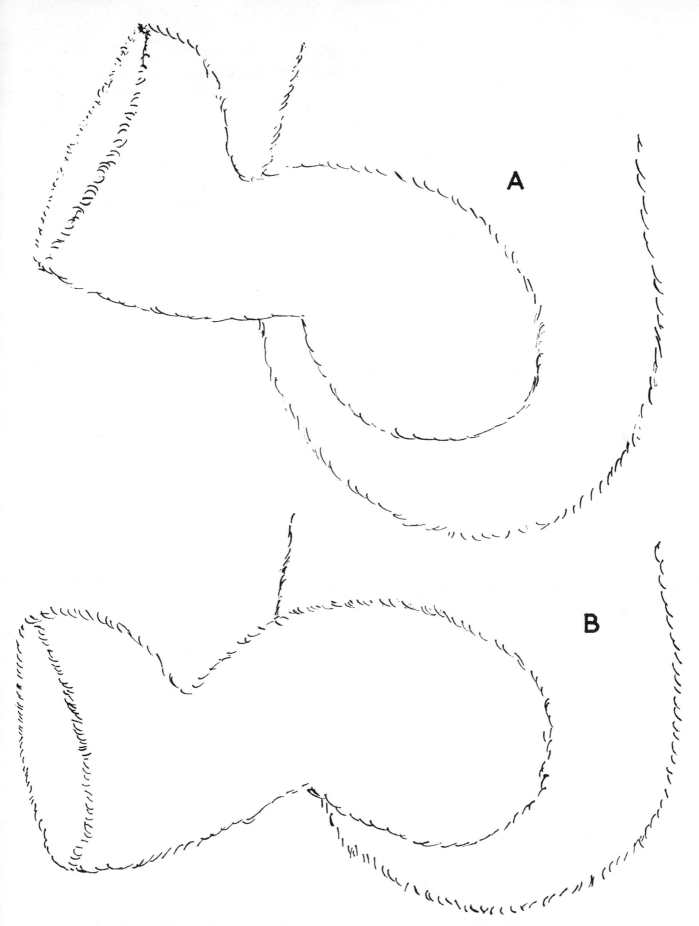

Fig. 28. Positions for inserting legs into a Bouncy Bear, according to how you wish him to sit.

95

PRAM TEDDIES[1]
Illustration Plate 16

These bears, although the same size as the Bouncy Bears (page 93), take the worker a stage farther in understanding the construction of a pattern. Darts at the top of the arms give a certain amount of shoulder shaping, and those at the top of the legs give shape to the hip and help to bring the legs inwards, as do the darts between the legs on the body pieces. Foam rubber may be used for filling if desired, but the original was stuffed with sheep's wool known commercially as "Sofwool". Terylene is also an ideal filling but of course is expensive. Contrasting footpads and paws are added to this bear. See page 93 for explanation of two arm patterns.

Height: standing, about 12 ins.; sitting, about 7 ins. *Weight:* approx. 4 ozs. Pattern pages 206–7, 228.

Materials

¼ yard fur fabric 48 ins. wide.
2 ozs. "Sofwool" or (see pages 65–6).
3 ozs. Terylene filling.
Brown, black and white stranded cotton for embroidering claws, nose and eyes.

Method

Cut out the body, outer limbs and paws as given on pages 206–7, and the inner limbs, head, head gusset, ears and footpads as given for the Bouncy Bear on pages 204–6. (21 pieces in all.) Second outer arm, if wanted, is on p. 228.

Make up exactly as given for the Bouncy Bear on pages 93–4, but when starting on the **Body** close dart X–Y–Z, and on the **Arms and Legs** close darts U–V–W before carrying out the rest of the instructions.

When **Inserting Footpads,** reverse the material so the wrong side is outside; this gives a pleasant contrast.

When **Assembling,** ease each limb into its hole, arranging any extra fullness evenly all round.

Paws

Hem these neatly to inner arms, tucking in the raw edge as you work, and using them with the wrong side of material outside so as to form a contrast and match the footpads.

Alternatively use chamois leather for paws and pads.

The pattern is specially cut to allow for very soft stuffing, but fill shoulders, nose and hips well!

Tie a bow of ribbon round the bear's neck.

Try a more ambitious eye; the bear shown on Plate 16 has eyes embroidered as shown by Fig. 14.

[1] For the benefit of my American friends, may I explain that "pram" is the English equivalent of "baby carriage".

11 Tedwina, the little girl glove bear, looks down at the jointed panda, Bruin bear, and the miniature woolly panda, while the Polar bear rolls on the floor.

(Reproduced in color on the inside back cover.)

"HONEY BEARS" FOR THE TEENAGERS

Teenagers are notorious bear lovers—it matters not whether they are still at school, office workers, shop assistants or débutantes! It is in this age group that character really counts in a toy, for any bears they acquire will be used to sit, stand or lie about in their bedrooms or bed-sitters. In these circumstances jointed Teddies are not ideal, but exciting effects can be achieved by careful cutting and modelling as in these Honey Bears, illustrated in the Frontispiece. Each one takes up a different attitude—two being specially designed to lie on a bed!

In this section, too, the worker goes on to yet another stage in bear making—the ears are inserted into a seam and slit instead of being sewn on after the bear is stuffed, an open mouth in the form of a tiny gusset is added and a rudimentary "tail" included in the shape of the seat. Felt is used for the eyes and nose and kapok for filling.

SITTING THINKING BEAR

(Illustration Frontispiece. This is the bear sitting on the log and holding a honey pot. The original was made in nylon and wool mixture, but any long-pile fur fabric is suitable.)
Height: sitting, about 11 ins. Pattern pages 208–10.

Materials

⅜ yard long-pile fawn fur fabric 48 ins. wide (¾ yard will make any three of the Honey Bears in this section).
Scraps of fawn felt for paws and footpads.
Scraps of brown, white and black felt for eyes and nose.
Scrap of pink felt for mouth lining.
About 4 ozs. kapok for stuffing.
Dark brown stranded cotton for claws.

Method

Cut out nose, eyes and body pieces (piecing foot on to this; see page 62); body gusset, inner legs and outer arms as given on pages 208–10; also inner arms, paws, mouth lining, footpads and ears as given on pages 218–21, for the Bear Lying on Tummy; and the head gusset as given for the Bear with a Bee on his Nose on page 211 (26 pieces in all).

Stitching

It is now assumed that "stitch" means first tack by oversewing, then stitch (Fig. 21 (1 and 2)).

†Arms

On outer arms, join darts at top, so that the A's meet and the B's meet. Join the paws to inner arms, matching letters C and D. Place each inner arm on top of an outer arm and, matching letters, stitch all round A–E, leaving the tops of arms open. Turn right side out and fit them into the armholes on body sides. Place the left arm with dart B at A on body pattern and the right arm with dart A at A on body pattern, so as to have them in different positions—one to rest on knee and one to cup the chin. Stitch both arms in place all round armholes.

Ears

Place the pieces together in pairs and stitch all round the outside curved edge E–F–G. Turn right side out and oversew E–H–G. Place ears into slits on head and stitch securely E–H. Curve H–G round and along top of head; oversew in place (see Fig. 21 (6)).

*Head gusset

Insert this piece, matching letters and stitching on both sides of body I–J–G–H–K, then stitch the two body pieces together K–M. There will be four thicknesses of material to stitch through from G–H. Now fold the short, straight, front edge of gusset in half, so that the I's meet (see Fig. 45), and stitch L–I–X (this makes the tip-tilted nose) and then Z–Q. Cut slit X–Y.

Mouth lining

Oversew raw edge X–Y–Z–Y–X to stop it fraying, then insert pink felt mouth lining (Fig. 29), folding it in half at Y–Y and oversewing, then backstitching all round X–Y–Z–Y–X. This is a fiddly job but will give your bear a very professional finish!*

Legs

Join each inner leg to the body gusset O–P. Then join these completed pieces to the main body piece, matching letters, stitch on both sides Q–O–R, then P–S. Lastly join the two body pieces together P–N. Turn right side out. If a stiff material has been used, this will take a little persuasion. Help the head down through the rather narrow neck with a blunt piece of wood. Push the "lips" well out from inside.

Stuffing

Stuff carefully, inserting a small quantity of kapok at a time and paying particular attention to the nose, paws, feet, lips and where the limbs join the body. When the bear is quite firm but not hard or heavy, invisibly ladder stitch the opening M–N.†

Modelling

Your bear will now be apparently gazing at the floor and may be modelled into almost any position you wish, owing to his long, slim neck. The original was definitely "a thinker". To achieve this, pull the head over to one side and slightly backwards, stitching it very firmly in place with a long needle and very strong thread. Embroider four brown strokes on the end of each paw and foot (Fig. 22) to denote claw divisions, then stitch elbow of right arm to the corresponding knee and right paw to side of chin—or arrange them how you prefer.

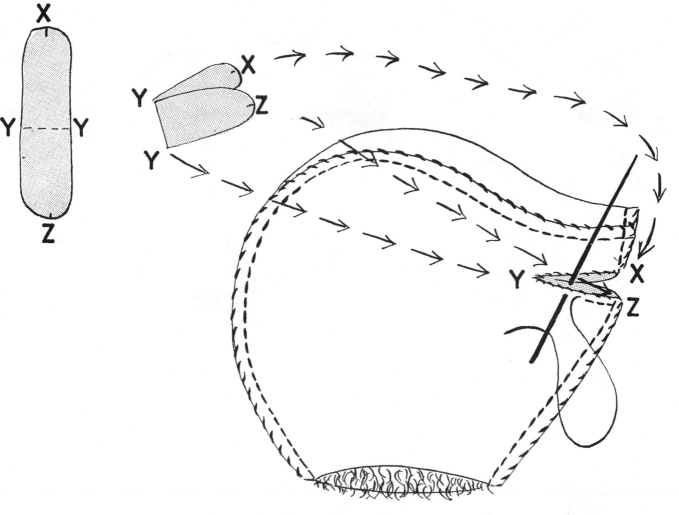

Fig. 29. Inserting "gusset" to make an open mouth.

Nose

On the wrong side, join the darts U–V–W. Stitch felt nose to tip of face at L (Fig. 49 B), darts on top, poking a tiny piece of stuffing into it so that it has a "pert" and tip-tilted appearance.

Eyes (Fig. 30)

Stitch each black circle to a brown (Fig. 30 A), then these two completed circles to a white (Fig. 30 B). Embroider white highlight (Fig. 30 C). Consulting Frontispiece and Fig. 30 D, hem each eye neatly to the head—low down and wide apart with the black pupils in the bottom left-hand corners so that the bear looks thoughtful. Just before completing the hemming stuff each eye firmly so that they are nicely rounded and firm, pushing the kapok in with a cocktail stick or slim scissor points (Fig. 30 E). If you do not like his expression,

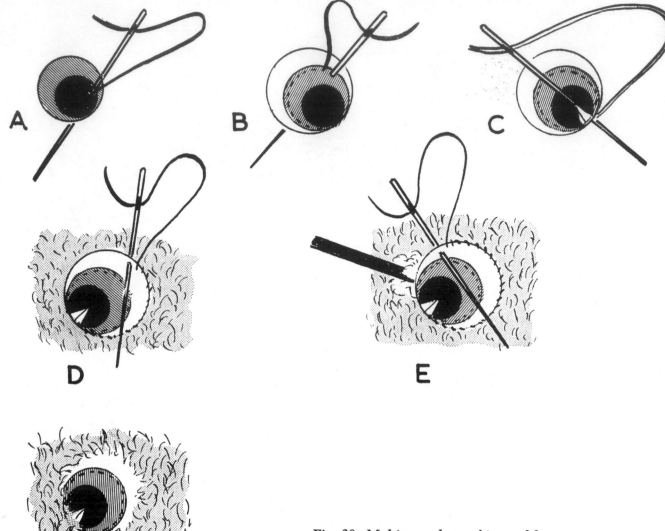

Fig. 30. Making and attaching a felt eye.

remove the eyes and start again—it's worth it! With the eye end of a large darning needle pull out any pile caught in the hemming and tucked under the eyes so that each eye is deeply embedded in fur (Fig. 30 F).

For the Honey Pot see page 105.

THINKING BEAR LYING ON TUMMY
Illustration Frontispiece and Plate 16

This is the bear in front of the log, lying on his tummy with his chin cupped in his hands, in the Frontispiece. The original was made in a nylon and wool mixture, but any long-pile fur fabric is suitable. For another view see Plate 16.

This bear is very quick to make—as most of the seams are long and straight. The arms are not inserted into holes, but added to the outside of the body after stuffing, so as to be sure to achieve the correct angle.

He looks enchanting lying on a teenager's bed!

Length: about 17 ins. Pattern pages 218–21.

Materials

Exactly as given for Sitting Thinking Bear on page 97, and a scrap of red felt for the tongue.

Method

Cut out the body (piecing the legs on to it as explained on page 62); inner arms, paws, mouth lining, footpads, ears, tongue and underbody (piecing the top end on to this as explained on page 62) as given on pages 218–21; also the head gusset as given for the Bear With a Bee on His Nose on page 211; and the outer arm, nose and eyes as given for the Sitting Thinking Bear on pages 208, 210 (25 pieces in all).

Ears

Make up and insert into head as given on page 98 for Sitting Thinking Bear.

Arms

Make up as given on page 98 for Sitting Bear but do not insert into body. Turn right side out, stuff and place on one side.

Head gusset

Work from * to * as given on page 98.

Underbody

Join this piece to the main body pieces S–M–S, then R–O on one side and R–P on the other so that there is an opening between P and Q for turning and stuffing.

Footpads

Insert these pieces into base of legs, matching letters and stitching all round S–R–S.

Stuffing

Turn right side out and stuff carefully, filling nose, "lips" and tail well. Close opening Q–O, then push in some final stuffing so that the neck is very firm. Continue closing opening O–P.

Lay the bear on his tummy and consulting the plates place the arms one on each side of body, ladder stitch them firmly in place, working twice round each one.

Nose and eyes

Make these up and attach to the bear exactly as given for Sitting Bear on pages 99–100, but have the pupils in an upward, cornerwise direction this time (Fig. 15 (9) shows a good position).

Finishing off

Embroider four brown claw divisions on each paw and foot (see page 84 and Fig. 22). Draw the head backwards a little and stitch in place with strong thread. Stitch one paw to each side of face. Slip the tongue into mouth, protruding forwards, and stitch into place. If you like, cock one leg into the air and with ladder stitch secure it in this position.

THE BEAR WITH A BEE ON HIS FOOT
Illustration Frontispiece

(The original was made in long-pile nylon, but any long-pile fur fabric is suitable.)

This entertaining creature sits "pop-eyed", licking his lips and about to pounce on the bee sitting on his foot!

Height: sitting, about 10 ins. Pattern pages 214–17.

Materials

Exactly as given for the Sitting Thinking Bear, page 97, and scraps of brown and white felt and yellow stranded cotton for the bee.

Method

Cut out the body (piecing on "seat" as described on page 62) as given on pages 216–17; the inner legs and body gusset on pages 214–15; the ears, tongue, footpads, mouth lining, paws and inner arms as given on pages 218–21, for the Bear Lying on His Tummy; head gusset as given for the Bear with a Bee on His Nose on page 211; and the eyes, nose and outer arms as given for the Sitting Thinking Bear on pages 208–10 (27 pieces in all).

Work as given for the Sitting Thinking Bear on page 98, working from † to †, but reversing the arms, i.e. placing the *right* arm with dart B at A on body pattern and the *left* arm with dart A at A on body pattern.

Nose and eyes

Work as given for Thinking Bear on page 99, but place his eyes with both pupils turned inwards and downwards so that he is staring at his foot.

Modelling

No modelling is necessary except to cross one foot over the other and stitch it securely in place.

Claws

Embroider four brown claw divisions on each paw and foot (see page 84 and Fig. 22), and stitch the tongue into mouth protruding sideways so that he is licking his lips at the thought of a tasty bee!

Make a bee (page 108), and stitch to the tip of his toe.

THE BEAR WITH A BEE ON HIS NOSE
Illustration Frontispiece

(The original was made in long, silky mohair, but any long-pile fur fabric is suitable.)

Leaning backwards to enjoy the sunshine—the peace of this bear has been disturbed by a bee settling on his nose. He is sitting very still, licking his lips and wondering what to do next!

Height: sitting, about 11 ins. Pattern pages 211–14.

Materials

Exactly as for the Bear with a Bee on His Foot, page 102.

Method

Cut out the body (piecing on the foot as described on page 62); body gusset, inner arms, paws, outer arms and head gusset as given on pages 211–14; the inner legs as given for the Bear with a Bee on His Foot on page 215; the nose and eyes as given for the Thinking Bear on page 208; the mouth lining, footpads, ears and tongue as given for the Bear Lying on His Tummy on pages 218–21 (27 pieces in all).

Work as given for The Sitting Thinking Bear on page 98, working from † to †, remembering that you are using a different pattern for his arms and when inserting these into the holes on body sides match dart A on arms with A on armholes instead of as given on page 98. This will seem an unnatural position, but if you look at the plate you will see that this bear leans backwards on his "hands"—paws flat on the ground and "hands" turned slightly outwards.

Nose and eyes

Work as given for Thinking Bear on page 99, but place the eyes in a "crossed" position, looking straight at the end of his nose.

Modelling

This bear needs quite a lot of modelling. Deal first of all with his legs, which will probably be too wide apart. Bring them a little closer together by stitching with very strong thread the top inside of the leg to the part of the body between the legs. Ideally, the "toes" should be about 6 ins. apart. Adjust the bear so that he is leaning backwards and, if necessary, stitch the inside of the arms to the side of the body about 3 ins. down from shoulder. Try to twist the head a little to one side. Make a bee and stitch it to the end of his nose (see page 108), and sew the tongue into the mouth protruding a little from one side.

THE SLEEPY BEAR
Illustration Frontispiece

(The original was made from long-pile nylon, but any long-pile fur fabric is suitable.)
This bear lies on his tummy, head turned to one side and resting on his arms. His eyes are half shut as though drifting into a lovely sleep.
Length: about 18 ins. Pattern pages 222–5.

Materials

Exactly as given for Sitting Thinking Bear on page 97, and a scrap of red felt for the tongue and fawn felt for lids.

Method

Cut out the body, head, eyelids and underbody (piecing on the end as described on page 62) as given on pages 222–5, the ears, footpads, tongue, mouth lining, inner arms and paws as given for the Bear Lying on His Tummy on pages 218–21; the nose, eyes and outer arms as given for the Sitting Thinking Bear on pages 208–10; and the head gusset as given for the Bear With a Bee on His Nose on page 211 (29 pieces in all).

Arms

Make exactly as given for the Sitting Thinking Bear on page 98. Turn right side out and stuff firmly. Place on one side.

Ears and head gusset

Work exactly as given for the Sitting Thinking Bear on page 98, but you will not have two body pieces to stitch together K–M this time—instead, stitch Q–O on neck. Turn head right way out and place on one side.

Body

Place one body side against the underbody and stitch R–P. Then place the other body side against other side of underbody and stitch R–P. Then stitch body to underbody along one leg S–T. Next stitch underbody to body along other leg S–T, then carry on stitching the two body pieces together T–N. Join U–M.

Footpads

Insert these pieces, matching letters and stitching all round R–S–R.

Neck join

Join head to body, stitching all round neck and matching letters K–U–O–P–K. Remember that the head is lying on one side (Frontispiece), so the centre back seam of head K will be in centre of neck on body at K—not as you would normally expect at U on body! (If you push the head, which has already been turned right way out, in at opening on body M–N, you can easily stitch all round the neck with the head inside the body.) Turn bear right way out by first pulling the head out through opening, then reversing each leg and the tail by pushing out with the wrong end of a pencil.

Stuffing and modelling

Stuff the bear firmly, paying particular attention to the "corners" such as nose and "lips". Very neatly close opening M–N. Look carefully at the plate for position of arms and stitch them in place so that the bear's head is resting sideways on his paws. Pin the arms to body first, so as to be sure to get them in the right place, then ladder stitch all round the top of each twice, using a long, slim darning needle and button thread. Place one foot on top of the other and stitch it in place.

Nose and eyes

Make up and attach these as given for the Sitting Thinking Bear on page 99, having the pupils and highlights to one side and slightly to the bottom. Place the lids over eyes so that these appear to be almost shut. Hem all round curved edge V–W as shown by broken line on pattern.

Embroider four claw divisions on each foot (see page 84 and Fig. 22). Add the tongue protruding forward and if necessary stitch head to arms in a "comfy" looking attitude!

MAKING A HONEY POT (Fig. 31)
Illustration Frontispiece

Materials

An empty reel (spool) from Sylko or other thread.
Scraps of yellow and white felt.
Black stranded cotton and natural coloured linen thread.

Method

1. Take an empty Sylko reel.
2. Saw off one of the wide "ends".
3. Cut a rectangle of white felt about $\frac{3}{4}$ in. × $\frac{1}{2}$ in. and using three strands of black cotton embroider "HONEY" on it.
4. Cut a strip of yellow felt to fit round the reel and stab stitch the "label" to the centre of this, rather low down.
5. Cut a circle of yellow felt to fit base of reel.
6. Place the strip round reel and oversew seam.
7. Oversew bottom circle in place.
8. Cut a circle of white felt, large enough to cover the top of the reel and hang down a little. Run a gathering thread round this at a place where it will come just under the "ridge" of the reel.
9. Put this white circle on to top of reel, pull up gathers and take a few stitches here and there all round to secure this piece to the top of the yellow strip.
10. Wind some natural coloured linen thread round top of "jar" for string.
11. Tie in a knot. If necessary trim round edge of white felt.

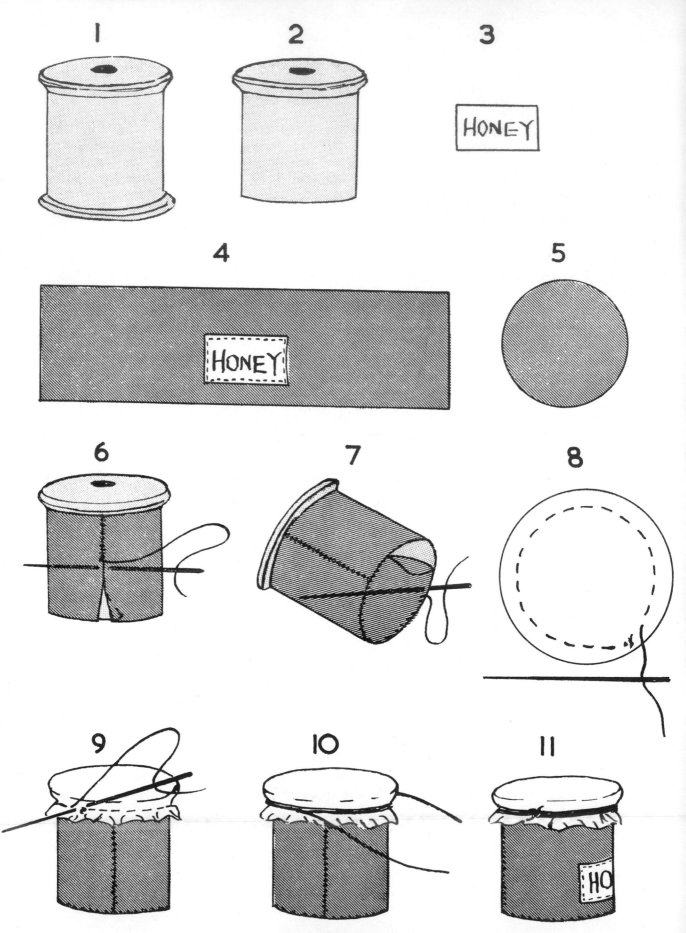

Fig. 31. Making a honey pot.

106

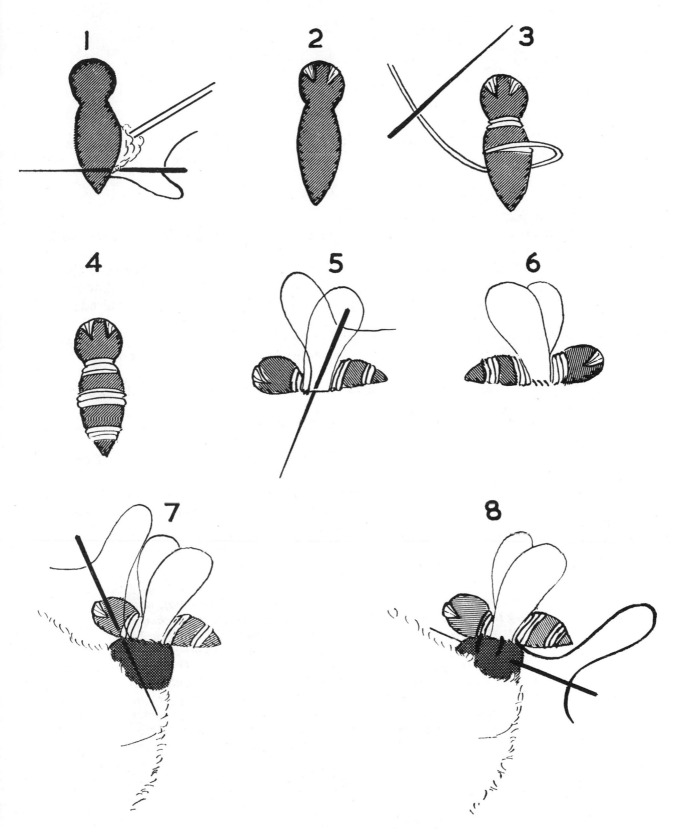

Fig. 32. Making and attaching a bee.

107

MAKING A BEE (Fig. 32)

Illustration Frontispiece

Materials

Scraps of brown and white felt.
White, yellow and black stranded cotton.
A tiny piece of kapok.

Method

Cut out the pieces as given on page 217.

1. Place the two body pieces together and oversew all round, stuffing firmly as you work.
2. Embroider two white "eyes".
3. Attach a length of yellow stranded cotton to the under part of the bee by taking a few stitches, then wind the cotton several times round the "neck" to make a yellow stripe. Take the thread farther down the body by pushing the needle through to the required place and repeat the winding.
4. Push the needle into the body again and bring it out farther down still. Wind again and then fasten off the yellow cotton securely on the under part of the bee. You now have three stripes.
5. Place a wing, curving backwards against side of body, and hem it neatly in place.
6. Hem the other wing on to the other side.
7. Stitch the bee securely to whatever part of the bear's anatomy you wish—in this case his nose!
8. With black stranded cotton take six stitches, three on each side of the body, from the bee to the bear's nose. These are the insect's legs.

Note. Be sure to have the bee's body a different shade of brown from the bear's nose or it will not show up. In case of difficulty use black felt and turn your bee into a wasp—this looks most effective.

Did you know that there is a family of five (now grown up), who every time they go to Rome return to St. Anthony's altar in the church of St. Maria-sopra-Minerva because of their childhood Teddy bear?

When they were small, the five children and their parents together with their Teddy, who was a pet of the whole family, made a long-awaited holiday-cum-pilgrimage to the Italian capital, but while there lost the bear. The children's grief was intense, but changed to joy at finding him sitting at the foot of St. Anthony's altar. He is, of course, the saint who "finds things" so the wise parents thought correctly that that would be the place he would be put if some kind person had picked him up.

Section Seven

GLOVE BEARS

These Glove Bears are completely soft and cuddly and, as such, should not be confused with puppets which have stiff linings to their necks and limbs and are designed for a theatre.

They are made to fit the hand of an adult, for their main purpose is for story-telling at bedtime, after which they can be taken off the hand and tucked up in bed to serve as a cuddly toy. A wisp of paper or a pair of socks stuffed up inside them will transform them into a sitting toy.

Again unlike a puppet—whose body is usually a plain bag—they are turned into lively animals by elastic, which draws in certain parts of each one and shapes it, and the addition of legs and feet except where a "skirt" would hide them.

Experiment has shown how useful these lively creatures can be in infants' schools and hospitals as an aid to gaining and keeping the attention of the very young and in various forms of therapy—particularly speech training.

Should you wish to make similar Glove Bears to fit a small child's hand the patterns can easily be reduced (see page 58).

Although koalas and pandas are, of course, not bears at all, the very young understandably enough always consider them as such, and because they are great favourites, they have been introduced here.

GLOVE TEDDY
Illustration Plate 15

This is a perfectly ordinary Teddy bear, but made as a glove, on the principles described at the beginning of this section. A long-pile, fawn nylon was used for the original, but he looks equally well made in a short pile material.

Pattern pages 226–9.

Materials

¼ yard long-pile, fawn nylon fur fabric 48 ins. wide. (This will not be sufficient for two bears but ½ yard will make three.)
Scraps of fawn felt for footpads and paws.
Brown and white stranded cotton for nose, mouth, eyes and claws.
Two or three large handfuls of kapok for stuffing head and legs.
An odd scrap of cotton material about 5 ins. × 3 ins. for lining head.
6 ins. or 7 ins. very narrow elastic for wrist.

Method

Cut out the pieces as given on pages 226–9, and footpads as given for the Babies' Bouncy Bears on page 204, using the fur fabric for all pieces except the footpads and paws which should be in felt (21 pieces in all).

P*

Body

Place the front and back pieces together face to face and stitch shoulder seams A–D and side seams B–E. Turn up a narrow hem all round the bottom edge, as marked on pattern, leaving a small gap into which to insert elastic later. Place on one side, still turned WRONG way out.

Arms

Neatly hem a felt paw to each inner arm where shown on pattern, then place each inner arm face to face with an outer arm and stitch all round A–C–B, leaving the short top ends open. Turn right side out and place on one side.

Legs

Place together in pairs and stitch front seam F–E and back seam H–G. Insert a felt footpad into the base of each leg, and matching letters stitch all round E–G–E. Turn right side out and place on one side.

Head and ears

Place the ears together in pairs and stitch all round R–U–T. Turn right side out and oversew R–S–T (Fig. 21 (1, 2, 3 and 5)).

On each head piece cut the slit for ears as shown on pattern. Insert an ear into each one of these, stitching it firmly from R to S on the wrong side. Then turn the rest of the ear forwards and oversew it along top of head, S–T (see Fig. 21 (6)). Join head gusset to one side of head, stitching N–O. Then join on the other side of head stitching from the other N–O. Take particular care between T and S, where you will have four thicknesses of material to stitch through. Fold end of gusset at nose end in half, so that the N's meet, and stitch R–N–Q. This gives the tip-tilted nose, and a glance at Fig. 45 will help you to see clearly how it is done.

Assembling

Turn completed head right way out and push it upside down into body (which is WRONG way out). Matching letters stitch all round Q–D–O–D–Q. Place each arm (right way out) inside the body (which is still wrong way out) and stitch each one all round A–B–A. Turn the bear right way out.

Stuffing head and lining the finger tube (Fig. 33)

1. Stuff the head very firmly, taking particular care over the nose, but all the time you are working, keep pushing two or three fingers up into the head so that there will be plenty of room for them to manipulate the bear.

2. Turn the body inside out, back over the bear's head, so that the stuffed head is upside down inside (as shown by broken lines on Fig. 33 (2)). Stitch the strip of cotton rag, hanging downwards, all round the neck.

3. Turn the rag upwards and turning in the raw edges, seam them together to make a "tube".

4. Run a gathering thread all round top edge of "tube", turning in a narrow hem as you work.

5. Pull up gathers to form a little "bag". Fasten off securely, taking several stitches through and across at this point.

6. Push this little cotton bag down into the cavity that you left when stuffing the head.

7. Turn bear right side out. The head cavity should now be neatly lined, keeping the kapok in the head and forming a convenient "finger tube" for manipulation later.

Finishing off

Stuff legs firmly and stitch each one to the front of body where shown on pattern, ladder stitching all round F–H–F. (Be careful not to stitch right through the hem at base.) Insert a piece of narrow elastic in the hem, so that it fits the wrist tightly, join ends and close opening in hem. P*

Eyes

Using dark brown stranded cotton embroider the eyes as explained on page 73 and in Fig. 13.

Nose and mouth

Embroider these as described on page 70 and in Fig. 12.

Claws

Embroider those on the feet as described on page 84 and Fig. 22, and those on the "hands" as described on page 87. C*

Tie a bright-coloured bow of ribbon round the bear's neck.

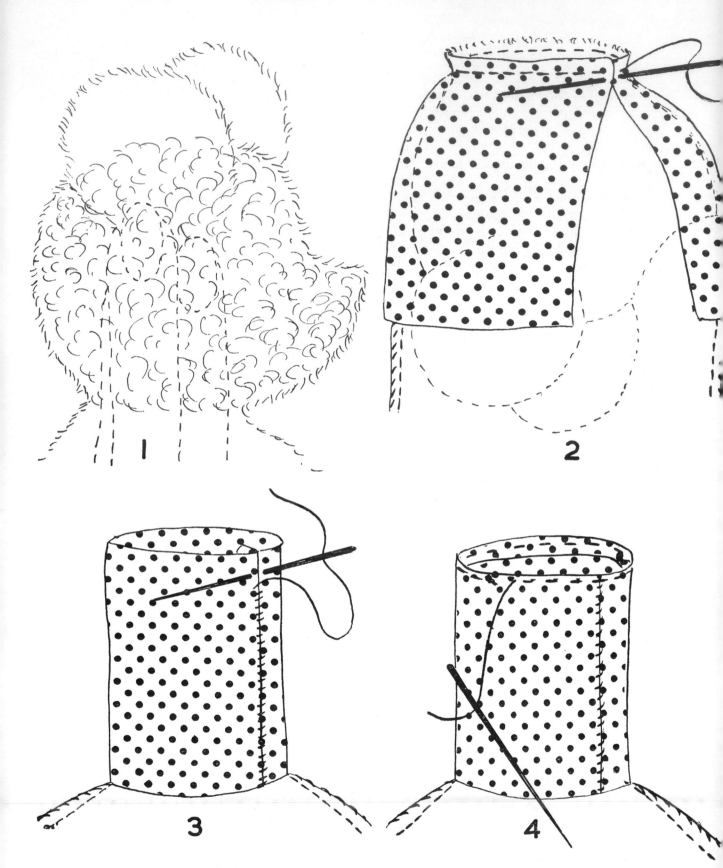

Fig. 33. Stuffing the head and lining the finger tube of a glove bear.

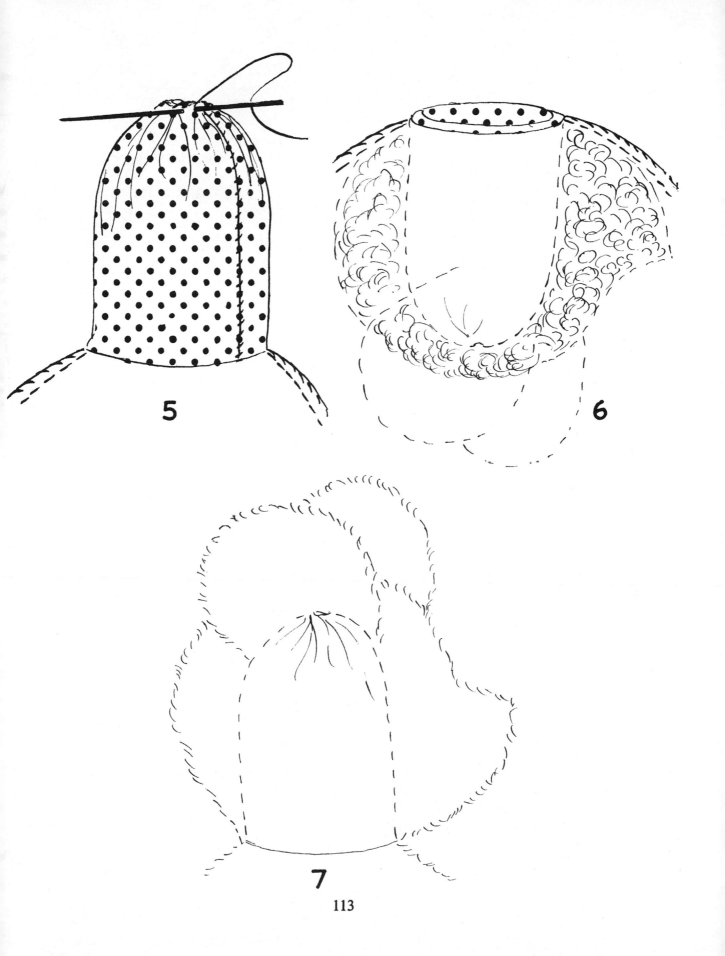

5

6

7

TEDWINA—A LITTLE GIRL GLOVE BEAR
Illustration Plate 11

This appealing person utilizes the fur fabric pieces over from the Glove Teddy on page 109—only small pieces being needed for her head and arms. The rest of her simply comprises a very full-skirted felt dress. Felt was chosen because it is strong and wears well, standing up to the wear and tear of being pulled on and off hands, but any strong cloth could be substituted, if a little more material were allowed so as to make a hem round lower edge of skirt (not necessary with felt).

In this bear the elastic is placed at the waist of the dress in order to draw it in and when the hand is placed inside the toy, comes at the base of the thumb round the widest part; there is none at the wrist. Scarlet felt, with white trimmings, gives a certain "crispness" which adds appeal.

Pattern pages 230–1.

Materials

Scraps of fawn, long-pile nylon fur fabric for head and arms.
Scraps of fawn felt for paws.
$\frac{1}{4}$ yard 36 ins. wide red felt for dress.
Scraps of white felt for collar and cuffs.
1 yard white tape $\frac{1}{2}$ in. wide for trimming dress.
Four small pearl buttons.
Brown and white stranded cotton for eyes, nose, mouth and claws.
6 ins. or 7 ins. very narrow elastic for waist of dress.
12 ins. of Prussian binding or tape for making hem for elastic.
A large handful of kapok for stuffing head.
An odd piece of cotton rag about 5 ins. $\times$ 3 ins. for lining head.

Method

Cut out the head, head gusset, ears and paws as given for the Glove Teddy on page 227; the collar, cuffs, sleeves, front and back of bodice and arms as given on pages 230–1; and a piece of red felt 36 ins. $\times$ $4\frac{1}{4}$ ins. for the skirt (24 pieces in all). If you have not a 36-in. length of felt available, several pieces may be joined. The seams will hardly show among the folds.

Head and ears

Make up as given for The Glove Teddy on page 110. Place on one side.

C*

Arms and sleeves

Place a felt paw on two of the fur fabric arms where shown on pattern and hem them neatly in place. Join an inner sleeve to each of these fur fabric arms all along X–X, making sure you reverse one of the felt pieces so as to make a "pair". Then join an outer sleeve to each of the two remaining fur fabric arms along X–X, once more making sure you reverse one of the felt pieces so as to make a "pair". Place each completed inner arm face to face with an outer arm and stitch together all round A–C–B, leaving the short ends open. Turn right side out. C*

Bodice

Place the front and the back together and on the wrong side stitch shoulder seams D–A and short side seams B–U.

Assembling

Join on head, insert sleeves and stuff head and line finger tube as given for Glove Teddy on pages 110–13.

Skirt

Machine a piece of white tape or trimming of your choice all along one long edge of the felt skirt piece about $\frac{1}{2}$ in. from the edge. Join the two short ends and seam them together. Run a gathering thread all round top edge of skirt. Pull up the gathers to fit base of bodice and fasten off securely. Placing the seam at centre back and distributing the gathers evenly, machine or backstitch the skirt to bodice on the wrong side all round U–U–U. Neatly, and so that your stitches are invisible on the right side, hem a piece of Prussian binding or tape all round lower edge of bodice. Insert a piece of elastic into this which fits the widest part of your hand *tightly* so as to pull in the waist of the bear's dress. Join the ends of the elastic and sew up the opening in the binding.

Eyes

Embroider these in dark brown stranded cotton as described on page 73 and in Fig. 13.

Nose and mouth

Embroider these as described on page 70 and in Fig. 12.

Claws on hands

Embroider these as shown in Fig. 22 and described on page 87.

Trimmings

Stitch each white collar piece round the neck, O–Q, turning upwards and having an "opening" at centre back and centre front. Turn the two pieces downwards and sew four tiny pearl buttons to the front of dress, using red Sylko for added decorative effect.

Sew a cuff to each arm where the sleeve meets the fur fabric at X–X, having the "gap" on the cuff at the lower arm seam. Sew on the cuffs while turned downwards over the fur fabric arms, then turn them up over the red felt sleeves.

If sufficient felt is available cut a strip about 1 in. × 14 ins., make it into a small bow with long flowing ends and stitch this to centre of back of dress at the waist. It gives a pleasant finish and looks like a sash, but, of course, it is not essential.

MISHKA—A BROWN GLOVE BEAR
Illustration Plate 14

Mishka is a sad-looking little brown bear of great charm. His white snout and body markings set him quite apart from the "Teddy" on page 109.
Pattern pages 232–3.

Materials

¼ yard short-pile brown nylon fur fabric 48 ins. wide.
Scraps of white fur fabric for snout and body marking.
Scraps of pinkish fawn felt for paws and footpads.
Black and white stranded cotton for nose, mouth, eyes and claws.
Two or three large handfuls of kapok for stuffing head and legs.
An odd piece of cotton rag about 5 ins. × 3 ins. for lining head.
6 ins. or 7 ins. very narrow elastic for wrist.

Method

Cut out the head, snout, head gusset, tip of gusset, body marking and lower half of front as given on pages 232–3; the ears and back of body as given for the Glove Teddy on pages 226–7; the inner and outer arms, paws, legs and footpads as given for the Glove Koala on pages 234–5 (25 pieces in all).

Preparing the pieces

C*

Join the white snouts to brown head pieces along broken lines 6–7. Place on one side.
Join the white tip of gusset to head gusset along broken lines 4–5. Place on one side. C*
Join the white body marking to brown lower half along 1–2–3. As there is a "point" involved, the easiest way to do this is to turn under a tiny hem along lower edge of white body marking. Place this on top of the brown lower half, over-lapping very slightly, and hem it in place 1–2–3. Place on one side.

Now make up exactly as given for the Glove Teddy, pages 109–13, but using black stranded cotton for eyes, nose, mouth and claws. The white markings and slightly different shaped "arms" and legs will give Mishka a totally different appearance from Teddy. A bow does not seem to suit him, but he looks well with a collar made from a watch strap or a strip of leather and a small buckle. Brass paper fasteners make decorative looking studs!

GLOVE KOALA
Illustration Plate 15

Koalas are such an extraordinary colour, being a sort of mottled greyish brown, that it is extremely difficult to find a suitable fur fabric from which to make them. Experiments showed that it was best to depart altogether from the real and accordingly a light-grey, short-pile fur fabric was used with white ear linings and pinkish-fawn paws and footpads.
Pattern pages 234–5.

Materials

¼ yard grey fur fabric 48 ins. wide.
Scraps of white fur fabric for ear linings.
Scraps of fawn felt for paws and footpads.
Scraps of black felt for nose and nose backing.
Tiny piece of grey felt for eyelids.
Pair of large brown glass eyes.
Black stranded cotton for mouth and claws.
Two or three handfuls of kapok for stuffing head and legs.
Odd piece of cotton rag about 5 ins. × 3 ins. for lining head.
6 ins. or 7 ins. of narrow elastic for wrist.

Method

Cut out all the pieces as given on pages 234–5, and the front and back of body as given for the Glove Teddy on pages 226, 229 (24 pieces in all).

Head

On each head piece cut a slit Y–Z. Run a gathering thread along X–Z and pull it up tightly so that X matches Y. Oversew, then backstitch Y–Z. This will give the koala his typical "puffy" cheeks. Sew one side of head to head gusset N–O. Then join on other side in the same way. Join under chin gusset to both sides of head N–Q. Turn right side out and place on one side.

Ears

Place together in pairs, a white with a grey, and stitch all round L–M–N. Turn right side out and ladder stitch L–N (Fig. 21 (1, 2, 3 and 4)). Place on one side.

Make up *Body*, *Arms* and *Legs* as given for Glove Teddy on page 110.

Assembling and stuffing head and finger tube

Work as given for Glove Teddy on pages 110–13.

Finishing off

Work as given for Glove Teddy on page 111.

Nose

Gather all round extreme edge of black felt nose; pull up those gathers so that they fit the nose backing and fasten them off. Stuff the nose firmly and stab stitch stuffed nose to backing. Placing N on nose to N on head gusset, hem securely to centre of face.

Eyes

Make two eyelids as described on page 82 and Fig. 20, and insert eyes as described on page 77 and Fig. 17, being very careful not to take threads through centre finger tube where they will get in the way.

Ears

Sew on as described on page 82 and Fig. 17 (7 and 8), consulting Fig. 34 for position.

Mouth

Consulting Fig. 34 embroider mouth—a rather "goofy"-looking one, in black stranded cotton, using stem stitch.

Claws

Embroider claws on feet and "hands" as described on page 87 and Fig. 22, using black stranded cotton.

Fig. 34. Head of glove koala.

GLOVE PANDA

No illustration s given for this toy as he will obviously look exactly like Peter the Little Boy Panda (Plate 13), but as with the Glove Teddy and Koala he has no clothes.
Pattern pages 236–7.

Materials

¼ yard black fur fabric (or a large number of small pieces) for the ears, eye patches, arms, legs and markings on the back and front of body.
¼ yard white fur fabric (or large scraps) for the head, head gusset and body.
Scraps of white fur fabric for the head and head gusset.
Scraps of black felt for paws, footpads and eyes.
Black stranded cotton for nose and mouth.
White stranded cotton for claws and highlights.
Two or three handfuls of kapok for stuffing head and legs.
An odd piece of cotton rag about 5 ins × 3 ins. for lining head.

Method

Cut out the head and head gusset in white fur fabric, the ears, legs, inner and outer arms in black fur fabric and the paws in black felt all as given for the Glove Teddy on pages 227–8; the footpads in black felt as given for the Babies' Bouncy Bear on page 204; the eye patches and eyes as given for Peter on page 238; the front, back and white V-shaped marking (shown by broken lines) in white fur fabric, and the markings for back and front in black fur fabric, as given on pages 236–7 (30 pieces in all).

Preparing the body

Back. Join black marking to lower white piece all along broken lines B–B. Turn a tiny hem back down the two pointed side of the V-shaped white piece and hem it invisibly in place where shown by broken line on pattern. Oversew this piece to the black base along D–O–D.
Front. Join black marking to lower white piece along broken lines B–B.
Now make up the panda exactly as given for the Glove Teddy on pages 110–11, working from P* to P*.

Nose, mouth, eyes and claws

Work exactly as given for Peter the Little Boy Panda on pages 121–2.
Tie a bow of brightly coloured ribbon round the panda's neck.

PETER—A LITTLE BOY GLOVE PANDA
Illustration Plate 13

This "humanized" glove panda is a good way of using up scraps of black and white fur fabric which you may have had over from the large jointed Panda on page 143. Small pieces of various coloured felt can also be utilized for his shirt and trousers.

Pattern page 238.

Materials

Scraps of black fur fabric for the ears, eye patches, arms and legs.
Scraps of white fur fabric for the head and head gusset.
Scraps of black felt for paws, footpads and eyes.
Scraps of white felt for collar, cuffs and eyes.
Small pieces of orange felt for shirt.
One 9-in. square of yellow felt for trousers and braces.
Black stranded cotton for nose and mouth.
White stranded cotton for highlights and claws.
Twelve small pearl buttons for trimming.
Two or three handfuls of kapok for stuffing head and legs.
An odd piece of cotton rag about 5 ins. × 3 ins. for lining head.
Two pieces of narrow elastic for wrist and waist each 6–7 ins. long.
A piece of Prussian binding or tape 12 ins. long for making hem for elastic.

Method

Cut out the head and head gusset in white fur fabric, the ears and legs in black fur fabric and the paws in black felt, all as given for the Glove Teddy on pages 227–8; the footpads in black felt as given for the Babies' Bouncy Bear on page 204; the arms in black fur fabric, inner and outer sleeves in orange felt, collar and cuffs in white felt, front and back of bodice in orange felt, all as given for Tedwina on pages 230–1; also the eye patches, eyes and trousers as given on page 238, and two strips of yellow felt 8½ ins. × ½ in. for the braces (39 pieces in all).

Make up the **Arms** and **Sleeves**, and the **Bodice** as given for Tedwina on pages 114–15.

Make up the **Head** and **Ears** as given for Glove Teddy on page 110.

Assembling

Join on head, insert arms and stuff head and line finger tube as given for Glove Teddy on pages 110–13.

Trousers

Join side seams U–E, and turn up a hem all round lower edge as shown on pattern, leaving a small gap to insert elastic later.

Join trousers to shirt (bodice) all round waist U–U–U, on the wrong side and while you have the work this way out stitch a piece of Prussian binding or tape all round lower edge of shirt for inserting elastic later.

Legs

Make up as given for Glove Teddy on page 110, and stuff and sew to front of trousers as given under "Finishing Off" on page 111. But do not insert elastic yet.

Nose and mouth

Using black stranded cotton embroider these as described on page 70 and Fig. 12.

Eyes

Turn a tiny hem back, all round each black eye patch, so as to get rid of the raw edges, and tack it invisibly in place. Consulting Plate 13 and Fig. 35, neatly hem one of these to each side of face. Place each black pupil on top of a white eye piece, to one side and stitch in place, embroider two white highlights. Stitch to eye patches as explained on page 99 and Fig. 30 D, E and F, but of course the eyes have no brown on them.

Fig. 35. Head of Peter the glove panda.

Braces

Neatly hem or backstitch the braces in place, starting one at each side of front where shirt and trousers join, and crossing them at centre back. Sew a tiny pearl button at each of the four points where the braces and trousers meet, and eight down centre front of shirt.

Collar and cuffs

Sew these in place as described under "Trimmings" for Tedwina on page 115. In this case the buttons will of course be already in place.

Claws

Using white stranded cotton embroider claws on feet as described on page 84 and Fig. 22, and on "hands" as described on page 87.

Elastic

Insert one piece of elastic in Prussian binding at waist, so as to bring this in. Join ends and close "gap". Insert the second piece of elastic in the hem at base of trousers. Join ends and close "gap". When the hand is inserted one piece will come at the base of your thumb where your hand is widest and one at your wrist—both should fit tightly!

GLOVE CIRCUS BEAR
Illustration Plate 14

This is useful toy for using up small pieces of fur fabric and felt, and almost any colour will do. The original was a brown bear with white snout and a grey and orange tunic.
Pattern pages 239–40.

Materials

Scraps of brown fur fabric for head, "hands" and feet.
Scraps of white fur fabric for the snout.
Scraps of fawn felt for paws and footpads.
Two 9-in. squares of grey and two of orange felt for the tunic and sleeves (or several odd
    pieces including some at least 8 ins. × 3¼ ins.).
Scrap of white felt for the hat.
Odd pieces of organdie or similar material for ruffs and bias binding for trimming.
A few "bobbles" from lampshade fringe.
Black and white stranded cotton for nose, eyes and claws.
A piece of elastic 6 or 7 ins. long for wrist.
Two or three handfuls of kapok for stuffing head and legs.
A piece of cotton rag about 5 ins. × 3 ins. for head lining.

Method

Cut out the head and head gusset in brown fur fabric and the snout and tip of head gusset in white fur fabric as given for Mishka on page 233; the ears in brown fur fabric, and the paws in fawn felt as given for the Glove Teddy on page 227; the arms in brown fur fabric, an inner and an outer sleeve in grey and one each in orange felt as given for

Tedwina on page 231; the backs and fronts as given on page 240; the footpads in fawn felt as given for the Glove Koala on page 235; and the feet and trouser legs as given on page 239 (34 pieces in all).

Preparation of body

Place the orange and grey back pieces together and on the wrong side join O–X. (Hardly any turning is necessary on felt.) Then join the orange and grey front pieces Q–X.

Head

Prepare the head pieces as given for Mishka on page 116, working from C* to C*. Place on one side.

Arms and sleeves

Make up these pieces as given for Tedwina on page 114, working from C* to C*. Place on one side.

Preparing legs

On the wrong side join a felt trouser leg to each foot along 1–2. (Making one pair grey and one pair orange.) Place on one side.

Body, arms, legs, head and ears, assembling, stuffing head and lining finger tube, finishing off, eyes, nose and mouth, claws

Work as given for the Glove Teddy on pages 110–11, starting at P* and finishing at C* but use black stranded cotton for the features instead of brown.

Hat

Make a clown's hat, stuff it and sew at a jaunty angle to head. (Instructions for hat, page 195.) Decorate this and the front of tunic with bobbles from lamp shade fringe or pompoms made from scraps of coloured fur fabric (as shown in Plate 14) exactly like the balls in Fig. 72 (1 and 2), using an egg cup to draw the circles.

Ruff

Make a ruff for the neck about 1½ ins. wide and one for each wrist about ¾ in. wide. Ruffs can be added to the ankles too, if liked. (Instructions for ruff, page 195.)

Did you know that of approximately 400,000 articles "lost" on London Transport vehicles each year about 250 are Teddy bears?

The Staff of the Lost Property office are human enough to notice that each bear on their shelves looks different, the more tattered the bear, the more doleful the look on its face. Happily, there are many joyful reunions but bears unclaimed for three months suffer the indignity of of being lotted with other soft toys and sold by public auction.

TRADITIONAL JOINTED TEDDY BEARS

The bears in this section are traditional and have been a "legend" with children since they first appeared on the market about sixty years ago. The design of an ordinary jointed "Teddy" has changed very little over the years, apart from the fact that they no longer have the rather ugly humped back of their ancestors.

All the bears in this section have a movable head and limbs. It is very important to see that these are very tight on a newly made toy, for they always wear looser during play. The eyes are of glass or plastic and if correctly inserted (see page 77) should be perfectly secure and run no risk of coming out. Gone are the bad old days when glass eyes on a spike were merely stuck into the head like a pin and secured with a dab of glue—wonderful, shiny objects which could easily be pulled out and as easily swallowed, complete with their spike of wire!

To keep to tradition noses and mouths are embroidered, but of course there is no reason why the individual worker should not use felt eyes and noses, adapting patterns given for the Honey Bears in Section VI.

Ears are sewn on after stuffing, to cover the knots holding the eyes in place. However, if preferred, they can be inserted into the head gusset and a slit, as given for the Honey Bears in Section VI, and the knots can be hidden in the "fold" of the ear.

After babyhood and right through childhood these bears are the "useful" ones, for being able to sit or lie in many attitudes they take the place of or intermingle with dolls and become part of every child's "family". Four sizes ranging from 2 ft. to 6 ins. are given, so that every worker can make the bear of her choice or perhaps embark on creating several generations.

THE TECHNIQUES OF JOINTING

Jointed Teddy bears, that is, those with a movable head and limbs, often frighten the needlewoman because they appear complicated. Naturally, they are more complicated than the simple washable bears, but they are not difficult to make if the mechanism and purpose of all parts of the joint set are thoroughly understood.

Plate 10 shows an X-ray of a jointed bear, illustrating the position of the joints and their purpose. It will be clearly seen that one disc is inserted into the base of the head and one into the top of each limb. A cotter pin is passed through a hole in these discs, through the fur fabric of the head or limb, then through the fur fabric of the body and through a hole in another disc, the ends then being tightly turned so that they form a spring to press the limb and body tightly together. All this being done, of course, while the body is still empty.

The act of turning the cotter pin successfully is a knack more than anything else and

124

once it has been achieved is never forgotten—rather like riding a bicycle! One knows automatically when the joint is tight, without even feeling it, and with a little practice most people can soon turn a pin with the pulling and twisting movement essential for the long life of the toy.

There are various types of joint sets on the market, obtainable from most good handicraft shops (postal addresses are given on page 68) and they are made in various sizes. It is important to choose a size which fits the head and limbs of the toy in question, or the parts will wobble badly. For all the bears in this book, suitable sizes are given under the materials list, but it would not matter if *slightly* smaller or larger discs were substituted.

TYPES OF JOINT SETS

Wooden joint sets (Fig. 36 (1))

These consist of two wooden discs, two small metal washers and a cotter pin. One small washer is needed to thread on to the pin first of all in order to hold it in place and avoid the possibility of the pin pulling right through the wooden disc—(an infuriating accident which sometimes happens and necessitates a lot of undoing and doing up again). The second one is only useful for protecting the wood round the hole on the disc in the body, and is better replaced by a larger one if available—a pot mender would be ideal. This protects the rather soft wood and prevents the end of the pin "digging in" and thus wearing it—however, this is not essential, and if you have no large washer just use the small one.

These wooden sets are usually sold with the cotter pin through the holes and bent backwards (as in Fig. 36 (1)). By the time you have straightened the pin in order to get it out, it is often bent, weakened and beyond using. It is therefore a good idea to keep a box of cotter pins by you as replacements, and as those provided with the wooden discs are often too short to turn correctly, buy your extra ones a little longer. Those used for the original Teddy bears were $1\frac{1}{4}$ ins. $\times \frac{7}{84}$ in mild steel; they are obtainable from any ironmongers (hardware stores) by the dozen, or a box of a gross costs very little. If not in stock ask for them to be ordered.

Metal joint sets (Fig. 36 (2))

These are usually sold packed in small transparent envelopes—a good way to buy them as the cotter pin is new and straight! They consist of two cardboard discs, two metal discs the same size (for extra strength) and a cotter pin.

Extra large joint sets (Fig. 36 (3, 4 and 5))

It is almost impossible to buy very large joint sets, like those needed for the large bear on page 133, the largest generally obtainable being $1\frac{3}{4}$ ins. in diameter. If you have a handyman about the house it is a simple matter for him to cut circles of hardboard or plywood for you, in any size required, and to drill a hole in the middle (Fig. 36 (5)). If this is not possible, use plywood bases sold for cane work (Fig. 36 (3))—3 in. circular ones being very suitable for the large Teddy on page 133. (Addresses on page 68.) These have holes punched all round the edge to hold the cane, but ignore them. You will need to drill a hole through the centre for your cotter pin. For these large discs, very long, strong pins are needed, the best size being $\frac{1}{8}$ in. diameter $\times$ $2\frac{1}{2}$ ins. long in mild steel (Fig. 36 (4)).

1. WOODEN JOINT SET.

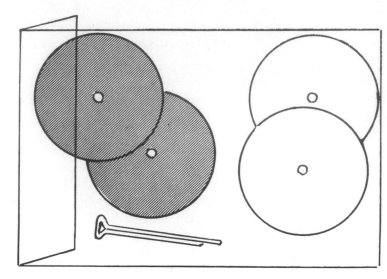

2. METAL JOINT SET.

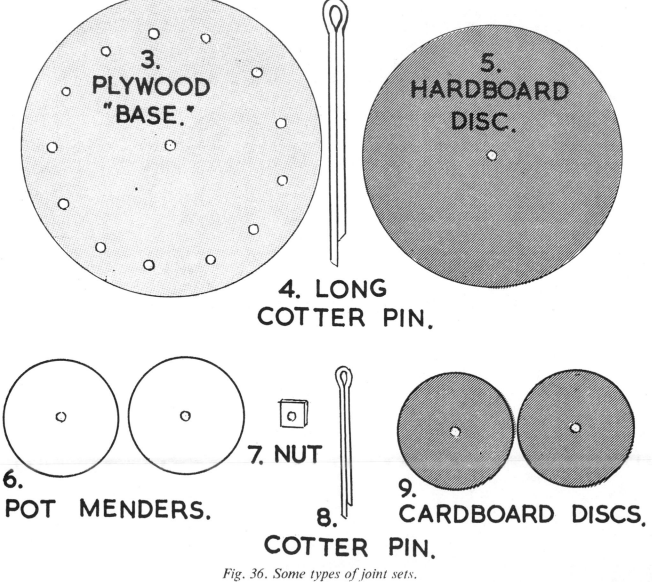

3. PLYWOOD "BASE."

4. LONG COTTER PIN.

5. HARDBOARD DISC.

6. POT MENDERS.

7. NUT

8. COTTER PIN.

9. CARDBOARD DISCS.

Fig. 36. Some types of joint sets.

Some home made substitutes (Fig. 36 (6, 7, 8 and 9))

As with the large joint sets, the smaller metal and wooden ones can also be substituted by cheaper versions. Plywood or hardboard discs may be cut and substituted for the bought wooden variety—while pot menders (Fig. 36 (6)) can be substituted for the metal ones. Unfortunately, pot menders are getting more and more difficult to obtain, their uses in this modern day and age being rather restricted. If you do find some in the shops (try Woolworths) they are usually sold on a card, each one consisting of six sets of discs, one large which serves for the head of the bear and five small, four of which do for the limbs. You will have one over. They are fixed to the card with tiny nuts and bolts—the nuts (Fig. 36 (7)) serving beautifully as washers! You will need to cut your own cardboard discs (Fig. 36 (9)) to strengthen these rather flimsy metal ones and to buy some cotter pins (Fig. 36 (8)). This is much cheaper and just as successful as buying prepared joint sets as long as the sizes are suitable for your bear but, of course, it is more bother!

Modern shop assistants seem astonished that anyone should want to buy pot menders these days and on one occasion the author's young son, sent to buy thirty-six cards of them from a multiple store, for use by a class of physically handicapped people, could hardly get out of the shop because of the curiosity of the staff. "What on earth do you want them for?" they eventually asked quite openly and as he made a hasty exit the small boy (infuriated by their "noseyness" as he afterwards explained), said airily: "Oh! my mother is going to turn all our sieves into saucepans!"

Preparing the discs

Whichever sort of joints you use it will be necessary to cut some circles of leather (old gloves, chamois leather or felt scraps are very suitable), slightly larger than the wooden or metal discs in question. These will be placed outside the hard discs, directly against the fur fabric body of the bear, and because they are larger than the hard ones, will roll over the edges and soften and mask them so that the wood or metal will neither wear the toy by constant movement, nor will be felt from the outside of toy (see Fig. 37).

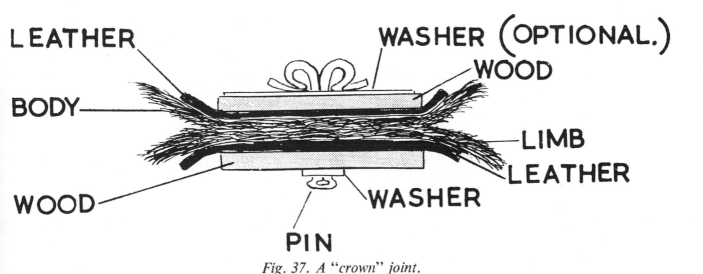

Fig. 37. A "crown" joint.

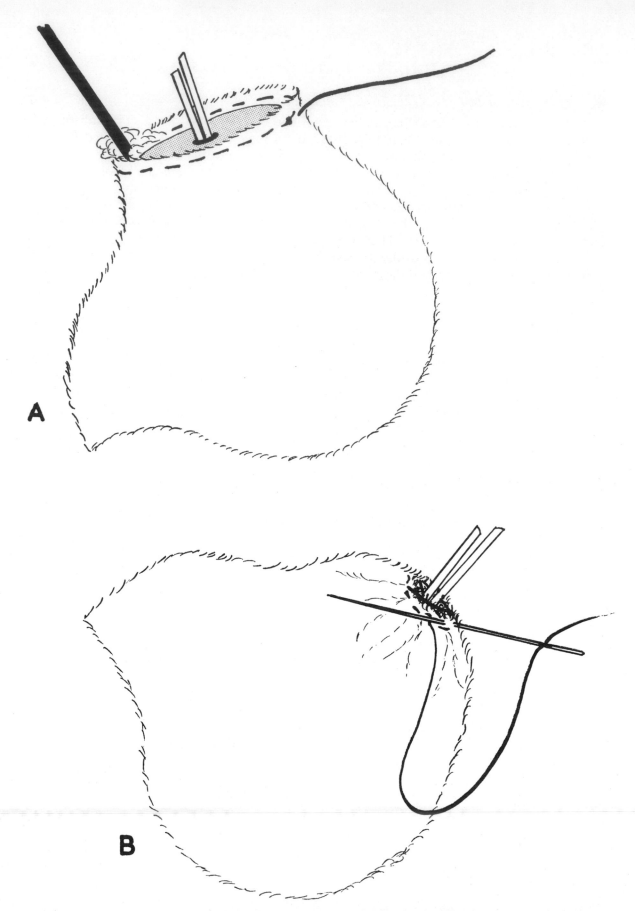

Fig. 38. Inserting the disc into a Teddy bear's head.

12 Goldilocks and the Three Bears.
(Reproduced in color on the cover.)

METHODS OF JOINTING

In the diagrams which follow, wooden discs were used. If you use metal ones remember that you will also need a cardboard circle for extra strength.

Jointing a head (Figs. 38 A and B, and 39)

Thread the appropriate size metal washer, wooden disc then leather disc on to the cotter pin, place upside down inside neck opening of stuffed head. Pack stuffing very carefully all round the *edge* of disc, so that no hardness can be felt from the outside (Fig. 38 A). Do not place any on *top* of the disc as this must be kept very flat. Pull up gathering thread and check that there are no empty "hollows" in the head, especially at nape of neck and beneath nose. If there are, loosen thread, remove disc and fill up any gaps carefully, using small pieces of kapok pushed among the wood wool. The head must be very firm, although there is no need for it to be heavy. When you are satisfied with it, fasten off the gathering thread very securely, taking stitches across and round the pin (Fig. 38 B), but not between the split ends. Push the pin through the hole formed by the gathers at top of body, thread on a leather disc, then a wooden one and if you have it, a large metal washer. Pull the body of the bear in all directions to make sure there are no double folds or "pleats" of material between the discs. Turn the bear upside down, standing on its head on a table and with SMALL snipe or round nosed pliers, grasp one end of the pin LOW DOWN and pulling upwards and outwards turn it away from you into the shape shown in Fig. 37. The bent cotter pin forms a "spring" and holds the head tightly in position. Turn the bear round and pull and twist the other half of the pin away from you and into a corresponding position (Fig. 37). Now try to move the joints; they should be so tight that it is difficult to do so, as they will inevitably wear looser in play. A Teddy bear with loose floppy limbs and a wobbly head is no fun to play with and will not sit up nicely. If your joint is loose, undo it, even if it means unpicking the head as well, to insert a new pin. It's well worth it. If you experience real difficulty try making a "sampler" by jointing two pieces of material together as shown by Fig. 37, keep undoing it and repeating the process until you have the knack. This is called a "crown" joint, because the shape of the turned pins resembles the top of a crown!

Some hints on jointing

1. Remember above all, to pull UPWARDS very hard all the time you are turning.
2. A pin merely bent like Fig. 36 (1) is *quite* useless, the limb cannot be made secure and will soon come off.
3. It must turn right in and touch the base of the cotter pin where this emerges from the hole as in Fig. 37 to give a good spring.
4. A second method of turning a pin is the "spiral" shown in Fig. 40. Some people find this difficult but sometimes it happens quite by accident when a "crown" joint is being attempted! If so, and if the discs are tight, leave it, it should be quite satisfactory.
5. It is unnecessary and a waste of time to aim at sharp angles when turning pins—indeed, it weakens them. Firm, round curves are simpler and stronger.

Jointing an arm or leg (Fig. 41)

Take the limb, partially stuffed. On to the cotter pin thread a small metal washer, the appropriate size wooden disc, and the larger leather disc. Push the cotter pin through the

Fig. 39. Sectional drawing of a head jointed to body.

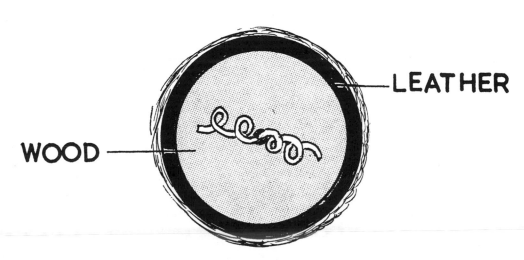

Fig. 40. A "spiral" joint.

130

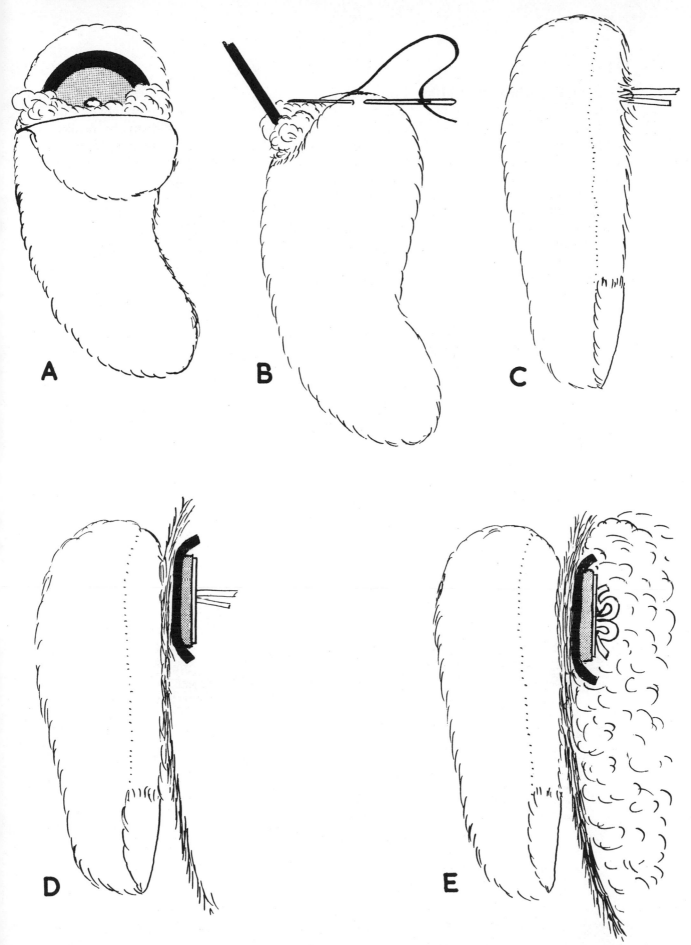

Fig. 41. Jointing a limb to a body.

INSIDE of arm where marked by X on pattern (Fig. 41 A). Stuff the top of limb firmly, using kapok, and start to ladder stitch opening (Fig. 41 B). Just before completely closing check to see that the limb is nicely rounded on the top, and that the hard discs are masked and padded so that they cannot be felt from the outside. If necessary push in more stuffing. Finish ladder stitching opening (Fig. 41 C). The limb should be completely flat on the inside, where it will press against the body, but well rounded on the outside.

Prepare the corresponding limb in the same way—making sure you have a *pair*, i.e. that both pins emerge on the INSIDE. Check, too, that the limbs are the same length from the pin to tip of paw, or toe, and from the pin to top of limb. Do not follow blindly the position marked by the X on the second limb, for if you have taken a slightly larger or smaller turning on the seams your limb will not match the first one exactly, and the position for inserting the pin may need adjusting. Push the pin of a completed limb through the bear's body at the appropriate X and slip on to it a leather disc, then a wooden one, and if you have it a large metal washer (Fig. 41 D). Turn the pin in exactly the same way as described under "Jointing a head" on page 129 (Fig. 41 E). Joint on the other three limbs in the same way, making quite sure they are level. If necessary, adjust the position of the X's for your own particular bear or you may find you have crooked "shoulders" or one leg longer than the other.

Note. It is easier to joint on first the head, then the arms and lastly the legs. In this order they get less in the way of each other than they otherwise would.

Extra padding for joints (Fig. 42)

It is sometimes difficult to place and keep the stuffing exactly round a joint so as to completely mask it, and the following method may perhaps be a help to those who experience this trouble.

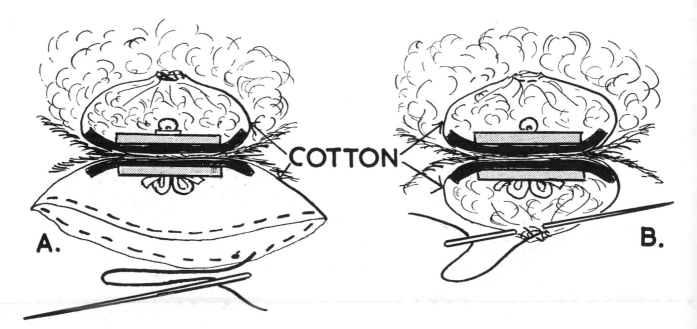

Fig. 42. A useful method of securing sufficient padding round discs.

Cut a large circle of some thin material such as cotton or silk, and when threading the discs on to the cotter pin, thread this between the leather disc and fur fabric of the limb. Pad all round the disc very carefully, then gather round the edge of the cotton circle and pull up tightly—this will enclose the stuffing and keep the joint firmly embedded. Then finish off stuffing in the normal way and push pin into the body. Thread another circle of material on to the pin inside the body before threading on the leather and wooden discs.

Turn the pin and after making sure it is quite tight, gather round the cotton, stuff all round the discs and pull up the gathers, just as you did inside the limb. Finish off the bear in the usual way.

Note. Always use strong discs, strong but flexible cotter pins and *small*-nosed pliers and you cannot go far wrong. $\frac{1}{8}$ in. in diameter is quite large enough for the nose of your pliers —if thicker you cannot possibly turn the pin properly.

LARGE JOINTED TEDDY BEAR

Illustration Plate 9

Height: about 2 ft. Pattern pages 244–51. *Weight:* about $2\frac{1}{4}$ lb.

Materials

$\frac{1}{2}$ yard long-pile fur fabric 48 ins. wide. (With careful cutting a miniature jointed bear can also be cut from this. Layout plan Fig. 43 A and B.)

One 9-in. square matching felt for paws and pads.

One pair "extra large" brown glass eyes (14 mm.).

Ten wooden or hardboard discs $2\frac{1}{2}$ ins.–3 ins. diameter.

Five extra large cotter pins $\frac{1}{8}$ in. diameter × $2\frac{1}{2}$ ins. long.

Kapok and wood wool for filling.

Black stranded cotton for nose and claw markings.

Note. See page 132 for stuffing technique and page 125 for these extra large joints.

Method

Cut out the pieces as given on pages 244–51, following the smooth outer lines for this size bear (21 pieces in all). Mark all ✳'s on the wrong side.

†Body

Place the two pieces together and join back and front seams A–B and C–D. Run a gathering thread all round the top A–D (Fig. 44 A). Pull up tightly (Fig. 44 B) and secure with a series of strong stitches going over and over and backwards and forwards through the gathers (Fig. 44 C). Turn right side out and place on one side.

Legs

Place the legs together in pairs and join front seams E–F and back seams G–H. Insert felt footpads, matching E and G, and sew all round. Turn right side out and stuff as far as opening, using a little kapok in the toes, then filling up with wood wool (see page 65). Place on one side.

Fig. 43. Layout plan for cutting one large and one miniature jointed Teddy bear from ½ yard 48 ins. wide material.

A. With the pile running DOWN *the material.*

B. With the pile running ACROSS *the material (opposite page).*

A

134

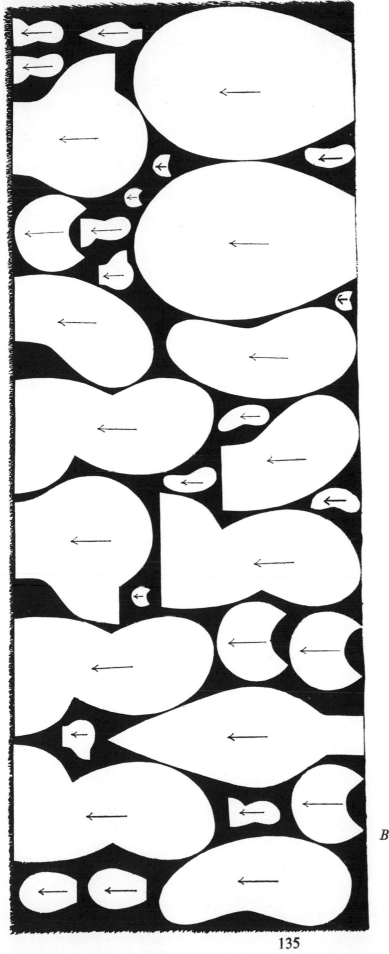

B

135

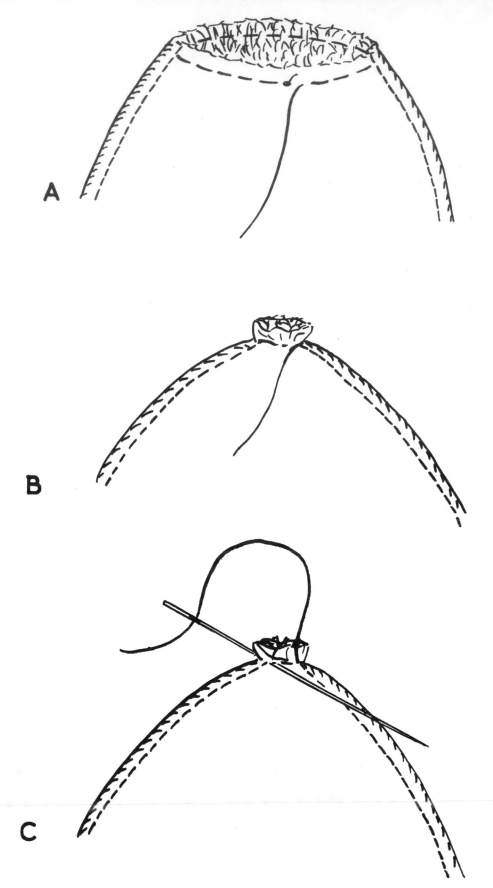

Fig. 44. Preparing the top of the body of a Teddy bear for jointing.

Arms

Join a felt paw to each inner arm, matching letters and stitching M–N. Then place one of these completed pieces on top of each outer arm and stitch together all round H–J–I. Turn right side out and stuff as far as opening. Place on one side.

Ears

Place the ears together in pairs and sew all round O–P–Q. Turn right side out and ladder stitch opening O–Q, making quite sure the raw edges are neatly turned in. Place on one side.†

Head

Join the two head pieces to the head gusset from E past L to F on both sides. Fold the gusset at E–K–E so that the E's meet and stitch front seam K–E–G. This fold gives the tip-tilted effect to the nose (Fig. 45). Run a strong gathering thread all round the neck F–G–F (Fig. 45) and turn right side out leaving the thread hanging. Stuff head very firmly, taking particular care to get the nose solid right to the tip by inserting small pieces of kapok before filling up with wood wool. Place on one side.

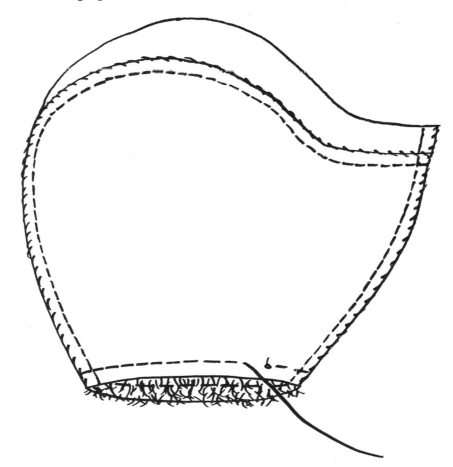

Fig. 45. Folding a head gusset to make a tip-tilted nose.

***Assembling

Using the extra large discs and cotter pins described on page 125, joint head to body as described on page 129 and Figs. 37, 38 and 39, pushing the cotter pin through the hole at top of body formed by gathering all round A–D: Next, pushing the cotter pins through ✳'s on patterns, joint first the arms, then the legs to the body as described on page 129 and Fig. 41. Make quite sure they are all *really* tight, so that it is quite difficult to move them. If one limb is at all loose it is worth while undoing it and starting all over again, even if it means taking the discs out of the limb in order to insert a new cotter pin. (It is rarely possible to straighten a pin sufficiently to use it again once it has been turned.)

Stuff the body *very* firmly, taking particular care over the shoulders, and making sure they are firmly "square" and well filled. Check that the legs and arms are level with each other and that they point forwards—towards the fat tummy A–B. Close opening between legs B–C, using strong thread and ladder stitch.

Nose

Clip a little pile away from the nose and mouth position (if you feel it is too long and will get in the way of your stitches). Embroider nose and mouth following Fig. 12 and working right over point formed by K on head gusset.***

Claws

Embroider four long strokes on back of each paw and four on each foot (Fig. 22 and page 84).

Eyes and ears

Prepare the eyes (Fig. 16) and insert (Fig. 17 and pages 77–80) roughly on the gusset seam 2½ ins. from tip of nose.

There can be no hard and fast rule for this, so experiment to see which is the best position for *your* bear. To make sure he looks pleasant, keep them *very* low down and wide apart. Ensure that they are tightly inserted and the shanks completely buried inside the head. Sew on the ears by ladder stitching in a curve first along the front of each one, then along the back. The ears will cover the knots attaching the eyes. If you think the ears stick up too much and therefore look too large, flatten them a little by stitching the backs to the head. It is well worth taking time and trouble over these details so as to get them just right, or you will never be really fond of your bear.

MEDIUM SIZE JOINTED TEDDY BEAR
Illustration Plate 9

Height: about 18 ins. Pattern pages 244–51. *Weight:* about 1 lb.

Materials

⅜ yard long-pile fur fabric 48 ins. wide (three miniature jointed bears can also be cut from this).
One 9-in. square matching felt for paws and pads.
One pair large brown glass eyes (12 mm.).

Five large joint sets (1¾ ins.).
Kapok and wood wool for filling.
Black stranded cotton for nose and claw markings.

Method

Cut out the pieces as given on pages 244–51, following the inner broken lines for this size bear (21 pieces in all).

Make up exactly as given for the large jointed bear on page 133, except that the eyes should be placed approximately 2 ins. from the tip of nose.

SMALL JOINTED TEDDY BEAR
Illustration Plate 9

Height: about 12 ins. Pattern pages 242–3. *Weight:* about 6 ozs.

Materials

¼ yard long-pile fur fabric 48 ins. wide. (This quantity will make two bears—layout plan, Fig. 46.)
Scraps of matching felt for paws and pads.
One pair medium brown glass eyes (10 mm.).
Five medium-size joint sets (1¼ ins.).
Kapok and wood wool for filling.
Black stranded cotton for nose and claw markings.

Method

Cut out the body, legs, outer arms, inner arms and paws as given on pages 242–3; and the head, head gusset, footpads and ears, as given for the Bouncy Bear on pages 204–5 (21 pieces in all).

Make up the body, legs and arms exactly as given for the Large Jointed Bear on pages 133, 137. Place on one side.

Ears

Place the pieces together in pairs and sew all round L–M–N. Turn right side out and ladder stitch opening L–N, making quite sure the raw edges are neatly turned in. Place on one side.

Head

Join the two head pieces to the head gusset N–O. Join short seam O–P. Fold the gusset at N–R–N so that the N's meet and stitch R–N–Q. This fold gives the tip-tilted effect to the nose (Fig. 45). Run a strong gathering thread all round the neck (Fig. 45) Q–P–Q and turn right side out, leaving the thread hanging. Stuff head very firmly, taking particular care to get the nose solid right to the tip by inserting small pieces of kapok before filling up the rest of the head with wood wool. Place on one side.

Assembling

Work exactly as given for the Large Jointed Bear on page 138. If preferred all kapok may be used for this bear as he is so small, and the wood wool omitted altogether.

Nose, claws, eyes and ears

Work exactly as given for the Large Jointed Bear on page 138, but place the eyes about 1¼ ins. from the tip of the nose.

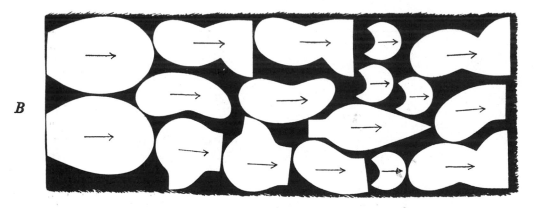

Fig. 46. Layout plan for cutting a small jointed bear from a piece of material 9 ins. × 24 ins. i.e. ¼ yard material cut in half widthwise). A. With the pile running DOWN the material. B. With the pile running ACROSS the material.

MINIATURE JOINTED TEDDY BEAR
Illustration Plate 9

Height: about 6 ins. Pattern page 242. *Weight:* about 2 ozs.

Materials

Odd scraps of fur fabric over from other bears—only very small pieces are needed.
Scraps of matching felt for paws and pads.
One pair small brown glass eyes (7 mm.).
Five very small joint sets ($\frac{5}{8}$ in.).
Kapok for stuffing.
Black stranded cotton for nose and claws.

Note. Small joint sets are obtainable in metal. Address page 68.

Method

Cut out the pieces as given on page 242 (21 pieces in all).
Make up the body, legs, ears and head exactly as given for the Large Jointed Bear on page 133 and place on one side.

Arms

Place a felt paw on a pair of the arm pieces in position shown by broken line on pattern and hem neatly in place. Now place each one of these on one of the other arm pieces and stitch all round H–J–I. Turn right side out and stuff as far as opening. Place on one side.

Assembling, nose, claws, eyes and ears

Work exactly as given for Large Jointed Bear on page 138, but use all kapok for stuffing and place eyes about $\frac{3}{4}$ in. from tip of nose.

Note. A small, white, jointed Teddy bear of a slightly different design will be found in *Modern Soft Toy Making.*

Did you know that not far from Ashridge in Hertfordshire a Teddy bear with a bullet in his chest is preserved in a glass case by a grateful mother?

The culprit was almost certainly a poacher who fired without any idea that he was near a garden in which was a baby in a pram cuddling a Teddy bear. The shot was spent and had just enough force to penetrate the Teddy's outer coat, so that it did not reach the child!

SOME FIRST COUSINS OF THE TRADITIONAL TEDDY

This chapter is devoted to altering the colours and contours of the traditional Teddy so as to turn him into a sort of first cousin of himself! No apologies are made to the zoologists among Teddy bear makers for including koalas and pandas in this category, they are here at the request of children, who as the Teddy Bear's Census (page 30) showed, regard them as bears.

The examples given here are just to whet your appetite, and it is hoped that you will go on to invent many more "cousins" to add to the family tree.

All the toys in this section are large, but are kept light in weight by careful stuffing. A smooth snout is introduced in the first example and the modern idea of an enormous head in the last one.

SNOUTY BEAR
Illustration Plate 16

Height: about 18 ins. *Weight:* about 1 lb. Pattern pages 253–4.

The best way to accentuate the snout of a bear is to use a smooth material for that part of his anatomy. Velvet is ideal for the purpose, but for the original, which was made in honey-coloured long-pile nylon, the wrong side of the material was used. This also served admirably for the paws and footpads and saved extra expenditure. (It should perhaps be emphasized that "honey" is *not* yellow but a glorious shade of dusty, beigy gold with a slightly pink tone—a lovely colour for bears!)

This bear has a fatter tummy than the traditional jointed bears and the original had an open mouth, although this is not essential.

Materials

$\frac{3}{8}$ yard long-pile fur fabric 48 ins. wide.
One pair large brown glass eyes (12 mm.).
Five large joint sets ($1\frac{3}{4}$ ins.).
Kapok and wood wool for filling.
Black or brown stranded cotton for nose and claw markings.
A scrap of red felt for mouth lining.

Method

Cut out the paws, outer arms, inner arms, legs, footpads and ears all in fur fabric, as given for the Medium Size Jointed Bear on pages 244–51; the body as given for Bruin

Bear on pages 260–1; and the head gusset, tip of gusset, head, snout and mouth lining, as given on pages 253–4 (25 pieces in all).

Preparation of head

Join the tip of gusset to the head gusset along broken line L–L, having the WRONG SIDE of the material on the outside in the case of the gusset tip. Place on one side.

Join each snout to a head piece along broken line L–G, having the WRONG SIDE of the material outside in the case of the snout pieces. Place on one side.

Body, legs, arms, ears

Make up exactly as given for the Large Jointed Bear on pages 133, 137, having the WRONG SIDE of the material on the outside in the case of the paws and footpads.

Head

Make up as given for the Large Jointed Bear on page 137 but when stitching down front seam stitch K–E–X, then Z–G separately. Cut slit X–Y and insert mouth lining working as given for the Honey Bear on page 98.

Assembling, nose, claws, eyes and ears

Work as given for the Large Jointed Bear on page 138, except that there will naturally be no pile to clip away from this bear's nose, and for a bear this size the eyes need to be approximately 2 ins. from the tip of nose.

If you think his mouth looks a little "naked", add a tiny red felt tongue protruding from one side.

JOINTED PANDA
Illustration Plate 11

Height: about 18 ins. Pattern pages 241, 252. *Weight:* about 1 lb.

To children, a panda is just a roly-poly black and white bear, and one of the first animals they ask to see when visiting the Zoo. Although not *truly* a close relation, in "toyland" he is certainly the Teddy bear's first cousin.

This model is based on the design of the Medium Size Jointed Bear on page 138 (except that he has a pointed head gusset) and is as easily made. It is only necessary to join the body pieces together before starting work so as to have the *front* black at the top and white at the bottom, and the *back* white with black "shoulders" coming to a point in the centre. The black eye patches are added after stuffing.

Materials

$\frac{3}{8}$ yard black fur fabric 48 ins. wide for ears, arms, legs, top of body and eye patches.
$\frac{1}{4}$ yard white fur fabric 48 ins. wide for lower half of body and head.
One 9-in. square of black felt for paws, footpads and nose.
Black stranded cotton for mouth.
White stranded cotton for claws.
Five large-size joint sets ($1\frac{3}{4}$ ins.).
One pair large brown glass eyes (12 mm.).
Kapok and wood wool for filling.

Method

Cut out the head as given for the Medium-sized Jointed Bear on page 250, and the head gusset on page 241, using white fur fabric. The legs, arms and ears as given for the Medium-sized Jointed Bear on pages 244–7, 251, using black fur fabric. The paws and foot-pads as given for the Medium-sized Jointed Bear on pages 244, 249, using black felt; the lower halves of body and tops of back as given on page 252, in white fur fabric; and the "shoulders" and eye patches as given on pages 241, 252, in black fur fabric (27 pieces in all: 16 in black fur fabric, 7 in white fur fabric, and 4 in black felt).

Assembling the body pieces

First of all take one set of body pieces and join the "lower half" to the "shoulders" Y–Z. Then join the "top of back" to these pieces Z–W. Place on one side.

Assemble the other set of body pieces in the same way and place on one side.

You will now have two body pieces the same shape as the pattern given for the Medium Bear on page 248, but they will be in two colours as Fig. 47.

Head

Take one side of the head and stitch to the head gusset E–L–F. Now join on the other side of head to the other side of head gusset E–L–F. Stitch E–G. Turn right side out and place on one side.

Body, legs, arms and ears

Make these up, assemble them, and work the nose and mouth exactly as given for the Large Jointed Bear on pages 133–8, working from † to †, and from *** to ***, but make the nose rather on the large side.

Eye patches

Turn a tiny hem back all round the edge of each patch, tacking it invisibly in place so as to lose the raw edges. Consulting Plate 11 for approximate position, pin, then hem, each patch neatly in place on the face.

Eyes and ears

Add these as given on page 138 for the Medium-sized Jointed Bear, placing the eyes towards the top of the patches, about 2 ins. from the tip of the nose. Curve the ears well, so that they look rather small. If you think they are too large turn the lower edges O–Q in a little more to make them smaller.

A scarlet bow round his neck gives the panda "that little extra something"!

If you decide to give him "claws" use white stranded cotton and work as described on page 84 and Fig. 22.

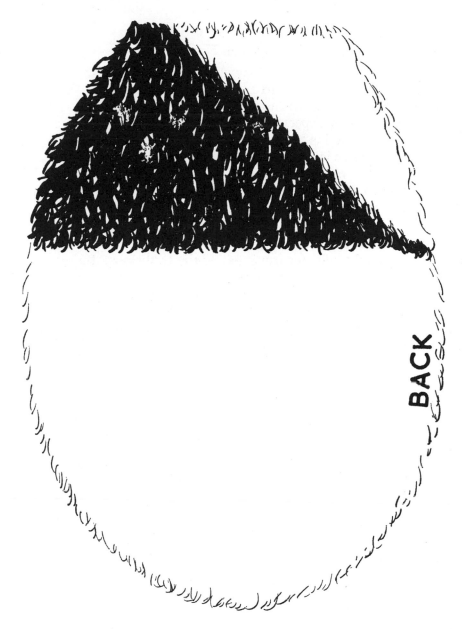

Fig. 47. Side view of panda's body.

JOINTED "BRUIN" BEAR
Illustration Plate 11

Height: about 18 ins. Pattern pages 258–62. *Weight:* about 1 lb.

Bruin bear is very closely related to the traditional Teddy, but he has certain extra "refinements" in the form of an open mouth, tongue, claws and footpads which simply ask to be tickled! One almost expects him to start to giggle when one scratches the bottom of his foot, so vulnerable do his "fleshy" pads appear.

He was created by the special request of a little boy who demanded "a real-looking bear cub with scratchy claws—not a Cissy one". Although not a "Cissy" he is certainly not fierce and resembles to a certain extent (and quite by accident) the bear cub which President Roosevelt refused to shoot, pictured on Plate 2.

For the best effect use fluffy dark-brown fur fabric as this shows up to advantage his white snout and claws and flesh pink "pads".

Bruin's shape is slightly different from that of the traditional Teddies in Section VIII, his head being broadened by a wider gusset and his "tummy" made much fatter. His ears are inserted into the head gusset instead of being sewn on afterwards. His arms are also quite different as the pads are inserted in the ends instead of on the inside. With all the detail of claws, pads, open mouth and felt eyes he naturally takes longer to make than an ordinary Teddy bear, but the results are well worth the trouble!

Materials

⅜ yard long-pile brown fur fabric 48 ins. wide.
Scraps of long-pile white fur fabric for snout.
One 9-in. square brown felt for soles, paws and eyes.
One 9-in. square flesh-pink or fawn felt for "pads" and mouth lining.
Scraps of white felt for claws and eyes.
Scraps of black felt for nose and eyes.
Scraps of red felt for tongue.
Five large-size joint sets (1¾ ins.).
Kapok and wood wool for filling.
Pipe cleaners for stiffening claws.

Method

Cut out the body, legs, claw pads, claws, head gusset, tip of head gusset, tongue, mouth lining, footpads, paw pads, head, snout, arms, soles, paws and nose, as given on pages 258–62; the ears as given for the Medium-sized Bear on page 247, but using brown fur fabric; and the eyes as given for the Thinking Bear on page 208 (98 pieces in all). The number of pieces is not quite so alarming as it sounds, for many of the pieces are very small, such as claws and paw pads! Mark all X's on the wrong side.

Body and ears

Make up exactly as given for the Large Jointed Bear on pages 133, 137, and place on one side.

Legs

Make up exactly as given for Large Jointed Bear on page 133, noting that you insert a "sole" into the base of each one, not a "footpad". Place on one side.

Arms

Place together in pairs and stitch the top seams I–M and lower seams H–N. Insert brown felt paws, matching letters and stitching all round N–M–N. Turn right side out, stuff as far as opening and place on one side.

Head

Join white snout to head piece—along broken lines and matching 1s and 2s. On the head gusset join the white tip to the main piece along broken lines, matching L's.

*Take the ears and insert each one into the slit on top of head piece oversewing, then backstitching in place O–3, then curving along top of head 3–Q and oversewing in place (Fig. 21 (6)). Join the two head pieces to the head gusset from E–L–Q–3–F. (*Note.* You will have four thicknesses to stitch through between Q–3 and this needs special attention!) Fold the gusset at E–K–E so that the E's meet and stitch front seam K–E–X. Cut slit for mouth X–Y, then stitch the rest of front seam Z–2–G.

Mouth lining (Fig. 29)

Insert this as given for the Thinking Bear on page 98 and Fig. 29.

Run a strong gathering thread all round the neck F–G–F and turn right side out leaving the thread hanging. Stuff head very firmly, taking particular care to get the nose solid also the "lips" well filled, using small pieces of kapok for these parts before filling up with wood wool. Place on one side.*

Claws and pads

Insert discs into the arms and legs, finish stuffing and ladder stitch the openings as shown on p. 129 and Fig. 41 A, B and C, but do not joint on to body yet. Make up the claws by placing them together in pairs and oversewing all round except for the short ends (Fig. 48 A). Push a piece of folded pipe cleaner (Fig. 48 B) into each claw—fold to the tip (Fig. 48 C)—and if necessary add a little kapok, coaxing it in with an orange stick so that each claw is firm and strong (Fig. 48 D). When finished there will be twenty; five for each limb. Sew the five claws firmly in place along the top edge of the sole of each foot and the paws (Fig. 48 E). Over the end of each one sew a pink claw pad, hemming them neatly all round the outside edge and pushing a little kapok under each one if you can persuade it in (Fig. 48 F). Now hem a pink paw pad to each brown paw, stuffing it so as to raise it (Fig. 48 G) and a pink footpad to each sole of foot, stuffing it in the same way (Fig. 48 H).

Assembling

Work exactly as given for Large Jointed Bear on page 138, but of course using the smaller joints.

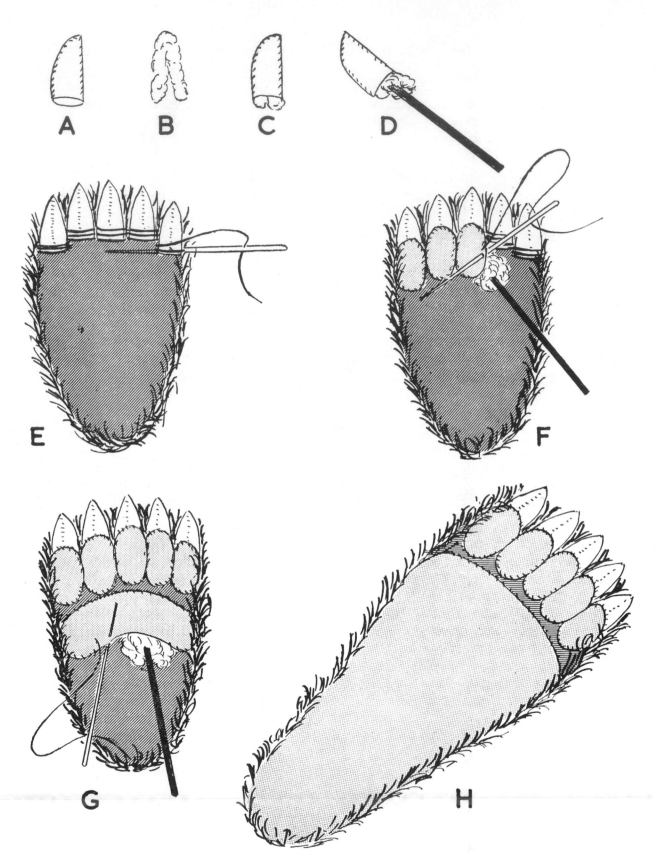

Fig. 48. Construction of realistic claws for Bruin bear.

148

Nose

Take two darts on the wrong side, as shown on pattern by broken lines T–U–V. Turn right side out and stitch on the *top* of head gusset at K, the darts to the front and forming nostrils and keeping the whole thing small—not spread out, pushing a little kapok in as you work. The nose turns up at a quite ridiculous angle! (Fig. 49 B).

Tongue

Place the two pieces together. Stab stitch all round except for the short end. Stuff firmly and close opening. Push into mouth, sticking out at one side and stitch firmly in place.

Eyes

Stitch each black circle to a brown, then these two completed circles to a white. Embroider a white highlight (Fig. 30). Consulting Plate 11, hem each eye neatly to head with the black pupils to one side, and pushing a little stuffing under each one to raise it. On the original the eyes were 1 in. from the edge of white snout, on the inside of the gusset line, but arrange yours to suit your own particular bear.

Bruin is not the type of bear to have a ribbon, but he looks good with a red dog collar. Try putting a red, felt ladybird on his foot. Instructions, page 153 and Fig. 50.

JOINTED POLAR BEAR CUB
Illustration Plate 11

Height: about 18 ins. Pattern pages 263–5. *Weight:* about 1 lb.

The simplest way to make a "Polar" Teddy bear is to use one of the patterns for the traditional bears in Section VIII, and make it up in white fur fabric! This will satisfy the very young. Here, however, an attempt has been made to fulfil the demand of a group of children who asked for either a "Teddyized Polar Bear", or a "Polarized Teddy Bear"—adding that they did not mind a bit *which* they had! It is not possible to emulate the thick neck of these enormous woolly creatures if the head is to be jointed, but by elongating and sloping the "snout", reducing the size of the ears and eyes and changing the shape of the arms, so that they flop downwards, a caricature of sorts can be achieved.

Materials

$\frac{3}{8}$ yard long-pile white fur fabric 48 ins. wide.
One 9-in. square white felt for paws and soles.
One 9-in. square black felt for "pads", claws and nose.
Scrap of blue felt for eye backing.
Scrap of pink felt for mouth lining.
Five large-size joint sets ($1\frac{3}{4}$ ins.).
One pair "Penguin's" eyes.[1] (Small white with black pupil.)
Kapok and wood wool for filling.
Pipe cleaners for claws.

[1] For address for obtaining these eyes, see page 67.

Method

Cut out the head, head gusset, arms, ears and eye backings as given on pages 263–5; the body, legs, claw pads, claws, soles, paws, nose, tongue, mouth lining, footpads and paw pads as given for Bruin Bear on pages 258–62 (91 pieces in all); but using white for all the fur fabric pieces, white felt for the soles and paws, and black felt for the pads and claws.

Note. If preferred, cut one arm as Polar Bear pattern and the other as for Bruin Bear on page 262. They will then be in two different positions—one hanging limp and one with paw raised as in Plate 11.

Mark all the X's on the wrong side.

Make up the **Body, Legs, Arms** and **Ears** exactly as given for Bruin Bear on pages 146–7. Place on one side.

Head

Make up and insert ears and mouth lining exactly as given for Bruin Bear on page 147, working from * to *.

Claws and Pads

Make and attach these exactly as given for Bruin Bear on page 147, but they will of course be all in black felt.

Assembling

Work exactly as given for Large Jointed Bear on page 138, but using the smaller joints.

Nose

Make up as given for Bruin Bear on page 149, but fit right over end of snout like a little cap and stitch in place with no stuffing (Fig. 49 A).

Tongue

Make up and insert as given for Bruin Bear on page 149.

Eyes

Prepare and insert these as described on page 77 and Figs. 16 and 17, but before making the shank slip the wire through a hole in the pale blue felt backing (Fig. 49 C). When inserting eyes the backings should have the points towards the nose. On the originals the pupil of each eye was slightly *below* the gusset seam and 2¾ ins. from the tip of the nose, but place yours to suit *your* bear!

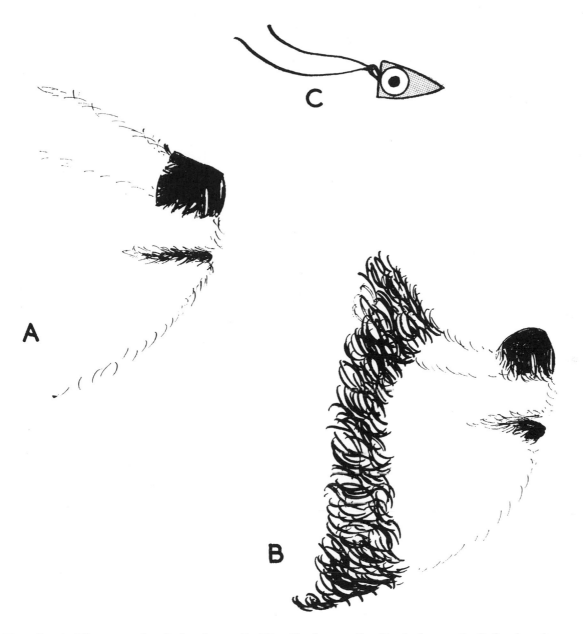

Fig. 49. A. Flat nose for Polar bear. B. Tip-tilted nose for Bruin bear. C. Polar bear's eye before inserting.

A CUDDLY CARICATURE KOALA
Illustration Plate 17

Height: sitting, about 12 ins. Pattern pages 255–7. *Weight:* about 1¼ lbs.

This toy *can* look a little grotesque with his ultra-large head, and care needs to be taken over his expression in order to avoid this. Use a very long-pile fur fabric to give the cuddly effect. The original was in grey and white.

Making this koala will show how to turn a pattern for a jointed toy into a "cuddly" one.

Materials

⅜ yard long-pile nylon 48 ins. wide in grey.
¼ yard long-pile nylon 48 ins. wide in white.
Scrap of black felt for the nose.
Scrap of grey felt for the eyelids.
One pair of extra-large brown glass eyes (14 mm.).
Kapok and wood wool for stuffing.
Black stranded cotton for mouth and claws.

Method

Cut out the arms and legs as given for the Medium-sized Jointed Bear on pages 245–51—one pair in white and one in grey fur fabric—the body as given for Bruin Bear on page 260, in grey fur fabric; the head gusset, two ears, footpads and head pieces in grey; two ears, the chin markings and underchin gusset in white fur fabric; and the nose and nose backing in black felt; all as given on pages 255–7 (24 pieces in all: 13 in grey, 9 in white and 2 in black felt).

Note. If preferred, the inner legs can be cut in two pieces, the top half white and foot part grey as in the illustration. The white tummy marking on the koala in the picture was added *after* making up and will be explained later. There are NO paws!

Preparing the head

Join white chin markings to head pieces along broken lines Y–N. Place on one side.

Head and ears

Make up as given for the Glove Koala on page 117, and place on one side.

Nose

Make up as given for the Glove Koala on page 117, and place on one side.

Arms, legs and body

Make up as given for the Large Jointed Bear on pages 133, 137, having the insides of the limbs white and outsides grey. Stuff all these parts completely and close the openings.

Assembling

Stuff the head, being careful to make it wide and to push out the puffy cheeks. Using strong thread, take a few criss-cross stitches across open base of head, then ladder stitch head to body, working round several times. Try to put it at an attractive angle—not staring straight ahead. Ladder stitch the legs and arms in place, working several times round the top of each one. Stitch nose to face matching N's and working round it several times with a long needle and black thread.

Eyes

Make two grey felt eyelids as described on page 82 and Fig. 20, and prepare and insert eyes as described on page 77 and Figs. 16 and 17.

Ears

Sew on as described on page 80 and Fig. 17 (7 and 8)—wide apart, about 4½ ins., and nicely curved. Plate 17 will help you.

Claws

Embroider four long strokes on the tip of each arm and foot using black stranded cotton (Fig. 22 and page 84).

Mouth

Embroider a "goofy" mouth as shown for the Glove Koala in Fig. 34.

White tummy marking

If you have any spare white fur fabric, cut a piece to fit the top of the front of the body and turning under the raw edges, neatly hem it in place.

Give him a bright-coloured bow.

MAKING A LADYBIRD (Fig. 50)
Illustration Plate 11

Materials

A scrap of red felt.
Black stranded cotton.
A tiny piece of kapok.

Method

1. Draw a small, oval shape on a scrap of red felt.
2. Using one strand of black cotton embroider six spots on the oval.
3. Cut out the shape.
4. Hem it neatly to the foot or paw of your bear, stuffing it with kapok as you work, so as to raise it well.
5 and 6. Embroider six tiny legs and two "feelers" using one strand of black cotton.

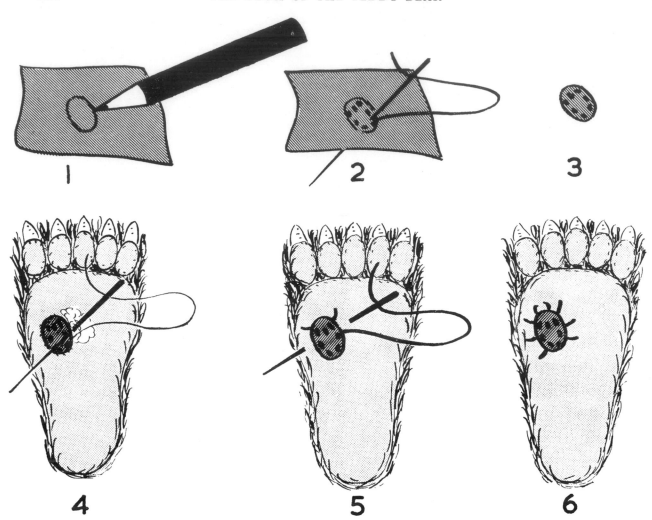

Fig. 50. Making and attaching a ladybird.

Did you know that "Ming", one of the first Giant Pandas to arrive at the London Zoo, was at one time housed in the Zoo Sanatorium, which in those days was situated some way away? Each afternoon she was driven to the gardens in a private car, sitting quietly in the front seat beside the driver, and as the car swept into the Zoo by the Timekeeper's Gate, she had a habit of lifting her paw to her face which looked exactly like a dignified salute!

TEDDY BEARS FOR THE TEDDY BEARS

Every self-respecting Teddy bear will enjoy having his own toys to play with, and among them he must of course have a Teddy bear of his very own. Mere human beings, especially the younger generation, usually find immense appeal in anything miniature, especially in comparison with a similar but much larger object. This is obviously the reason why *Gulliver's Travels*, written as a political satire, has automatically turned into a much-loved children's book, the young people ignoring the satire and finding only in the tale, all the delights of contrast in scale so necessary in a fairy story. If more proof were needed we need only to look at the popularity of Alice, growing and shrinking with such rapidity, Jack and the Giant he finds at the top of the beanstalk, and at the appeal of both Tom Thumb and Thumbelina!

The tiny bears in this section, illustrated on Plates 9 and 11, are only two inches high and will fit into any pocket. What a comfort it can be in times of stress, such as the first day at school, or a visit to the dentist, to have a private treasure hidden away in one's pocket which can be secretly handled from time to time.

They are not difficult to make but are fiddly and are more suitable for the nimble-fingered worker. Six varieties are given, a Teddy in felt and one in wool, a woolly panda, and a variation on each of these in which they are jointed with press studs (snap fasteners). The "hairy" effect on the woolly animals is achieved by taking a series of stitches to completely cover the body, using darning wool—and very effective it is.

Fig. 51. Miniature felt Teddy.

MINIATURE FELT TEDDY BEAR
Illustration Fig. 51

Height: sitting, 2 ins. Pattern page 278.

Materials

The tiniest scraps of fawn felt.
A small handful of kapok.
An orange stick for stuffing.
Black and white stranded cotton for eyes, nose and claws.

Method

Cut out the pieces as given on page 278. Work in stab stitch close to the edge and on the right side, using matching Sylko and a fine needle (size 11). The stab stitching must be very small and neat.

Body

Place the two pieces together and stitch all round A–B–C. Stuff the body very firmly so that it is fat and "podgy". Place on one side.

Head

Stitch head gusset to one side of head D–G, then join on other side of head D–G. Fold the tip of gusset in half so that the D's meet and stitch E–D–F. This will give him a turned up nose! Stuff the head very firmly, filling the nose up well and pushing out the cheeks *sideways* to make his face broad and fat, not long and narrow. Place the open end of the head on to the open end of the body, with the head either looking straight forwards or turned a little to one side, and ladder stitch the two together all round the neck (i.e. one stitch on the head and one on the body alternately).

Note. The front of the body is the fat part C–B.

Arms

Place the pieces together in pairs and stitch all round except for a small opening at top H–I. Stuff both arms firmly and close opening by continuing with the same stab stitch. Ladder stitch one arm to each side of body, placing them at different and interesting angles —e.g. one up and one down.

Legs

Place the pieces together in pairs and stitch front seam J–K and back seam L–M. Open out the base of foot and insert footpad, matching letters and stitching all round M–K–M. Stuff both legs firmly and close opening L–J by continuing the stab stitching. Pin the legs in place and test to see that the bear sits firmly; if he does, ladder stitch them to body.

Ears

Stitch the ears wide apart, one to each side of head, curving them well and making quite sure they look attractive. The bear's appearance will be spoiled completely if they stick up in the air, and if this happens, take a stitch or two pulling them down backwards, in other words, flattening them a little.

Finishing off

Embroider two tiny round black eyes low down and on the seam of head gusset and add a white highlight to each. Add a nose and mouth, then four claw markings on each limb. Use *one* strand of cotton only for all this work and a very fine needle. The beginnings and endings can usually be "lost" behind the ears, in the neck or between the two pieces of felt forming the "ridge" seam.

Tie a piece of bright-coloured, ¼-inch-wide ribbon round your bear's neck.

Fig. 52. Miniature jointed felt Teddy.

MINIATURE JOINTED FELT TEDDY BEAR
Illustration Fig. 52

Height: sitting, 2 ins. Pattern page 278.

Materials

As given on page 156, also five tiny press studs (snap fasteners), size 000.

Body and head

Make up as given on page 156, and after stuffing cut two tiny circles of felt, one to fit the open end of the head and one the body. Place each circle over the appropriate open end and neatly oversew it in place. Sew one half of a press stud to the circle on top of body and the other half to the circle on base of head and snap the two together.

Legs and arms

Make up and stuff as given on page 156. Sew one half of a press stud to the top of each limb where shown by broken line on pattern, and the other half to the appropriate place on the body, making quite sure that you place the legs so that the bear sits down. The press studs will have formed joints, so that the Teddy's head and limbs move in an attractive way. There is an inevitable small "gap" between the limbs and side of body, but this cannot be avoided.

Sew on the **Ears** and **Finish off** the bear as given on page 157. A ribbon round his neck will hide this "gap"!

Fig. 53. Miniature woolly Teddy.

MINIATURE WOOLLY TEDDY BEAR
Illustration Plate 9 and Fig. 53

Height: sitting, 2 ins. Pattern page 278.

Materials

As given for Felt Bear on page 156, also two or three skeins of darning wool to match the felt.

Method

Make up the **Head** and **Body** and join them together as given on page 156 for the Felt Bear, and sew on the ears. Place on one side.

Legs and arms

Make these up as given for the Felt Bear on page 156, but do not join to body.

Making the hair (Fig. 54)

Thread a length of darning wool into a *fine* darning needle and using it double take a series of stitches about ¼ in. long, all intermingling with one another to cover the bear's body, head and ears completely, so that you can no longer see the felt. These stitches are his "hair" and should run the way the pile would run on a normal size Teddy, i.e. downwards. Take your stitches up over the top of each ear—Figs. 53 and 54 should help you to understand how to work.

Then cover each limb in the same way, leaving the felt showing where there should be a paw and footpad (Fig. 53). Now stitch each limb in place at attractive angles, then continue with more woollen stitches so as to blend in where the top of the limbs join the body.

Finishing off

Work as given for Felt Bear on page 157.

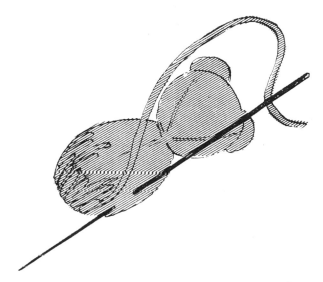

Fig. 54. Making the "hair" for a miniature bear.

MINIATURE JOINTED WOOLLY TEDDY BEAR
Illustration Plate 9 and Fig. 55

Height: sitting, 2 ins. Pattern page 278.

Materials

As for Woolly Miniature Bear on page 158, also five tiny press studs, size 000.

Method

Make up all the pieces—**Head, Body, Legs** and **Arms,** as given for Jointed Felt Bear on page 157, but do not sew on any of the press studs. Sew on the ears. Cover the six pieces separately with woollen stitches as described above, remembering to leave the felt footpads and paws exposed. Then sew on the press studs and finish off the bear as given for the Jointed Felt Bear on page 157.

Fig. 55. Miniature jointed woolly Teddy.

Fig. 56. Miniature woolly panda.

MINIATURE WOOLLY PANDA
Illustration Plate 11 and Fig. 56

Height: sitting, 2 ins.

Materials

Tiny scraps of felt in black and white.
A small handful of kapok.
An orange stick for stuffing.
Black and white and brown stranded cotton.
Two skeins of white and two of black darning wool.

Method

Cut out the pieces as given on page 278, using white felt for the head, head gusset and body, and black for the arms, legs, ears and footpads.

Make up all the pieces as given for the Felt Teddy on page 156, working through **Body**, **Head**, **Arms** and **Legs**, but do not sew on the limbs. Sew on the ears.

Making the hair (Fig. 54)

Cover the limbs with black woollen stitches, as described under "Making the hair" on page 158. Cover the head with white woollen stitches, embroidering two black eye patches, and the ears with black stitches. Cover the lower half of the body with white stitches, the top of the front with black (Fig. 56) and make a black V on top half of back (Fig. 57). Stitch the limbs in position and work a few more woollen stitches to "blend" in the place where they join the body.

Eyes, nose, mouth and claws

Embroider small brown eyes with a white highlight, and black nose and mouth and if liked, tiny white claws.

MINIATURE JOINTED WOOLLY PANDA
Illustration Fig. 57

Height: sitting, 2 ins.

Materials

As given for the Miniature Woolly Panda on page 160, also five small press studs, size 000.

Method

Make up exactly as given for the Jointed Woolly Teddy on page 159, but use the appropriate panda colours and markings as described under the Woolly Panda on page 160.

Fig. 57. Miniature jointed woolly panda.

Have you ever heard of The Teddy Bears' Preservation Society? Founded in about 1955 and housed in New Malden, Surrey, it collects and preserves old Teddies so that the older types may not be thrown away when homes are broken up, or people no longer want to keep an old family favourite.

GOLDILOCKS AND THE THREE BEARS

SOME FACTS ABOUT THE STORY

No book on Teddy bears would seem complete without the inclusion of some nursery rhyme or fairy tale characters, yet because these tales are old and as we have seen in Section I the Teddy bear is a mere "stripling" of sixty-odd years, he naturally does not appear in them. For this reason and so that some such characters may be included, Goldilocks has been turned into a rag doll and the three bears into Teddies (see Plate 12), instructions for making them appearing on page 165. This well-known story has an interesting history and could indeed constitute a book in itself!

Brought up as most of us were on the tale of a golden-haired little girl finding the home of the three bears, it is something of a shock to read older versions of this tale and find that instead of Goldilocks it was . . . "a little old woman" who visited the cottage.

The beginnings of the story are, like most fairy tales, shrouded in mystery—pure folklore, handed down by word of mouth from one generation to another. However, the first known *written* version is by Eleanor Mure, an intriguing little volume in the Osborne Collection of early children's books, in "Boys and Girls House" at Toronto Public Library. The story is metrically related and is illustrated with the quaintest water colours. The dedication page reads:

"The celebrated nursery tale of The Three Bears, put into verse and embellished with drawings, for a birthday present to Horace Broke. Sept. 26. 1831."

Horace Broke was apparently the author's nephew and the setting she gave the story has been identified from the illustrations as being "Cecil Lodge", her father's beautiful home in Hertfordshire. One of the enchanting water colours shows the end of the story (which is unusual in that the bears try to punish the old woman): in it the bears are depicted standing round a lake, each one holding an enormous pole with which to push the old woman under, while she, complete in bonnet and mittens, struggles helplessly in the water. The text tells us that:

". . . On the fire they throw her, but burn her they couldn't,
In the water they put her but drown there she wouldn't;
They seize her before all the wondering people
And chuck her aloft on St. Paul's churchyard steeple,
And if she's still there when you earnestly look,
You will see her quite plainly—my little Horbook!"

One wonders if "little Horbook" (alias Horace Broke) begged to be taken at once to St. Paul's, to see if his aunt had, in fact, got the end of her story correct.

The tale is also told by Robert Southey in Vol. IV of his *The Doctor* (1837). An explanation for the finding of a child's story in a book of this type is also given and we are told that:

". . . books which at once amuse and instruct, may be as useful to servant men and maids, as to their masters and mistresses. . . ."

chapters were therefore included—

". . . for the closet, for the boudoir, for the drawing room and for the kitchen. . . ."

and a final reminder is given that—

". . . so should there be one at least for the nursery. . . ."

—hence the inclusion of The Three Bears. This time we are introduced to a

"Little, Small, Wee Bear; a Middle-sized Bear, a Great, Huge Bear and a little, old woman—an impudent, bad, little old woman."

The end of the story is no less harrowing than Eleanor Mure's version:

". . . Now the window was open, because the Bears like good tidy Bears, as they were, always opened their bed chamber window when they got up in the morning. Out the little old woman jumped; and whether she broke her neck in the fall or found her way out of the wood and was taken up by the constable and sent to the House of Correction for a vagrant as she was, I cannot tell. But the three bears never saw anything more of her."

Even at this early date the dialogue between the bears is set up in Large, Medium and Small print and the children obviously had the tale read to them in the still approved fashion of suiting the reader's voice to the bear, for at the end of Southey's version, what almost amount to stage directions are found:

"O dear children, you who are in the happiest season of human life, how you will delight in the Story of the Three Bears when Mamma reads it to you out of this nice book, or Papa, or some fond Uncle, kind Aunt or doting Sister! Papa and Uncle will do the Great, Huge Bear best; but Sister and Aunt and Mamma will excel them in the little, small, wee Bear with his little, small, wee voice. . . ."

One person at least, seemed worried by the fact that, by being included in *The Doctor*, a book meant mainly for adults, "The Three Bears" was unlikely to reach the younger generation for whom it was really intended, and thus we find that the dedication of *The Three Bears and Their Stories* by "G.N." and dated July 1837 (a book which is also in the Osborne Collection) reads as follows:

"Unknown author of *The Doctor*,
Great original concoctor
Of the rare story of the bears
Their porridge pots and beds and chairs . . .
But fearing in your book it might
Escape some little people's sight
I do not like that one should lose,
What will them all so much amuse."

"G.N." is obviously mistaken in thinking that Southey as the author of *The Doctor* was the "original concoctor" of this old tale, for there already existed Eleanor Mure's version, and the fact that she herself mentions in her dedication "the *celebrated* nursery tale" proves that even she was not the originator!

"G.N.'s" book is planned in an interesting and unusual way, for after telling the story of "The Three Bears", the author tells us that while he was visiting the three bears in their home (known as "Bearwood"), the Wee Bear read him the story of "The Wolf and the Seven Kids" in German from a book of stories by the Brothers Grimm, and he relates this tale. The third story is the Great Bear's story—"The Vizier and the Woodman" and the rhyming introduction dated "Bearwood June 1840" and signed "Yours faithfully the Bear", contains a pun:

> "Call it not doggerel though it be
> For sure it's bearable from me!"

Thus many versions have been written and no doubt many new ones will continue to appear. Tolstoy's is fascinating because here we have the familiar little girl instead of the old woman, and the bears, which are of course Russian, have names—Michael Ivanovitch, Nastasia Petrovna and Mishutka. We are left with the ending we all know so well, of the little girl running away into the forest, the bears being unable to catch her.

Fashions change in fairy tales as in everything else and in discussing this story, Stanley Unwin's version of "Goldiloppers", usually told of course to an adult audience, cannot be left out. Mr. Unwin kindly wrote this shortened version[1] specially for *The Book of the Teddy Bear*.

"Once apon a tyto there was Goldiloppers and out she went in the early mordey to visit her granmardy in the deep forrey. She had a baskey egg and buttery and soapy deterger and a packet of tablets for granmardy after dinner indegeps or burpypardlo powder. Well, she tripped up on the crazy pave and grazed her kneeclabbers and had to rub it on vaselubrious for a quick healey-hup. Then off she went and get lost-it in the deep forrey. Oh folly!

"Soon she came to a little cottage with the thatchey-roof and with chimney-poggers with smoke curling up to heavenly-bode and she knocked on the door and nobody said come in so in she went. On the tabloid were three base-loaders of porrey. One large she dippy fingold in and taste with a flabe of over salty and she went s-p-t! Then she flabed the middle size one and no flabe at all! But the little one was just right and she gollopped it all up without so much as a burpy-pardle. Then she went upstairs for a lay down and tried the big bed but too hardly and a coil-spring came out doing-ng-ng in the backgrove, so she tried the little cot with donald dukkery on the side and snrrrrr fast asleep! Then the bears came hode.—Who's been flaben my porrey and sp-t! all over the tabloid? Mother bear stood all akimbold. Baby said O lookit someone's gollop all my porrey without so much as a burpy-pardle! Then they went upstairs and Father said deeply voice, Who's been jumping on my bedders and dirty footmarks on the quilting and a spring came out all doing-ng-ng? But baby saw Goldiloppers all snrrr in his cotty and with golden tresses all a-dangly and said Oh! There's Goldifastasleeves in my cot! But Goldi wokit-up all a frightfold and out from the window jumpen and quickly thro' the forrey to mum and they had a cuffa-low teadey at four a clobbers with two plop-lumpers!"

[1] The story in its entirety has been recorded by Mr. Unwin on PYE record No. NPL. 18062—"Rotatey Diskers With Unwin".

GOLDILOCKS
Illustration Plate 12

Height: 12 ins. Pattern pages 266–7.

This little rag doll is completely soft and pliable with a simple face embroidered in stranded cotton. Her charm lies in her full, short skirts and flying pigtails.

Materials

Odd scraps of flesh-pink stockinette (or $\frac{1}{4}$ yard) for body.
About 2 ozs. kapok (or washable filling—*not* foam rubber) for stuffing.
Crêpe hair or yellow 2- or 3-ply wool.
A piece of a wooden meat skewer about 3 ins. long (or three cocktail sticks).
Blue, white and red stranded cotton for features.
Scrap of coloured or white stockinette for socks.
Scrap of coloured felt for shoes.
Scrap of fawn felt for soles.
Odd pieces of *small*-patterned cotton material for dress and panties.
Odd piece of plain-coloured cotton material for apron.
Very small press studs (size 000) for fastening dress and shoes.
Round elastic for sleeves and panties.

Method

Cut out all the pieces as given on pages 266–7, *except* the body, arms, legs and soles. Also a piece of cotton material 5 ins. × 36 ins. for the skirt of dress. (If insufficient material is available cut several lengths and join them. The joins will not show among the gathers.) For the apron cut out a piece of plain-coloured cotton material $3\frac{1}{4}$ ins. × $2\frac{3}{4}$ ins. for the bib, a piece 12 ins. × $3\frac{1}{2}$ ins. for the skirt and two strips $10\frac{1}{2}$ ins. × 1 in. and two $4\frac{1}{2}$ ins. × 1 in. for the strings.

Body

For all body stitching use pure silk or Sylko which exactly matches stockinette.

Place the cardboard template for the body, arms and legs on the double stockinette, making quite sure the "grain" runs *down* the parts and the stretch *across* them or you will have a doll that is horribly long and thin. Pencil round the templates, leaving a little space between each. DO NOT CUT OUT. Using a fine needle in your sewing machine (a thick one cuts the stockinette and makes holes) stitch all round the body and head *on* the pencil line, leaving A–A at the base open. Stitch all round each arm leaving the top end A–A open, and similarly all round each leg—always stitching on the pencil line. Now cut out the pieces about $\frac{1}{4}$ in. from the stitching. Turn them all right way out, pushing out arms and legs with the blunt end of a pencil. Stuff the head and body quite firmly, trying to push out one side of the oval-shaped head more than the other to make a "chin". At the same time push a piece of wood or three cocktail sticks Sellotaped together and bound with a piece of rag (Fig. 58 A and B) into the neck to stop the head from wobbling. (If making a washable doll use plastic cocktail sticks and omit the Sellotape.) Turn in the raw edges A–A and oversew along B–C–B.

Stuff the legs firmly as far as D–E. Stab stitch or machine across D–E. Turn in the

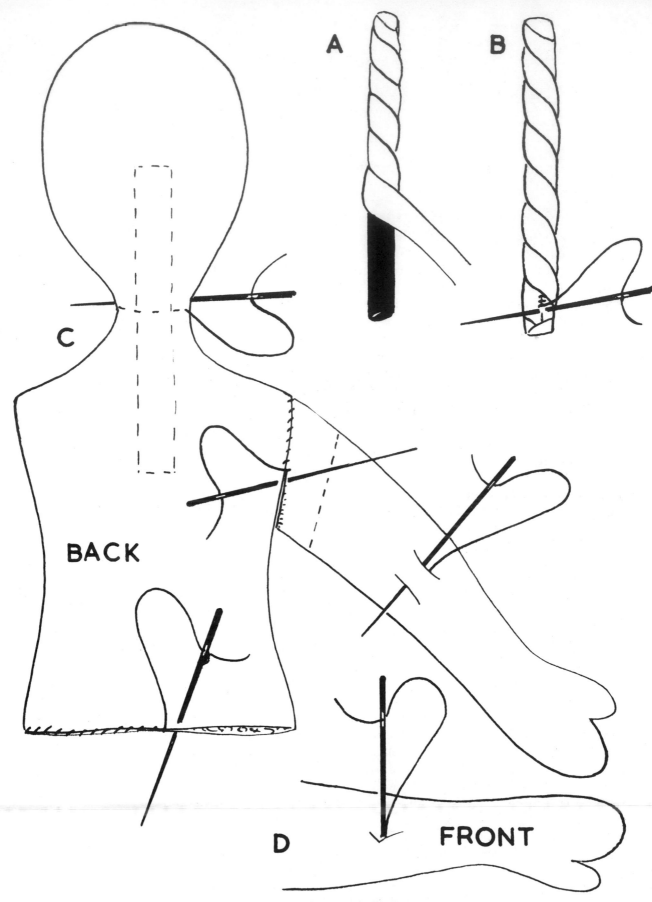

Fig. 58. Construction of Goldilocks' body.

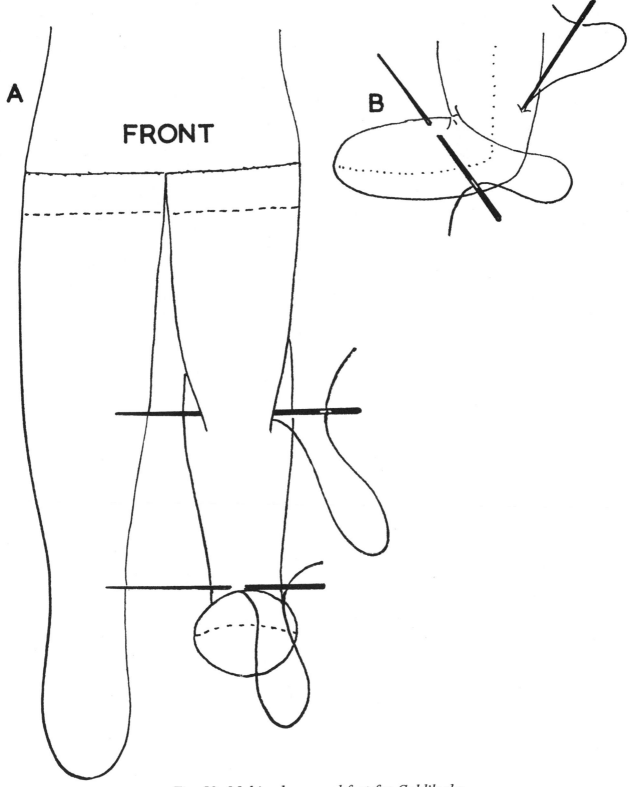

Fig. 59. Making knees and feet for Goldilocks.

167

raw edges A–A and oversew, taking only a tiny turning so that the tops of legs are now at B–C. Oversew each leg to the body of the doll, matching letters and working in each case from C–B on the back of the doll (Fig. 59 A). The empty piece at the top of each leg acts as a "hinge" so that Goldilocks will be flexible and able to sit down. Stuff the arms firmly as far as F–G. Stab stitch or machine across F–G. Turn in the raw edge A–A so that H–I is now the top of the arms. Oversew each arm to the body, matching letters and working from I–H on the back of the doll. Again the "empty" section at the top of each arm will allow them to move backwards and forwards (Fig. 58 C).

Finishing off

Run a gathering thread round the neck and pull it up tightly to make the neck slim, taking a few stitches backwards and forwards through the rag which is wrapped round the stick in the neck before fastening off (Fig. 58 C). Turn up about $1\frac{1}{4}$–$1\frac{1}{2}$ ins. at end of each leg to make a foot and ladder stitch it in place (Fig. 59 A and B). Take a few stitches through the back of base of each leg, pulling tightly to make an ankle (Fig. 59 B). Take a few stitches halfway down front of each leg to make a knee (Fig. 59 A). Take a few stitches from front to back halfway down arm and then from side to side at the back of arm in the same position to make a dimple at front of arm and small elbow which sticks out at the back (Fig. 58 C and D).

Fig. 60. Goldilocks' head.

Face (Fig. 60)

Using one strand of embroidery cotton and a very fine needle (size 11), embroider the face using just straight satin stitches. Red mouth and nostrils, blue eyes (bright blue—a pale colour will make an anaemic looking little girl), and yellow brows to match the hair.

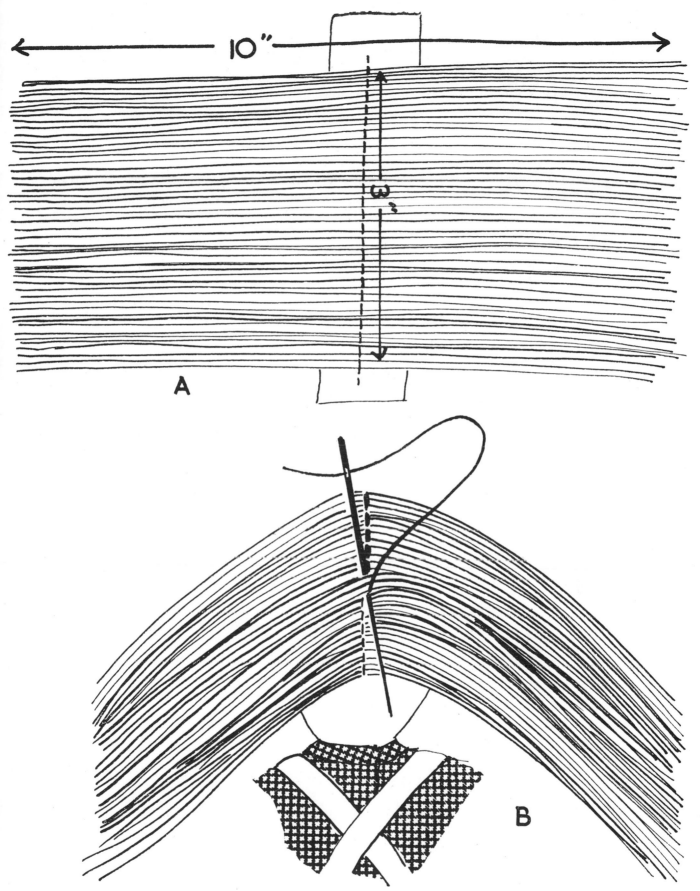

Fig. 61. Construction of Goldilocks' hair.

Beginnings and endings of threads can be on a part of the head which will eventually be covered by hair. Keep the features very low down in order to make Goldilocks look young. If you draw an imaginary line halfway down the face and keep everything under it you will not go far wrong, but if the features come above it, she will begin to age!

Hair (Fig. 61 A and B)

Naturally, the hair must be golden (although Goldilocks has sometimes been known as "Silver-Hair"). Try to choose a pleasant soft shade and to avoid harsh yellows. Do not use "doll's hair", made specially for the purpose. Short lengths of this pull out and cover the doll. It is never very satisfactory. For the original, theatrical crêpe hair was used (address page 68) or 2- or 3-ply wool is very satisfactory. Unravel the crêpe hair and tease it out flat so that it is 3 ins. wide—this is the length of the centre parting. Lay a length of about 10 ins., spread out to 3 ins., on a piece of paper and machine down the centre and back again—this is the parting. Try it on your doll and if the hair is too sparse so that the head shows through add a little more crêpe hair and machine again. If adding more be sure to add the full 10-in. length, but do not add the whole *thickness* of the plait—half is quite sufficient or your doll's pigtails will be much too "fat" in proportion to her head. If using wool, work in just the same way (Fig. 61 A). Tear the paper away and placing the hair on the doll's head, backstitch neatly down centre parting to keep it firmly in place (Fig. 61 B). Pull the hair tightly to each side of head and stitch in this position. Plait very tightly indeed until you have the required length. Bind and stitch the end of each pigtail to keep the hair neat, then tie a narrow bow of ribbon over the stitches. Cut off surplus hair. (*Note.* Tight plaiting makes the pigtails slim and also makes them "curl" so that they stick up in the air (see Plate 12 and Fig. 60). If you like, stitch a short length of "hair" to centre front of parting to soften the face a little.

On all the clothes, either use a *very* tiny hand-sewn French seam, or machine seams on the wrong side and overcast raw edges. It should be remembered that no two dolls are ever quite the same size because of variations in size of turnings and amount of stuffing used, so it may be necessary for you to make slight alterations. Do make sure that your doll's dress is very short indeed and that it fits her tightly at waist and neck.

Panties

Place the two pieces together and stitch side seams J–K and short seam between the legs L–L. Take a tiny rolled hem round each leg K–L–K. Turn back a $\frac{3}{8}$ in. hem all round top. Insert a piece of elastic to fit your doll's waist—"Shirlastic" used double is best, if not use round hat elastic. (You will not get a bodkin round the hem so use a tiny gold safety-pin.)

Dress

On the bodice, join side seams M–N and shoulder seams P–O. On the sleeves join underarm seams M–S. Run a gathering thread round top edge of sleeve M–X–O–X–M. and pushing gathers to the top, so that they mostly come between X–O–X, insert the sleeve into armhole of bodice stitching all round M–O–M. Make and insert the other sleeve in the same way. Turn up a $\frac{3}{8}$ in. hem all round base of sleeve, including in it as you work a piece of "Shirlastic"—used double. (It is easier to work this way than insert elastic afterwards, as the "circle" of base of sleeve is so small.) Fasten off elastic so that it fits the doll's arm very tightly and finish off hem. The sleeve should be fully "puffed". Run a gathering thread along the edge of strip cut for the skirt. (*Note.* 36 ins. seems a lot, but this length makes a beautifully full skirt. You could, however, use less if you wished.) Pull up gathers to fit base of bodice, and spacing them evenly, stitch on the wrong side T–R–N–N–R–T. Before doing this pull the gathers away so that on both sides of back there are no gathers on skirt between T and R, because the dress opens all the way down centre back and this piece is now going to be turned in. Turn back a hem all down both sides of centre back so that Q–R is now the edge of bodice and continue on down to bottom of skirt. Bind the neck with a *very* narrow, double strip of bias cut from the self material. Try the dress on the doll and pin up a wide hem so that the dress is about 1–1½ ins. above the knees. Slip stitch this hem invisibly. Sew three or four press studs at back, overlapping it so that the dress really fits.

Apron (Fig. 62)

On the "skirt" piece make a ⅜ in. hem along the two short and one of the long sides and run a gathering thread along the top of the other long side, leave the thread and place on one side.

On the "bib" piece make a ⅜ in. hem along the two short and one of the long sides. Pull up the gathers on the skirt piece to fit the raw edge of bib and, spacing them evenly, stitch one to the other on the wrong side. Take the four strips for strings and turning in the raw edges stitch all round so that each strip is now ⅜ in. wide. Stitch a long string to each side of the waist of the apron, and a short one to each top corner of bib. At the end of these last two, fold back about ¾ in. and stitch it in place, thus forming a loop. These strings cross over at centre back and each of the waist strings passes through one of them before tying in a bow with long "tails" at centre back of waist.

Socks

Make sure you cut these with the stretch of the stockinette going *across*. (Good tops of children's socks or cuffs of cotton cardigans, or T-shirts, are useful for making these.) On the wrong side oversew down centre back seam V–W and back again. If you have a raw edge at top turn back a tiny rolled hem all round. Turn right side out and put on doll.

Shoes (Fig. 63)

Cut two cardboard "soles" for shoes and two pieces of fawn felt about ¼ in. larger all round. Run a gathering thread all round outside edge of felt pieces and placing a cardboard sole on each (Fig. 63 A), pull up the gathers and secure by a few criss-crossed stitches (Fig. 63 B). On shoe sides, slit along A–B–C to form ankle strap. On the wrong side join seams A–D (centre front of shoe) (Fig. 63 C) and E–F (centre back) (Fig. 63 D). Turn right side out and placing shoe on top of sole (felt side of sole outwards) and matching letters, stab stitch all round D–E–D, forming a neat "welt" (Fig. 63 E). Cut two other sole shapes in white postcard, felt or chamois leather, making them very slightly smaller than the first two. Slip one into each shoe to neaten the insides, keeping them in place with a small amount of Copydex or similar adhesive. Sew a tiny press stud to each side of ankle strap so that it fits your doll's leg tightly. Sew the little bow trimmings to the top of the shoes.

Try making one of the bears in Section X for Goldilocks to play with—they just fit her!

Note. Other patterns for dolls, also dresses and shoes, will be found in *Dolls and How to Make Them.*

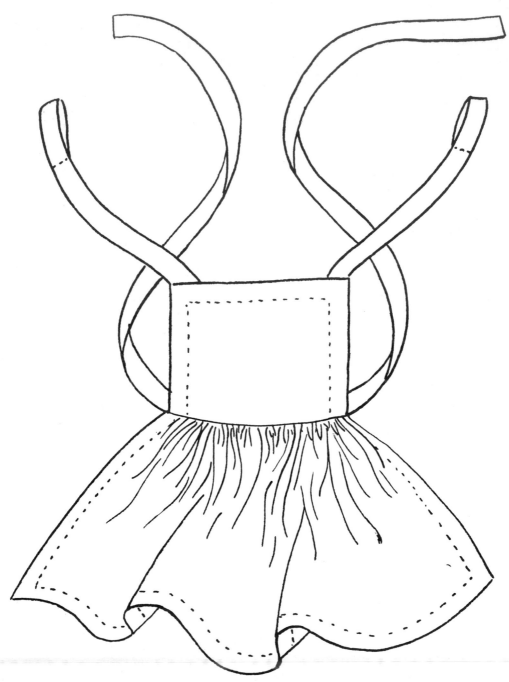

Fig. 62. Goldilocks' apron.

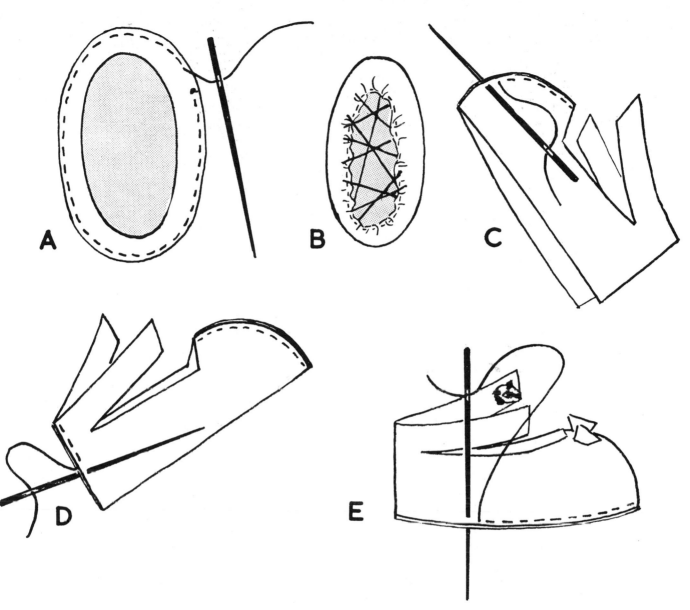

Fig. 63. Construction of Goldilocks' shoe.

THE BEARS

In order to "match" the rag doll which is Goldilocks and so as to introduce yet another type of Teddy bear, a simple, swing-legged design has been used. These are quickly and easily made up, yet can be full of character. They could easily be made washable with a little thought as to stuffing and the material used for footpads and paws, and they all wear the minimum of easily removable clothes, which do up down the centre back.

LITTLE, SMALL, WEE BEAR
Illustration Plate 12

Height: 12 ins. Pattern pages 268–9.

Materials

¼ yard fur fabric 48 ins. wide (long-pile nylon in "Honey" shade was used for the original).
Scraps of matching felt for paws and footpads.
About 2 ozs. kapok for stuffing.
Dark brown and white stranded cotton for eyes, nose, mouth and claws.
Approx. ¼ oz. 2-ply white wool for jersey.
One 9-in. square blue felt for trousers.
Tiny press studs for fastenings.
A wooden meat skewer for stiffening neck.
Note. ⅝ yard material makes all three bears.

Method

Cut out the pieces as given on pages 268–9 (23 pieces in all).

Legs

Place the pieces together in pairs and stitch seams A–B and C–D. Insert footpads, matching letters, and stitch all round B–D–B. Turn right side out. Stuff each leg as far as broken line X–O–X. Now flatten the leg at top so that the X's touch and stitch across O–X–O. Turn in the raw edge at top so that A touches C and oversew across E–AC–E. The unstuffed piece at top will later form a "hinge" so that legs swing and the bear will sit down. Place legs on one side.

Arms

Place the felt paws in position as shown by broken line on pattern and hem neatly all round; remember to make a pair! Then place the arm pieces together in pairs and stitch all round F–G–H. Turn right side out and stuff both arms as far as broken line X–X. Turn in raw edges F–H and oversew. Place arms on one side. Stitch across X–X.

Ears

Place together in pairs and stitch all round I–J–K. Turn right side out and oversew raw edges I–L–K (Fig. 21 (1, 2, 3 and 5)).

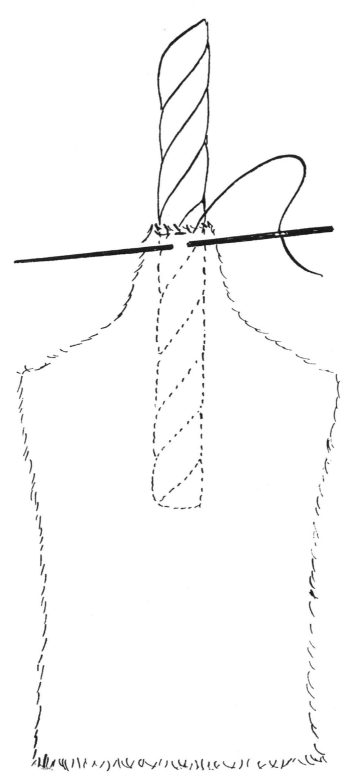

Fig. 64. Stiffening the necks of the Three Bears.

175

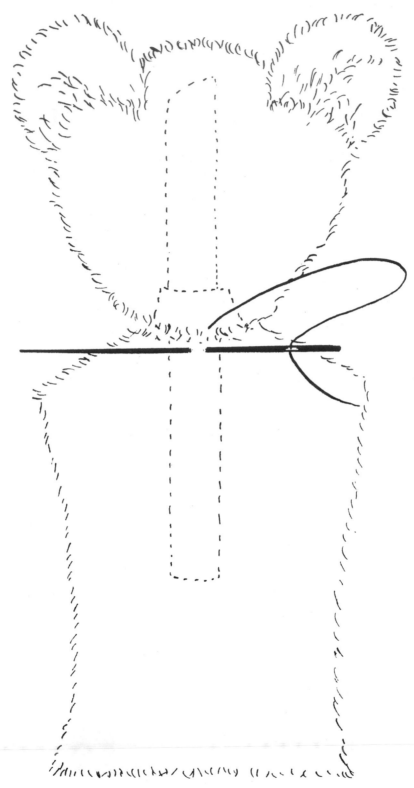

Fig. 65. Attaching the heads of the Three Bears.

176

13 Peter the Little Boy Panda.

14 The Glove Circus Bear and Mishka.

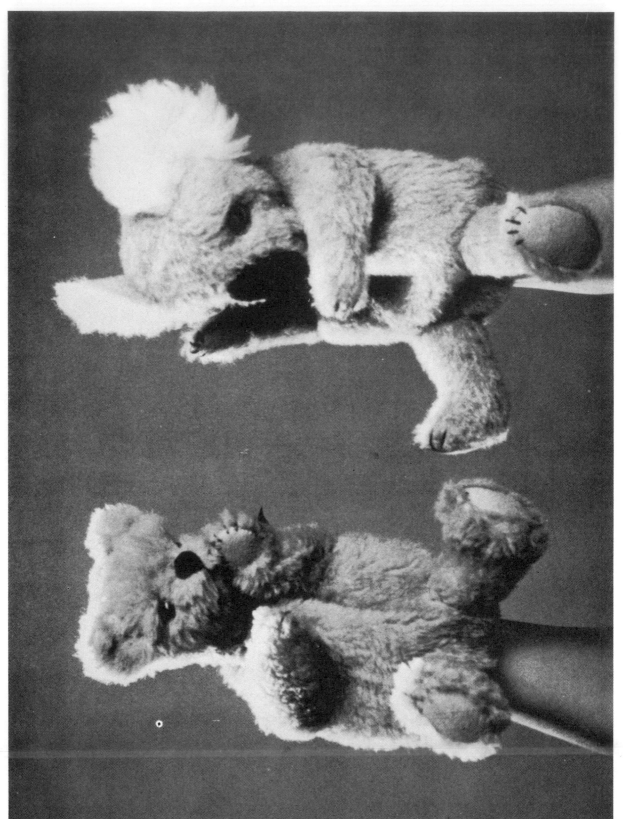

15 Glove Teddy and Koala.

Head

Cut slits L–K and insert ears into these, matching L–K. Tack, and stitch L–K (Fig. 21 (6)). Oversew other halves of edges of ears L–I along top of head, matching letters (Fig. 21 (6)). Insert head gusset, stitching on both sides M–N–I–L–P. (Take special care between I and L where there are four thicknesses of material.) Fold end of gusset in half so that the M's meet and stitch down front of head Q–M–R (Fig. 45). Turn head right way out, stuff and place on one side.

Body

Place the body pieces together and stitch all down S–T–U–V on both sides, leaving S–S and V–V open. Turn right side out. Stuff very firmly, turn in and oversew V–V, still leaving S–S open. Take the wooden meat skewer and bind it with an odd piece of rag as shown for Goldilocks (Fig. 58 A and B). Push this halfway into body through the hole at S–S (Fig. 64). Add more stuffing so that the skewer is firmly embedded. Gather round S–S, pull up to fit skewer and stitch firmly to the binding rag (Fig. 64). Place head on to body so that S–T (i.e. the "neck") and the other half of the skewer disappear right up into head and R on head is at R on body pattern. With the point of your scissors tuck the raw neck edge of head R–P–R up inside head and stitch firmly all round here, working round and round several times for safety (Fig. 65). (If you want your bear to look sideways, it is a simple matter to turn the head before stitching.)

Assembling

Working at the back of the bear, oversew each arm to the top of the body, as shown for Goldilocks, Fig. 58 C, and each leg to the base in the same way as shown for Goldilocks, Fig. 59 A, using strong thread.

Claws

Embroider these as described on page 84 and Fig. 22.

Eyes, nose and mouth

Embroider these as described on pages 70–4 and Figs. 12 and 13. A suitable size is shown on the pattern page and the eyes look well about $1\frac{1}{4}$ in. apart and about $\frac{1}{2}$ in. up the gusset seam from the nose.

Modelling

This type of bear *is* inclined to look a little like a signpost with his arms stuck out on either side! If you object to this they can easily be modelled and curved. Fold each arm as you want it and with a long, slim needle and strong thread, take long, invisible stitches to keep it in place (Fig. 66).

Jersey

This simple jersey has a shoulder fastening so that it slips easily over the bear's large head. With 3-ply wool and two knitting needles (gauge 12 or U.S. 1) cast on 28 stitches. Work in K2, P2 rib for 6 rows.

Work 34 rows in stocking stitch.

Next row: K8, cast off 12 for neck, K8.

Work 8 more rows of stocking stitch on these last eight stitches for overlap on shoulder fastening. Cast off.

Join wool on to other eight stitches and work 16 rows in stocking stitch for shoulder. Cast on 12 stitches for neck.

On separate needles cast on 8 stitches for underlap of shoulder fastening and work 7 rows in stocking stitch. Now, with the needle containing the rest of the jersey, knit right across these 8 stitches (28 stitches on needle).

Work 33 rows in stocking stitch.

Work in K2, P2 rib for 6 rows.

Neck: Treat the square neck as a round and with the right side of the work facing you pick up and knit 38 sts. all round here.

Work 6 rows in K1, P1 rib. Cast off in rib.

On the open shoulder, overlap one side over the other so that the work is double and the 16 rows become the same length as the 8 on the other shoulder. Oversew them in place on outside (sleeve) edge.

Sleeves: With the right side of the work facing you pick up and knit 32 sts. along the edge—16 on each side of the "shoulder".

Work 20 rows in stocking stitch.

Work 6 rows in K2, P2 ribbing. Cast off.

Make the other sleeve in the same way.

Making up: Press work flat under a damp cloth. Sew up sleeve and side seams in one. Reinforce edges of shoulder openings with narrow white tape hemmed neatly to the wrong side and fasten with three tiny press studs (size 000).

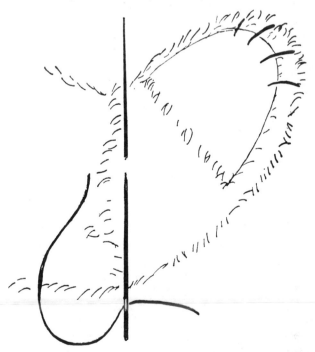

Fig. 66. Modelling the arms of the Three Bears.

Trousers

Fold each piece in half and join leg seams B–C. Then place the two pieces together and stitch down centre front seam and up the back A–B–D. Try on bear and if they are the correct size for the amount of stuffing you have used, join two darts E–F and two darts H–I. If too large at waist make these darts a little larger. Turn right side out. Turn up base of trousers and press—making "cuffed" legs. Cut a strip of matching felt $\frac{1}{4}$ in. wide and stab stitch this in place all round top edge of trousers. Then stab stitch all round the lower edge of this strip.

Cut two more strips of felt about $\frac{5}{8}$ in. wide and 8 in. long for braces. Turn about $\frac{1}{8}$ in. back on either side, stab stitch all down each edge, leaving the finishing braces $\frac{3}{8}$ in. wide, with a neat row of stitching down the sides. On the wrong side, stitch one to each side of back of trousers on the outer side of darts, as shown on pattern, and at an angle so that they cross easily at centre back. Put on to the bear and crossing the braces adjust them to fit, fastening them to the trousers with a small press stud (on the inside).

MIDDLE-SIZED BEAR
Illustration Plate 12

Height: about $14\frac{1}{2}$ ins. Pattern pages 270–3.

Materials

$\frac{1}{4}$ yard fur fabric 48 ins. wide (long-pile nylon in "Honey" shade was used for the original).
Scraps of matching felt for paws and footpads.
About $3\frac{1}{2}$ ozs. kapok for stuffing.
$\frac{1}{2}$ oz. 3-ply wool for the shawl.
Dark brown and white stranded cotton for eyes, nose and claws.
$\frac{3}{8}$ yard soft wool or cotton material 36 ins. wide for dress and panties.
$\frac{1}{4}$ yard or odd pieces of checked gingham for apron.
Tiny press studs for fastenings.
A wooden meat skewer for stiffening neck.
Note. $\frac{5}{8}$ yard material makes all three bears.

Method

Cut out the pieces as given on pages 270–3 and a piece of material $6\frac{1}{2}$ ins. × 34 ins. for the skirt, and one $5\frac{1}{2}$ ins. × 11 ins. for the apron (27 pieces in all).

The Bear

Make her up exactly as given for the Little, Small, Wee Bear on page 174. Note suggested sizes for her eyes and nose are given on page 273.

Panties

Make up exactly as given for Goldilocks on page 170.

Dress

Slit one bodice piece U–T. This is the back. Join shoulder seams O–P and side seams M–N. The dress is sleeveless and does up down centre back from top to bottom. Bind the armholes with a narrow strip of the same material, cut on the cross. Gather the skirt strip along one of the long edges, adjust gathers to fit lower edge of bodice and space them evenly all round, pulling them away from the extreme edges at T, so that a hem can be turned all down back opening later.

Stitch skirt to bodice all round T–N–N–T. Turn back a very narrow hem U–T bottom of skirt, on both sides, and stitch. Turn up a hem all round bottom of skirt, so that the dress is about 2 ins. from ground. Sew four or five small press studs down centre back opening to fasten it.

Apron

Turn back a very narrow hem all round the two short and one long edge of apron. Run a gathering thread along the other long edge and pull it up so that this edge is 3½ ins. long. Fasten off gathers.

Cut a strip of gingham 15 ins. × 3 ins. for apron strings. Place the centre point of this to centre of gathered edge of apron on the right side and stitch all along top edge. Turn the strip over on to the wrong side and turning in the raw edge slip stitch all along. (The gathered edge of the apron is now bound.) Working on first one string and then the other turn in the lower raw edges so that each string is the same width as this binding (about ⅜ in.) and oversew right along these edges and across ends.

A tiny pocket and hankie can be added for an extra attraction and rows of cross stitch worked along the bottom edge of apron and top of pocket for a decoration (see Plate 12). Gingham is ideal material for this as the checks act as a guide.

Shawl

With size 8 needles (U.S. 6) and 3-ply wool cast on 3 stitches. Work in garter stitch (plain knitting).

Increase one stitch at the beginning and end of every row until there are 53 stitches on the needle. Knit 16 rows. Cast off loosely.

Crochet an edge all the way round if you wish, and place on the bear with the point at centre back and front corners crossed and tucked into the top of the apron.

GREAT, BIG, HUGE BEAR
Illustration Plate 12
Height: about 17 ins. Pattern pages 272–7.

Materials

⅜ yard fur fabric 48 ins. wide (long-pile nylon in "Honey" shade was used for the original).

Scraps of matching felt for paws and footpads.

About 5½ ozs. kapok for stuffing.

Dark brown and white stranded cotton for eyes, nose, mouth and claws.

Two 12-in. squares of grey felt for trousers.

One oz. 4-ply wool for jersey.

Note. ⅝ yard material makes all three bears.

Method
Cut out the pieces as given on pages 272–7 (23 pieces in all).

The Bear
Make him up exactly as given for the Little, Small, Wee Bear on pages 174–7. Note suggested sizes for his eyes and nose as given on pages 274–5.

Spectacles
If you would like to give your bear a pair of pince-nez spectacles as shown in Plate 12, take a piece of wire about the thickness of a 12–14 gauge knitting needle (U.S. 1–0) and with your pliers bend it to the shape shown in Fig. 67. Place these on the nose and stitch in place at either side of bridge.

Fig. 67. Plan for spectacles for the Great, Big, Huge, Bear.

Trousers
Fold each piece in half and on the WRONG side join seams A–B (oversewing will do well for this or stab stitch very near the edge). Then on the RIGHT side continue these seams from B–C. (This is so that the wrong side of seam will not show when the "turn-up" is made.) Turn back to the WRONG side. Place the two pieces together and join all down centre front and back seams G–A–G. Make a ½-in.-wide hem all round the waist leaving a small "gap" for elastic later. Turn RIGHT side out, fold the trousers flat and turn up the bottoms, B–E–B. Press under a damp cloth to form "creases". Insert a piece of elastic in the top hem to fit the bear's waist.

Polo-necked jersey
In order to get this over the bear's large head it has an opening down centre back.
You will need: one pair knitting needles size 10 and one pair size 8.
Front and Back:
    Cast on 32 stitches on size 10 needles (U.S. 3).
    Work in K2, P2 rib for 6 rows.
    Change to size 8 needles (U.S. 6).
    Work 36 rows in stocking stitch ending with a P row.
    K10, cast off 12, K10. (Leave the first 10 stitches on a spare needle.)
    Continue on the last 10 stitches:
    *Work 5 rows in stocking stitch ending at neck edge.

Cast on 9 stitches (19 stitches). Continue on these 19 stitches:

Work 36 rows of stocking stitch, but always knit the 3 stitches at inside edge, i.e. all down back opening, so as to keep this firm.

Change to size 10 needles (U.S. 3) and work in K2, P2 rib for 6 rows. Cast off.*

Return to the 10 stitches left on the spare needle.

Join in the wool and work down this side of the back (i.e. from* to *) to match the other—keeping the three knitted stitches at the opposite end of the rows.

Sleeves: With the right side of the work facing and size 8 needles, pick up and knit 28 stitches along one of the outside edges of jersey, 14 on each side of the "shoulder".

Work 21 rows in stocking stitch. Change to size 10 needles, work 6 rows in K2, P2 rib. Cast off.

Work the other sleeve in the same way.

Collar: With the right side of the work facing and size 10 needles, pick up and knit 44 stitches all round edge of neck. Work 15 rows in K2, P2 rib. Cast off in rib.

Press the work flat, using a hot iron and damp cloth. Sew up side and sleeve seams all in one. Sew eight small press studs all down the back opening, including the collar. Put on to bear, fasten all down back and turn down collar.

Did you know that "Winnie-the-Pooh" had been translated into Latin? This must surely be the only book about a Teddy bear to have this distinction.

Dr. Alexander Lenard, who is of Hungarian birth and lives in Brazil, translated the story into German before he embarked on the Latin version which took him seven years. In 1958 Methuen produced a limited version of "Winnie Ille Pu", but the book was brought out properly in 1960.

Dr. Lenard is said to have read his way through 36½ shelf-inches of Latin classics, Juvenal, Pliny, Ovid, etc., while searching for the exact sentences or phrases for "Pu"!

A CHAPTER FOR CHILDREN

If you like sewing and have been watching Mummy make Teddy bears, you may have been wishing you could make one for yourself. This chapter is specially for YOU and contains instructions for making two different sorts of Teddies—easy ones that you will be able to do alone. One is made from two flat pieces of fur fabric and the other from seven circles made into large pompoms. Ask Mummy for some odd pieces of her material and borrow the book for a little while. You'll find them both fun to do.

A BEAR FROM TWO FLAT PIECES
Illustration Fig. 71

Height: 7½ ins.

Turn to page 279, where you will find a pattern for this bear. Trace it on to a piece of cardboard and cut out the shape. Place this cardboard shape on the WRONG SIDE of a piece of fur fabric and with a soft pencil draw all round it. Do this twice and cut out the two pieces; one is for the front and one for the back. If you can manage it, have the pile on the fur fabric (that is, the fur itself) so that it strokes downwards on your bear in the way the arrow points on the pattern. If you stroke your kitten or puppy you will feel that the fur or hair grows downwards, away from his head—he would look very funny if it grew upwards!

Now follow Fig. 68 and directions 1 and 2 on it. (The oversewing is just a good way of tacking fur fabric.) Then Fig. 69 and directions 3, 4 and 5. (If you can use a sewing machine you will save a lot of time. If not, be sure to backstitch very tightly.) Then follow directions 6, 7, 8, 9, 10, 11, 12 and 13 on Fig. 70, any kind of stuffing will do, and push it in with the wrong end of a pencil or a wooden meat skewer. Pull up the gathers at the neck tightly, to make it slim and when stitching across the base of ears and limbs use ordinary, small, straight stitches stabbing the needle right through from the front of the bear to the back, so as to separate each part.

Lastly, follow directions 14, 15, 16, 17 and 18 on Fig. 71. This bear has a very flat face, which doesn't really matter as he's nice and small to slip into your pocket, but if you would rather he had a "snout" make a pompom as shown by Fig. 72 (1 and 2) and described on page 189, using an egg cup for drawing the circle, and stitch it to the lower part of the front of his face, as shown by Fig. 72 (4). Then embroider the nose on this pompom, as in Fig. 72 (5).

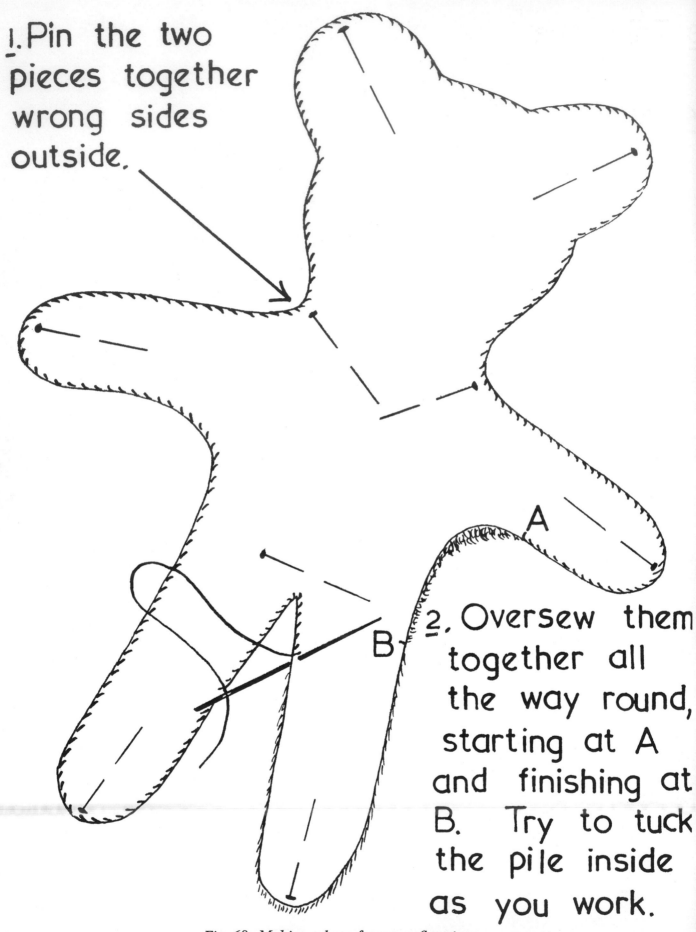

1. Pin the two pieces together wrong sides outside.

A

B

2. Oversew them together all the way round, starting at A and finishing at B. Try to tuck the pile inside as you work.

Fig. 68. Making a bear from two flat pieces.

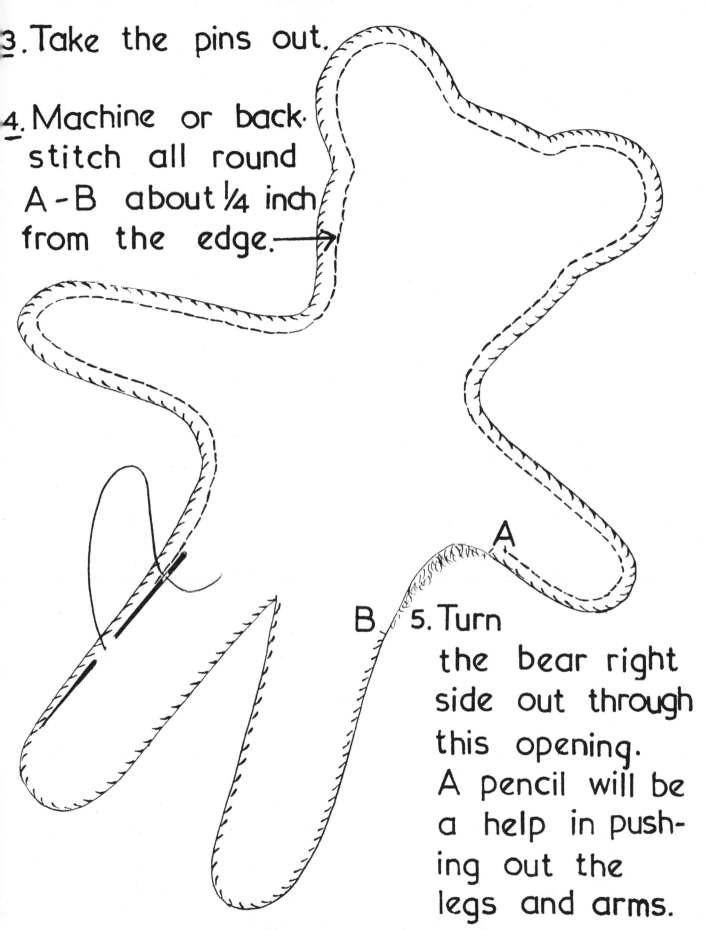

3. Take the pins out.

4. Machine or back stitch all round A – B about ¼ inch from the edge. ⟶

A

B

5. Turn the bear right side out through this opening. A pencil will be a help in pushing out the legs and arms.

Fig. 69. Making a bear from two flat pieces (contd.).

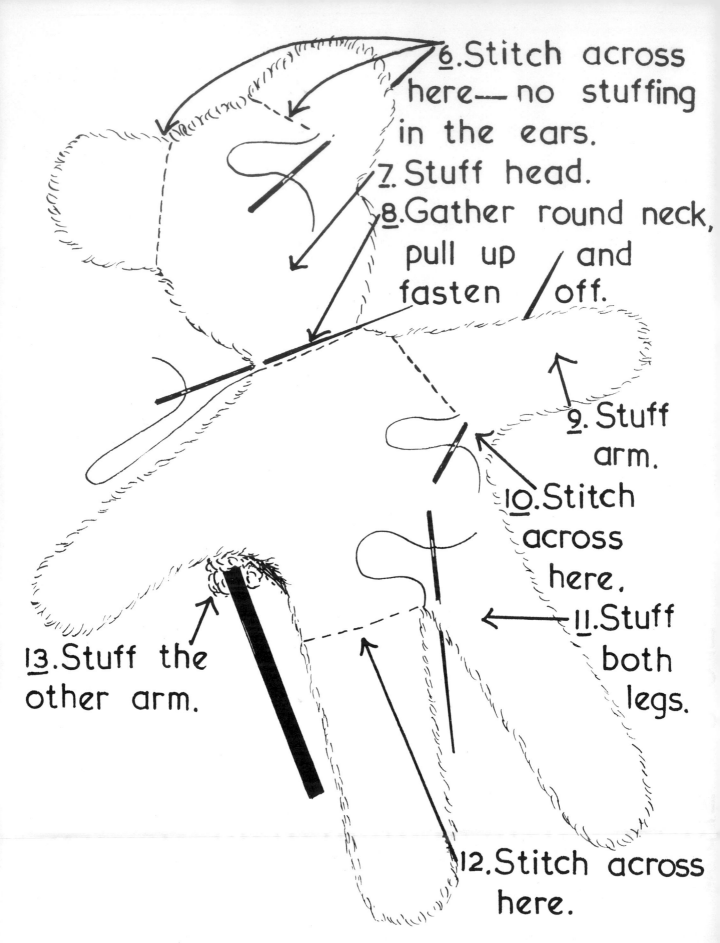

6. Stitch across here—no stuffing in the ears.

7. Stuff head.

8. Gather round neck, pull up and fasten off.

9. Stuff arm.

10. Stitch across here.

11. Stuff both legs.

12. Stitch across here.

13. Stuff the other arm.

Fig. 70. Making a bear from two flat pieces (contd.).

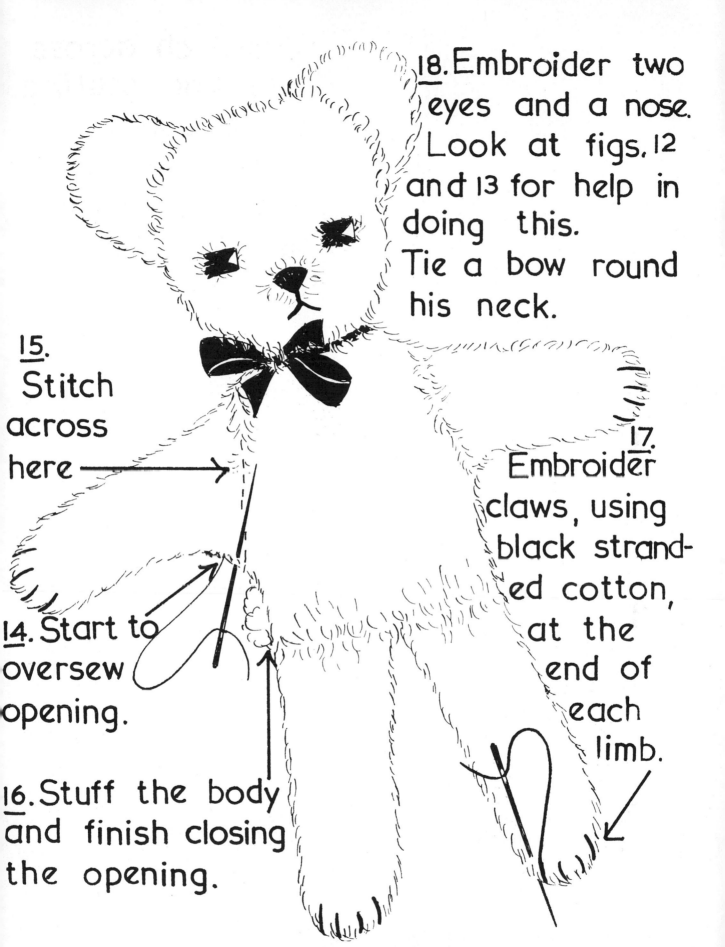

18. Embroider two eyes and a nose. Look at figs. 12 and 13 for help in doing this. Tie a bow round his neck.

15. Stitch across here ⟶

14. Start to oversew opening.

16. Stuff the body and finish closing the opening.

17. Embroider claws, using black stranded cotton, at the end of each limb.

Fig. 71. Finishing off a bear from two flat pieces.

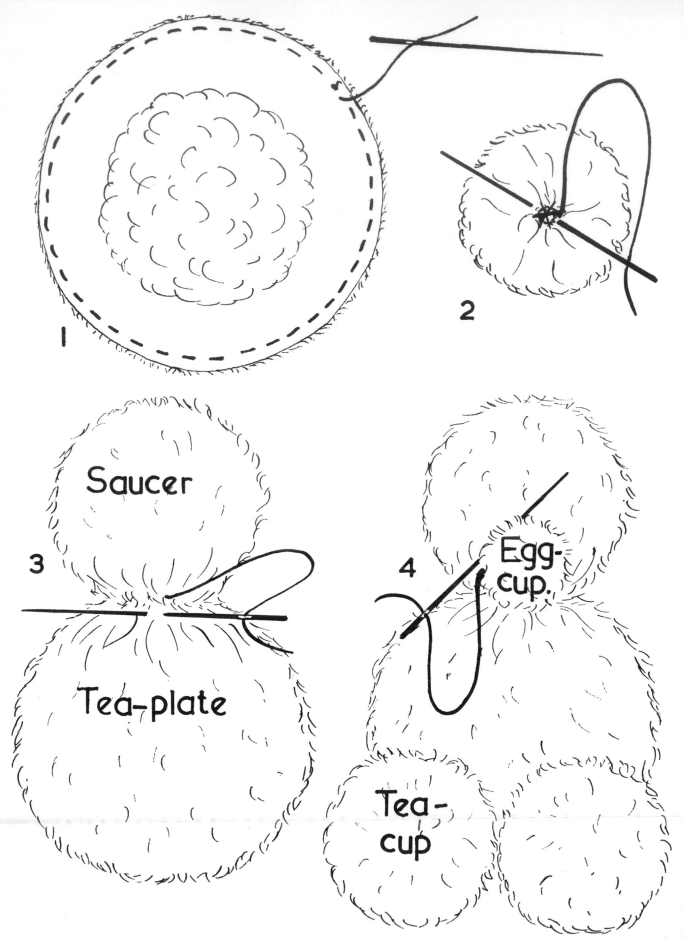

1

2

3   Saucer

Tea-plate

4   Egg-
    cup.

Tea-
cup

Fig. 72. Making a bear from circles.

188

A BEAR MADE FROM CIRCLES
Illustration Fig. 72

Height: about 4 ins.

Place a small plate, about 6 ins. across, on the back of a piece of fur fabric and pencil all round it. Cut out the circle—this is for the body. Then cut one circle the size of a saucer for the head, four the size of a teacup for the arms and legs, and one the size of an egg cup for the "snout". Make each one of these circles into a ball by gathering all round the outside edge and placing some stuffing in the centre of it (Fig. 72 (1)), then pulling up the gathers and fastening off (Fig. 72 (2)). Sew the saucer- and plate-sized ones together, with the gathered up parts inside where they will not show, and join them by stitching round and round several times, taking a stitch first on one ball, then on the other (Fig.

72 (3)). Join on the egg-cup-sized ball to make a "snout" (Fig. 72 (4)) and two of the tea-cup-sized balls for legs (Fig. 72 (4)).

Join on the other two teacup-sized balls for arms (Fig. 72 (5)).

Trace the ear pattern on this page and cut out two pieces this shape, using felt which matches the fur fabric as nearly as possible. (Mummy may have some over from making footpads on her bears.) Stitch the ears to the head in a nice curved position. Look at Fig. 12 for help and embroider the nose and mouth, then at Fig. 13 and embroider the eyes, using thick, black, stranded cotton. Don't forget to give both eyes a little white highlight, it brings the bear to life.

VARIATIONS

The bear in the picture was fawn, he was made from pieces of material over from the Honey Bears in the first picture, but any colour would do, even pink or blue. Brown fur fabric with a little piece of white for a snout makes a lovely cuddly bear, and if you have black and white pieces you could try making a panda (both shown in Fig. 73).

Pattern for ear.

Panda's eye patch.

Fig. 73. An idea for a brown bear and a panda made from circles.

191

HAVING A TEDDY BEARS' PICNIC

Have you ever had a Teddy Bears' Picnic instead of an ordinary party?
Parties are hard work for Mummies and there is a lot you could do to help if you tried.
A party is always more fun if you have planned it yourself.

Invitations

Naturally, you will need to send an invitation to each of your friends AND her Teddy bear. An idea for a design is given in Fig. 74. Trace the picture from here on to a card and paint it. Write your address on the back.

Fig. 74. A design to trace when making invitations to a Teddy bears' picnic.

Food

Mummy probably has a Teddy bear pastry cutter and will be able to make you biscuits this shape. If not, trace the shape in Fig. 75 on to a clean postcard and ask her to place this on her rolled-out biscuit mixture and cut round it with a sharp knife. *You* can put currants on them for eyes, nose and mouth. Ask Mummy to make a chocolate sponge, then decorate it yourself. To do this, trace and cut out in postcard the Teddy shapes in Fig. 75 and put them on top of the cake (which has NOT been iced). Sieve a thick layer of icing sugar all over the top of the cake, then very carefully lift off the postcard Teddies. Their shape will be left brown and showing up clearly among the white icing sugar.

Of course, you must have HONEY to eat as well.

16 The Snouty Bear and Pram Teddy seem to be "cooking something up", watched by the Thinking Bear Lying on His Tummy.

17 Two clown and two little boy bears having fun, watched by the caricature Koala.

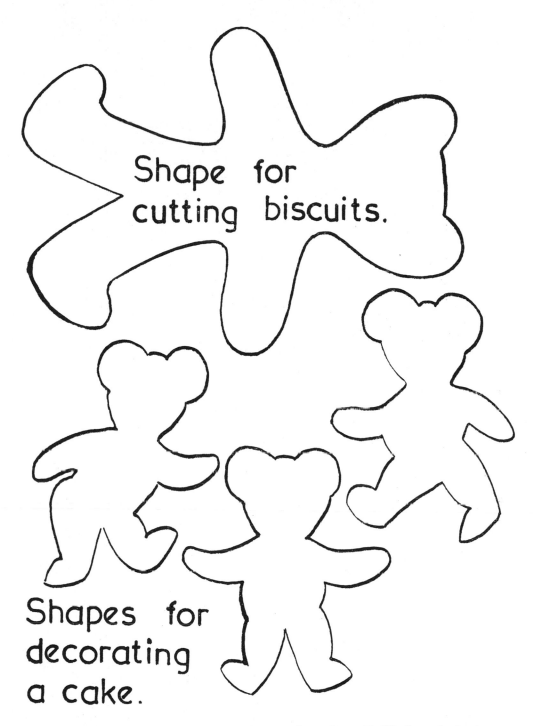

Shape for cutting biscuits.

Shapes for decorating a cake.

Fig. 75. Designs to help you when cooking for a Teddy bears' picnic.

Fig. 76. A design to trace when making place cards for a Teddy bears' picnic.

Place cards

Trace these from Fig. 76 on to a postcard, paint them and cut out the shape. Write each friend's name on a card and her Teddy's name. Cut a strip of card as shown in Fig. 76, bend it along broken line and stick this piece to the back of the bear so that he stands up.

Presents

If you want a little present for your guests, try to think of something connected with Teddy bears. Perhaps you could make them each one of the bears described in this chapter, especially if someone helped you. Chocolate Teddy bears would be fun, you can buy them from most sweet shops, or the little booklet *The Story of the Teddy Bears' Picnic* (see page 281). A tiny jar of honey would make a lovely present for each Teddy bear, or a new bow for his neck (page 200 gives an idea for making these as ribbon is expensive).

BEARS FOR BAZAARS

Stocking bazaar stalls can be quite a problem, for understandably enough, customers openly seek only real bargains, and only articles which are really attractive as well as useful are snapped up. We are all too familiar with dreary stalls full of drab bits and pieces, and everyone makes an immediate beeline for something with real appeal! There is no doubt that Teddy bears (but only those with nice expressions) are best sellers.

Usually, one finds oneself with lots of bits and pieces of material but very little time in which to sit and sew, but there are, of course, the folk with all the time in the world for sewing and who would love to help but who do not possess and cannot afford to buy the necessary materials. A little passing round and sorting out can usually put this right.

Bits and pieces over from other toys are obviously the things to use for Bazaar Bears. It does seem such a complete waste of time to spend hours and a lot of money making beautiful toys which barely recover the cost of the materials used. One feels it would surely be less worry to give the amount one's material would have cost to the cause concerned and save oneself the unnecessary work.

TWO-COLOUR CLOWN BEARS
Illustration Plate 17

Often one finds oneself with sufficient material to make half a bear but not enough for a whole one. The solution is to cut out two halves in different colours (the bigger contrast the better) and put them together to make a clown. Fig. 77 shows diagrammatically three ways of arranging the pieces. A and B are shown made up in Plate 17. Some thought and care are needed when cutting out, especially if using the arrangements shown in Fig. 77 B and C, or you will find you have some of your parts facing the wrong way! Footpads and paws can be of leather, felt or in the same fur fabric as the rest of the bear.

Almost any pattern will do, but for the originals the Pram Teddy (page 96) was used. Washable stuffing must be *bought*, so is rather extravagant for a bazaar bear and finely cut up fur fabric pieces over from other toys will help out.

It takes 5 ozs. of cuttings to fill this bear, so it is rather heavy when finished.

The eyes of the bears illustrated in Plate 17 are one in felt and one embroidered.

The ruffs are straight strips of material or wide ribbon edged with bias binding. They need to be really full to look nice—about 18 ins. long. Make a narrow hem at each short end, then run a gathering thread lengthwise down the centre, pull up to fit the neck exactly and fasten off. Sew a press stud at back to fasten. They need to be removable for washing and ironing.

A pattern for a clown's hat is given on page 239, but this can be extended or shortened to vary the size. Cut out in felt. Join seam A–B. Turn right side out, stuff and sew to head. To make pompoms, cut a circle of fur fabric, gather all round the edge, place a tiny knob of stuffing in the centre, pull up gathers and fasten off (Fig. 72, 1 and 2). Alternatively, use bobbles off an odd piece of lampshade fringe.

Fig. 77. Placing colours when making clown bears.

Fig. 78. Placing colours when making little boy bears.

"LITTLE BOY" BEARS IN TWO COLOURS
Illustration Plate 17

Another way of using up small pieces of different coloured fur fabrics is to make them into little boy bears. Fig. 78 shows two ideas diagrammatically, and if you look at Plate 17 you will see that one is a little boy in "trunks" and the other a bear wearing a pair of "leggings". For this one the footpads should be of the same material as the legs.

You will think of many more ideas of your own.

BEAR'S HEAD RATTLES
Illustration Fig. 79

If you have just enough material for the head of a bear, try making a rattle. Make up a small head—the Bouncy Bear is very suitable; before stuffing it place a small tin, containing a few dried peas or beans and sealed with adhesive tape, inside the head, then stuff carefully all round this so that the tin is completely embedded (Fig. 79 C). Take a piece of wood such as an old dish-mop handle or a piece of dowelling 9 or 10 ins. long, and cut a strip of fur fabric to cover it. Stick the material in place with just a trace of Copydex or similar rubber-based adhesive so that the wood will not "swivel" inside the material (Fig. 79 A). Then, turning in the raw edges, oversew along one end and down the length of the handle, drawing the fur fabric tightly round the wood (Fig. 79 B). Run a gathering thread round the neck edge of the head, turning in the raw edges (Fig. 79 C). Pull up the gathers tightly, pushing the covered wood inside. Push the handle *right* up into the head to make it firm and fasten off the gathers, stitching head securely to handle. (Instead of using a tin for a rattle you could sew two tiny bells to the ears—but remember these COULD come off and be swallowed!)

Finally, add the ears, embroider nose, mouth and eyes and if you wish, sew a bow of ribbon or felt at the neck (Fig. 79 D).

Note. The stick could be covered with felt if you are short of fur fabric.

OTHER IDEAS FOR BAZAAR BEARS

The two bears given in the chapter specially for children (page 183) are very quick to make up and the one cut from two pieces is a best seller, especially if given a "snout" as described on page 189. A large quantity of these can be made in a short time, they make an attractive display and can be priced low.

Tedwina, the Little Girl Glove Bear (page 114) can also be made cheaply, as only small pieces of fur fabric are needed for her head and paws. It would, of course, be too expensive to use felt for her dress, but checked gingham or any pretty cotton material you might happen to have by you could be used instead. While cotton material is ideal for the skirt it really is not quite thick enough for the bodice and sleeves. If a second bodice is cut from something strong like an odd piece of old sheet and the two materials are used together, so that the sheeting backs the gingham, sufficient extra strength will be added.

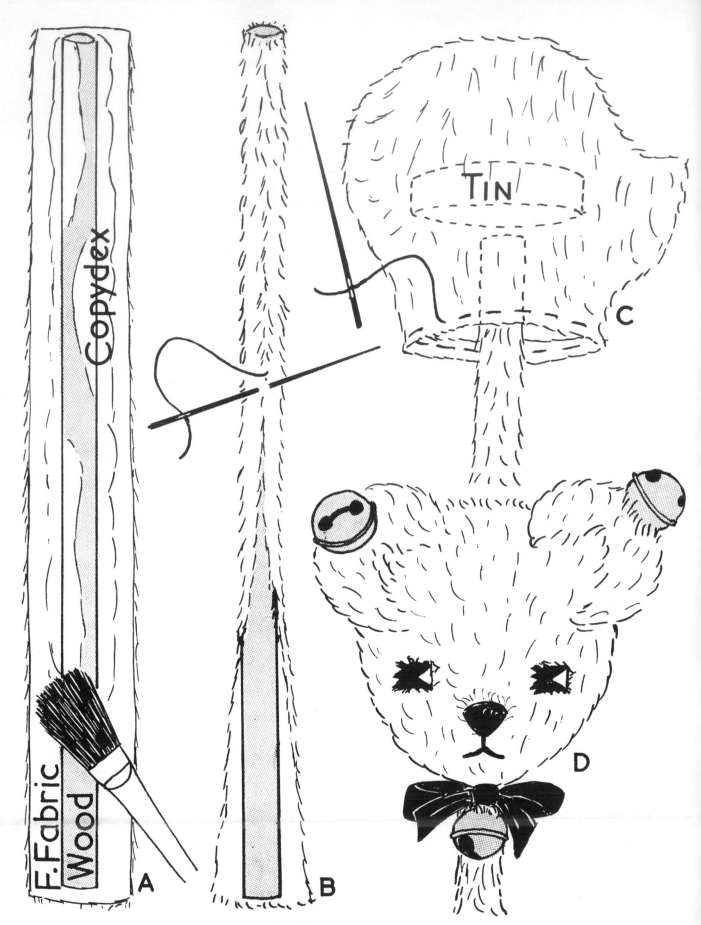

Fig. 79. Making a bear's head rattle.

RUNNING A TEDDY BEARS' HOSPITAL

When you have mastered the techniques of jointing, inserting glass eyes, etc., your talents will be much in demand as a repairer of neighbours' and friends' Teddy bears. Such services can be put to good use by running a Teddy bears' hospital at your local bazaar, fête or show. The first thing to do is to make sure the hospital is well advertised, not too far in advance or people will forget all about it and not too close to the date or there will not be time for would-be patients to be "got out", their odd limbs found and arrangements made for them to be brought for repair. Local papers are normally very helpful over anything a little unusual and if approached will probably give your effort a useful write-up. The following is an example recently used to advertise such a hospital run by a County Federation of Women's Institutes—gaps have been left for you to fill in dates, places, etc., to suit your own needs.

A TEDDY BEAR'S HOSPITAL AT THE   SHOW

It seems that the Teddy bear population are complaining of the shortage of hospitals where the many casualties among them can receive treatment. The main need appears to be for more ophthalmic and orthopaedic departments willing to tackle the ever growing queues of out-patients. Anxious as usual to help fill such gaps and as another step towards building Jerusalem in England's green and pleasant land, the   of   are running a hospital specially for Teddy bears in their tent at the   Show this year, where all injured and disabled bears are invited to attend for examination and, if possible, treatment.

Modern Teddy surgery can work miracles and is far in advance of that used on mere human beings. Instead of just doing a corneal graft, the surgeons on duty will be able to actually insert completely new eyes! In the same way, limbs which have become severed can be rejoined to the body, a feat only very rarely possible in the human species.

Please bring your bears early in the day and leave them while you visit the rest of the show. An up-to-date recovery room will be installed and your bear will be able to rest quietly while awaiting your return. Patients' next of kin are asked to pay the cost of the materials used (only a few pence) and it will be appreciated if they will also donate a small amount to the funds as a thank offering for the hospital's services. The out-patients department will be open to the public for the two days of the show—all visitors being welcome to watch the doctors and nurses at work. Operations are quite painless and medicines (which always taste of honey) are delicious, so your bear will be sure to enjoy his visit and will go away looking and feeling very much better for it. Please bring him to see us no matter how old and we will do our best to rejuvenate him, indeed geriatrics will be specially welcome!

Plenty of table space is needed and if possible some shelves as a background, everything being in spotless white! It is necessary to obtain a large supply of eyes and joints in every possible size, which can be on show in large glass jars. These can usually be had on sale or return. Stick a label with the price of the articles *under* each jar where it will not show or you will be in a muddle later. Stuffings can be stored in polythene bags under the tables and out of sight. Tools such as pliers, large needles and scissors can be on show, arranged in kidney dishes, and tiny bottles of medicine (lemonade coloured red) can be neatly labelled and available for patients to take home. Smarties or similar sweets make excellent pills!

Depending upon the size of the event one or two "nurses" (appropriately dressed, of course) and a doctor (in white overall with a borrowed stethoscope hanging round her neck) will be needed. One of the "nurses", handpicked, of course, for her ability to talk to children and enter into the spirit of the thing, receives the patients, labels them so that no muddles occur, arranges what time they shall be called for and puts them to bed to await treatment. She can also help by looking out the appropriate size "bits and pieces", and having them ready for the doctor, threading needles, opening seams, removing stuffing, etc. The "doctor" operates all the time, which makes an interesting demonstration for those unfamiliar with Teddy bear anatomy. The second nurse bandages the patients after treatment, sees that there is medicine for them to take home, puts them to bed to await collection and sees that the owners sign for them when taken away—this avoids confusion.

The hospital can be made attractive with a row of beds, all with matching counterpanes and small vases of flowers by each bed, also a tiny book and a doll's-size glass of water.

Two tins are needed for money, one to hold the payments for materials used and the other for contributions to the funds.

There is no doubt that such a hospital fills a very real need, is a good "draw", and is immense fun for all concerned.

SOME HINTS ON MAKING BEARS FOR BAZAARS

1. It is more fun and much quicker to work with others than alone. A series of "get togethers" over a cup of tea, when friends work on a "conveyor belt" system, usually works wonders. Seated round a large table one person tacks, one stitches, one stuffs, one does the faces, etc., etc.

2. If your bears are washable, label them as such. They are worth more and should fetch a much higher price.

3. Ribbons can be expensive, so make them by machining very narrow hems round odd strips of crisp taffeta or cotton materials. Be sure to make them wide enough. The bears in Plate 9 are wearing home-made "ribbons" of checked green-and-white gingham. If you *do* buy ribbon, avoid satin. Its slippery texture makes the bows constantly come undone. Nylon is much more satisfactory.

4. If selling Glove bears on a stall, have someone specially deputed to wear one on her hand and show its possibilities. They look empty and depressing lying in a heap and to the casual "looker round" it is not always apparent that they *are* glove bears.

Did you know that "Brumas", Polar bear cub of "Ivy" at the London Zoo, and who became so famous, was not in fact Ivy's first cub? Ivy produced cubs every year for some time, but never succeeded in rearing them. The raising of Brumas was a great achievement which caught the imagination of the public and brought 3 million visitors to the Gardens—a rise of a million on the average annual attendance.

THE PATTERNS

N.B. f.f. = fur fabric.   fe. = felt

x and * show position of joints.

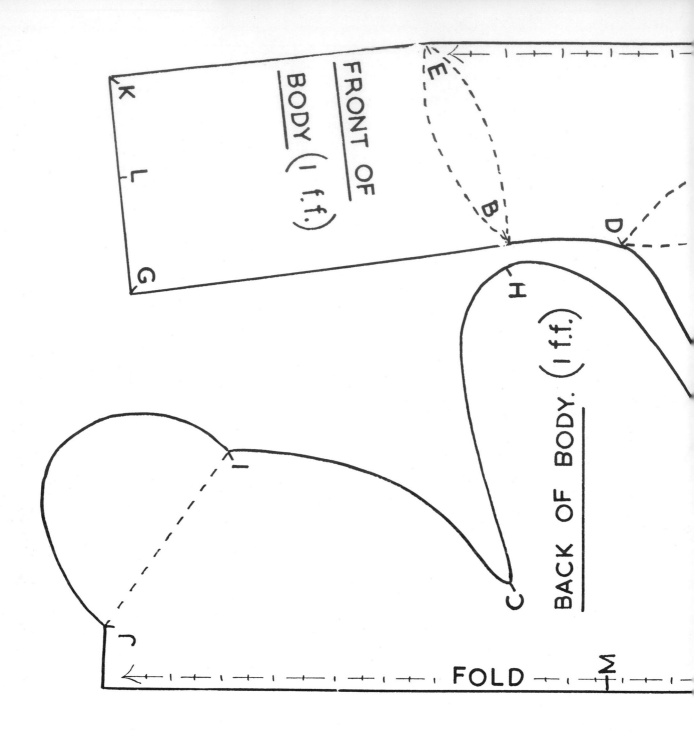

FRONT OF
BODY (i f.f.)

K   L   G

E   B   D

BACK OF BODY. (l f.f.)

H

C

I

J

FOLD

M

suggested size for eye.

202   SIMPLE BED-

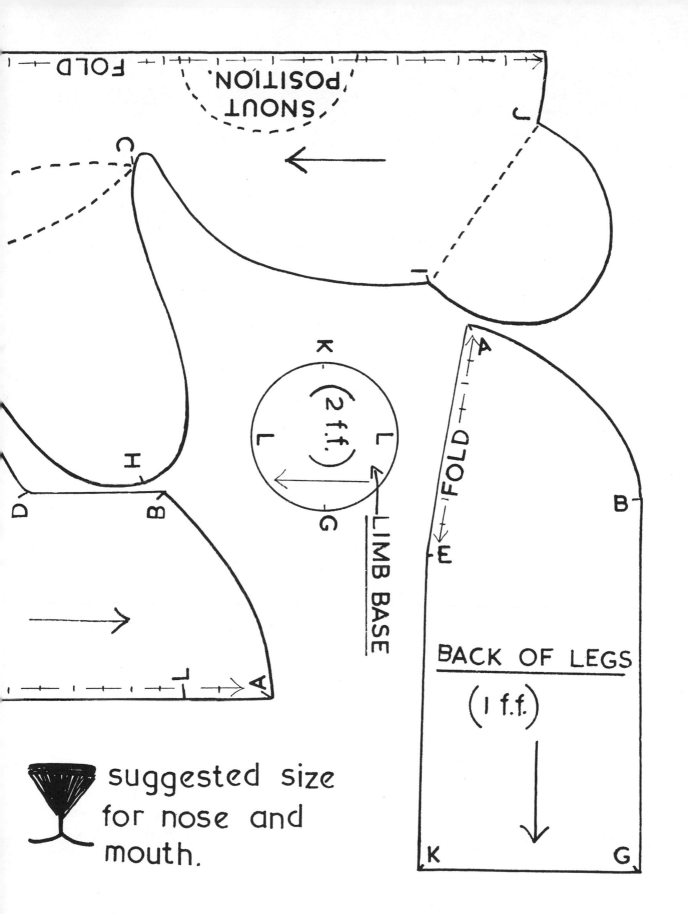

FOLD

SNOUT POSITION

C

H

D   B

LIMB BASE

K

(2 f.f.)

L   L

G

A

FOLD

E

B

BACK OF LEGS

(1 f.f.)

K   G

suggested size for nose and mouth.

TIME TEDDY.

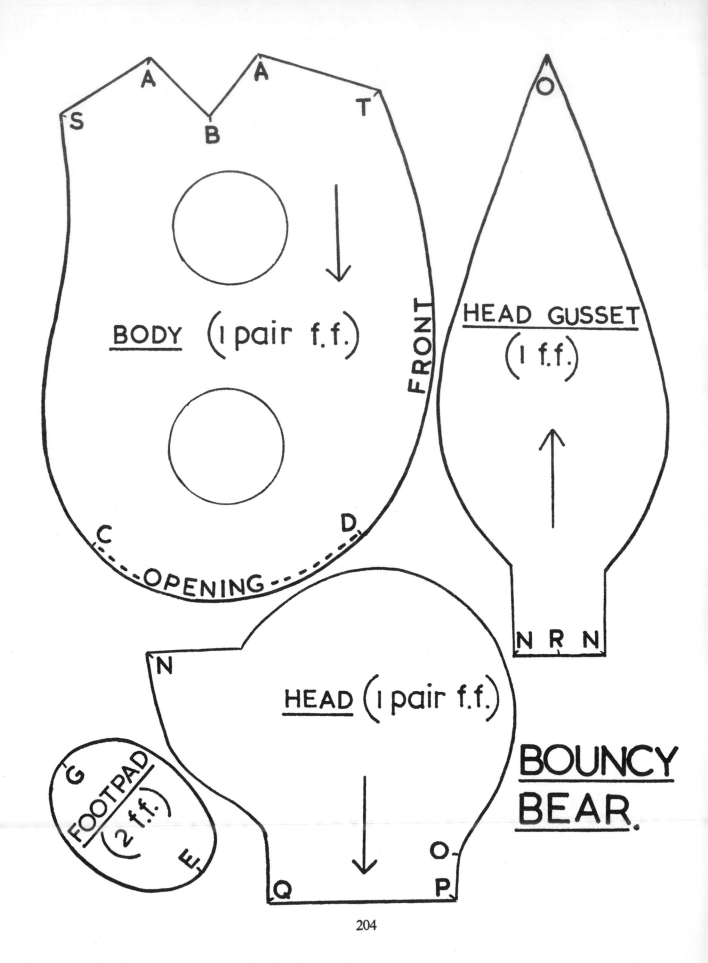

BOUNCY BEAR.

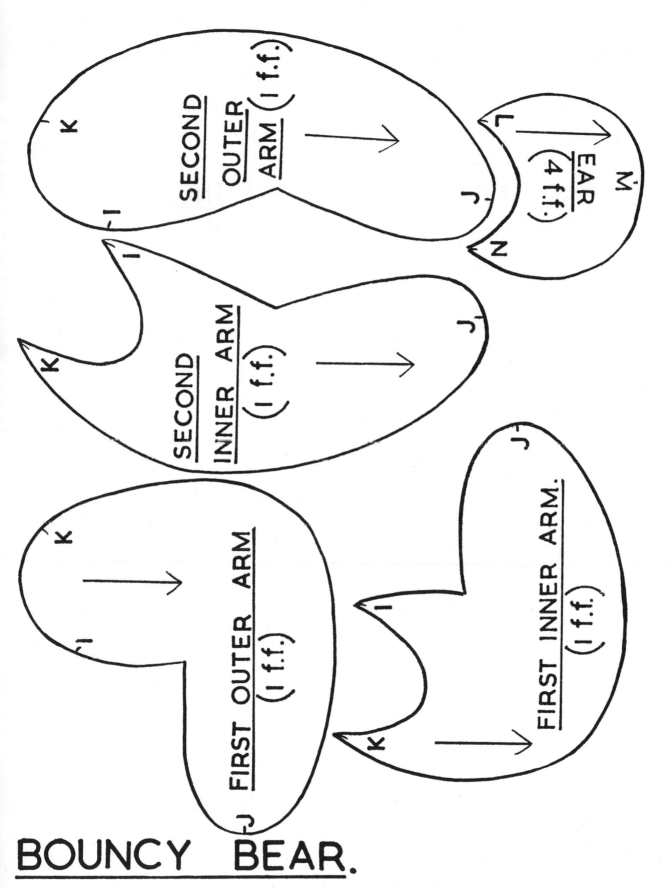

BOUNCY BEAR.

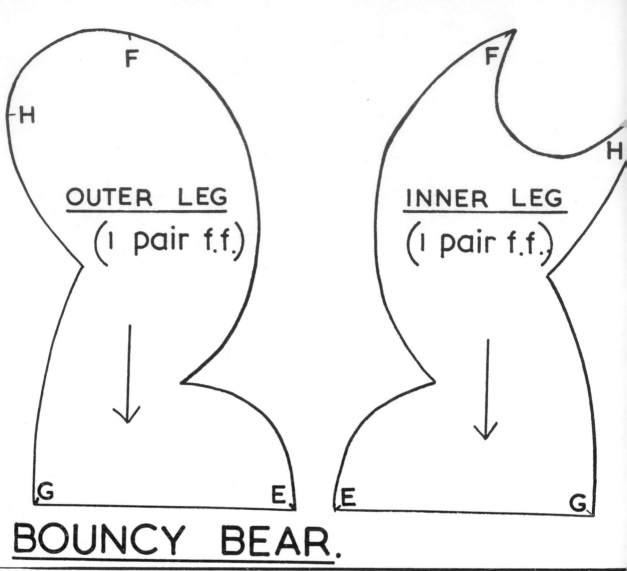

BOUNCY BEAR.

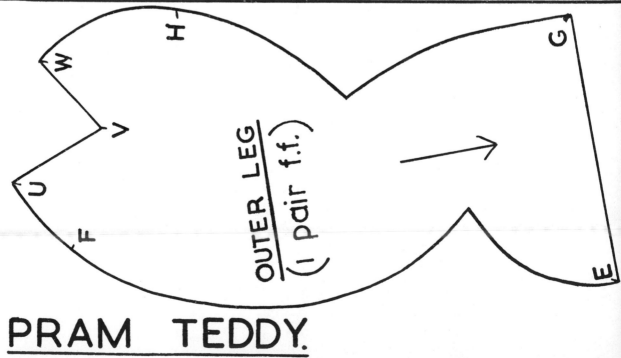

PRAM TEDDY.

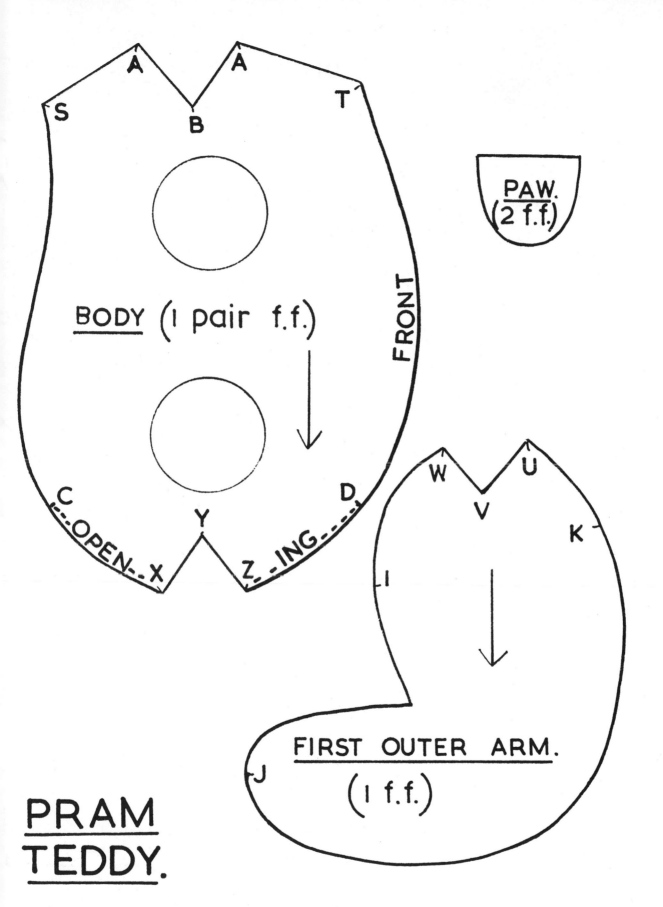

BODY (1 pair f.f.)

FRONT

PAW.
(2 f.f.)

FIRST OUTER ARM.
(1 f.f.)

PRAM
TEDDY.

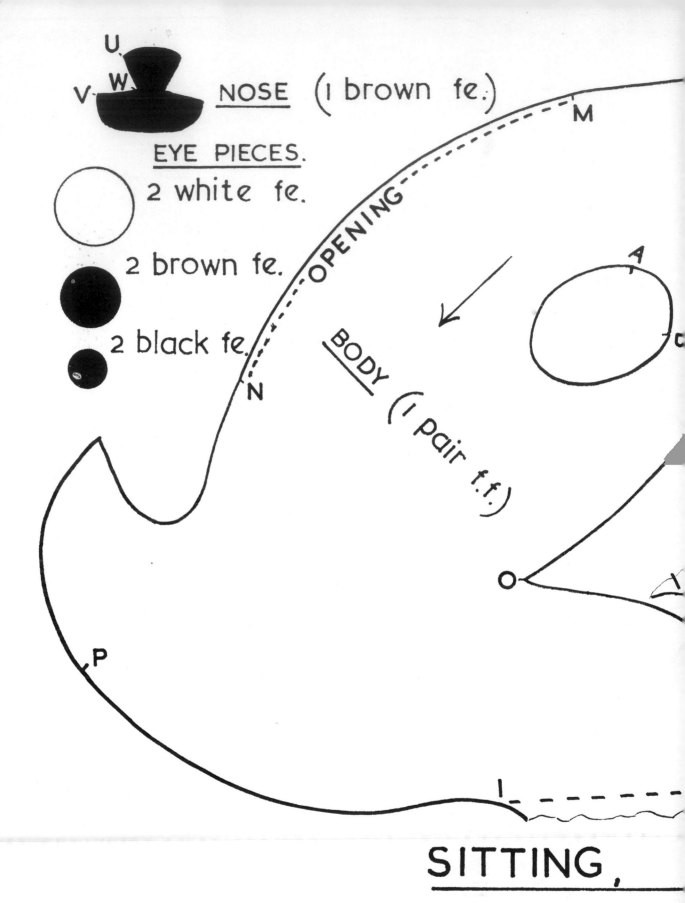

NOSE (1 brown fe.)

EYE PIECES.

2 white fe.

2 brown fe.

2 black fe.

U.

V. W.

OPENING

M

BODY (1 pair f.f.)

A

N

O

P

I

SITTING,

208

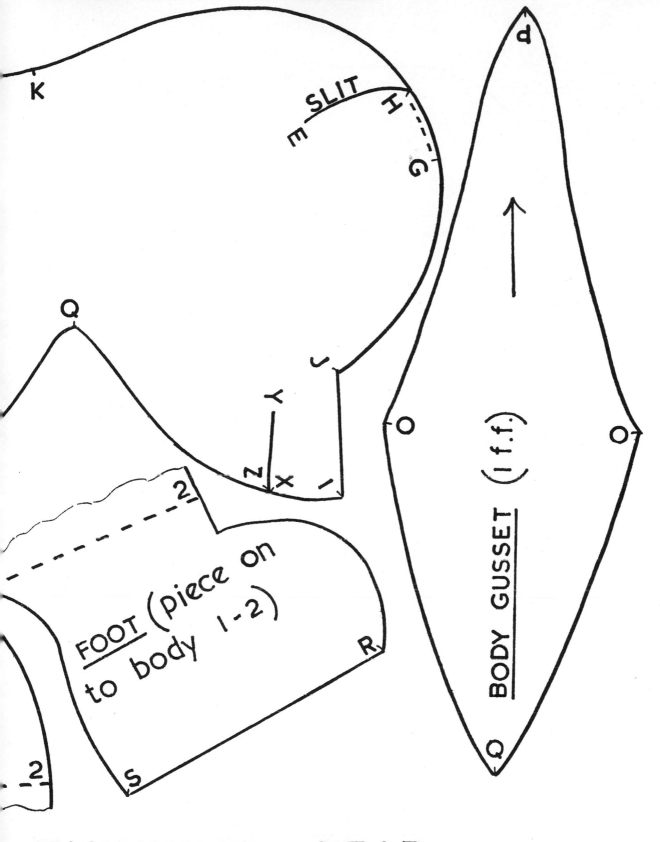

SLIT

FOOT (piece on to body 1 - 2)

BODY GUSSET (1 f.f.)

THINKING BEAR.

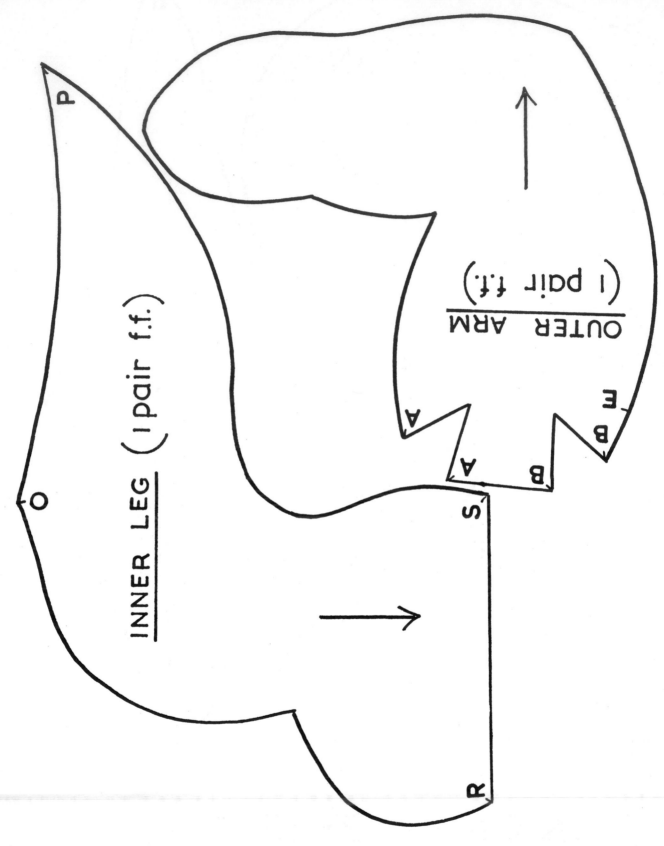

INNER LEG (1 pair f.f.)

OUTER ARM (1 pair f.f.)

P

O

A

B

E

A

B

S

R

SITTING, THINKING BEAR.

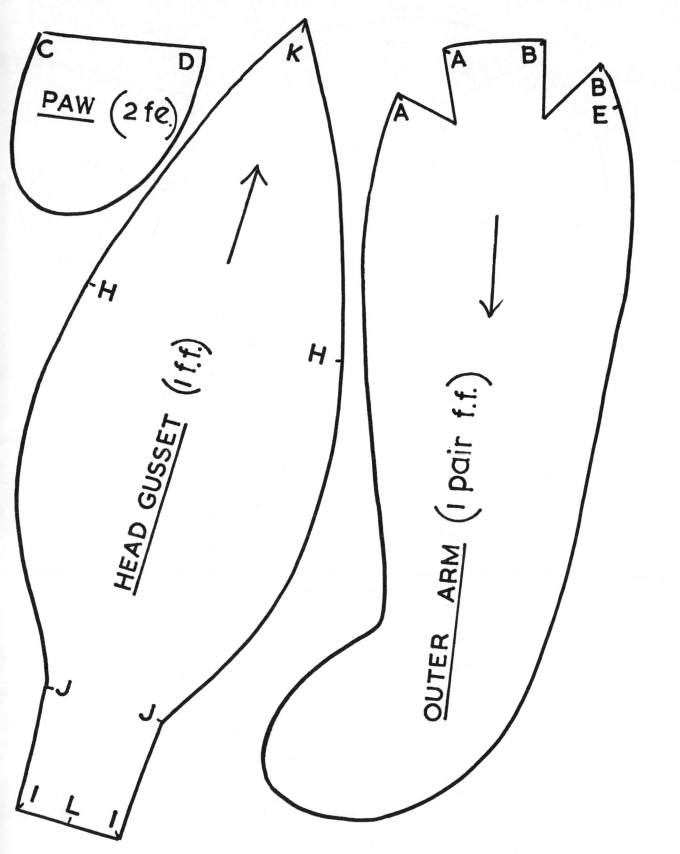

PAW (2 fe.)

HEAD GUSSET (1 f.f.)

OUTER ARM (1 pair f.f.)

BEAR WITH A BEE ON NOSE.

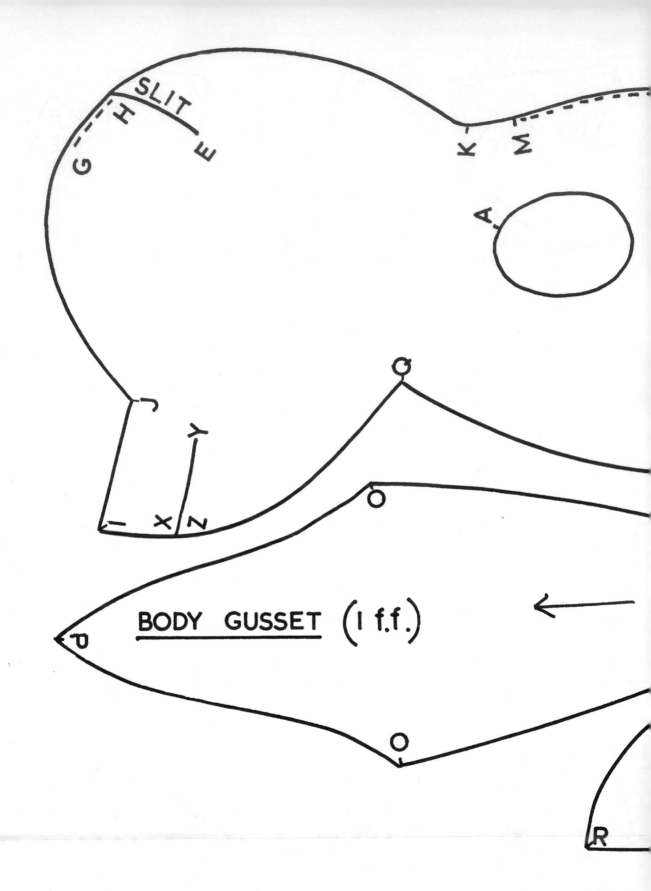

SLIT

G H E

K M

A

J Y

X Z

BODY GUSSET (1 f.f.)

P

O

O

R

BEAR WITH A BEE ON

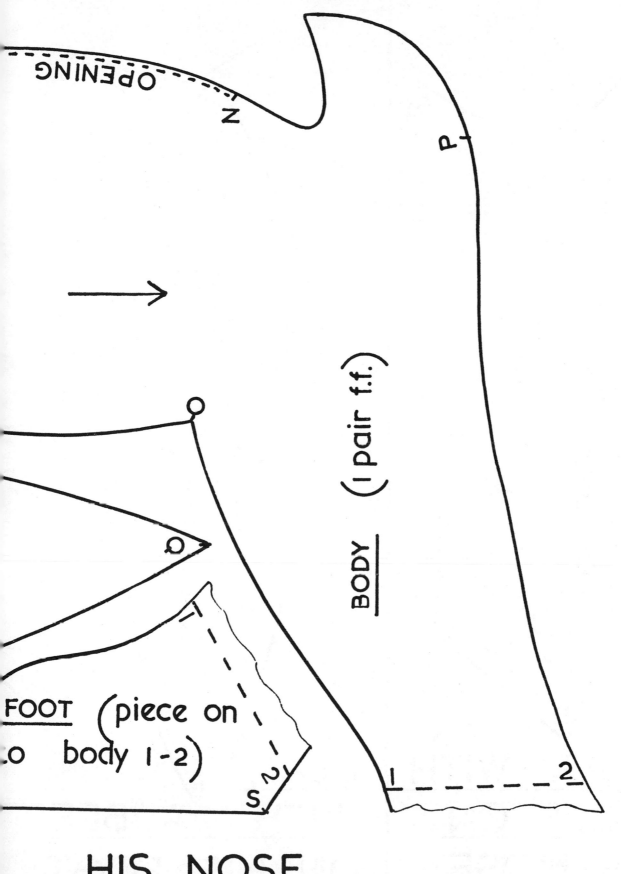

OPENING

N

P

BODY (1 pair f.f.)

O

Q

FOOT (piece on body 1-2)

T

2

S

1

2

HIS NOSE.

213

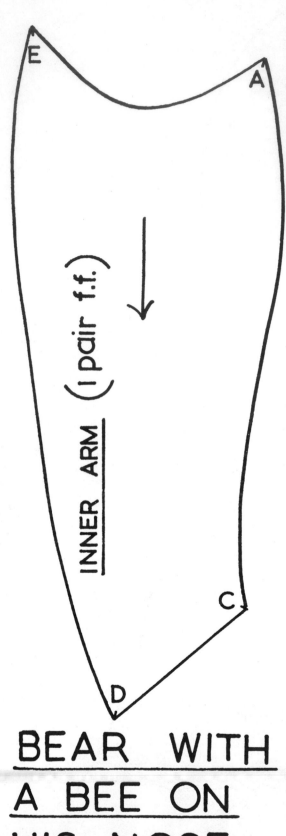

INNER ARM (1 pair f.f.)

BEAR WITH A BEE ON HIS NOSE.

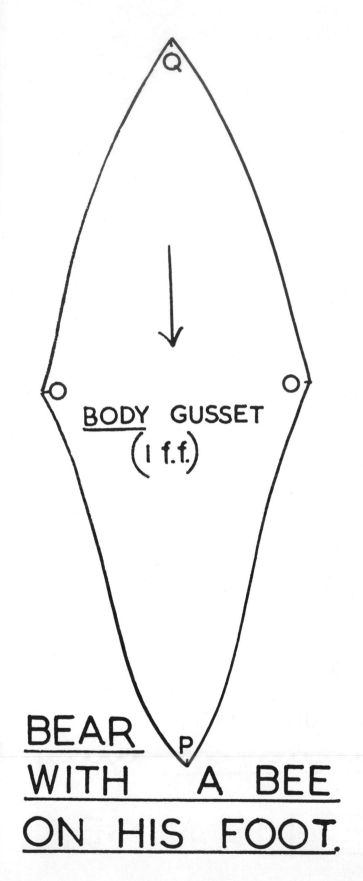

BODY GUSSET (1 f.f.)

BEAR WITH A BEE ON HIS FOOT.

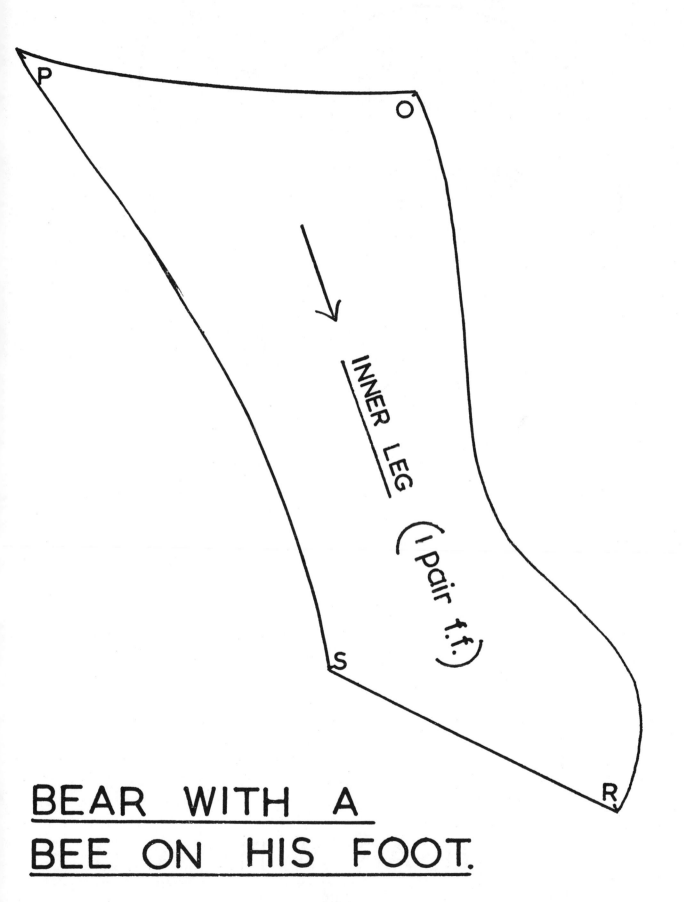

P

O

INNER LEG

(1 pair f.f.)

S

R

BEAR WITH A
BEE ON HIS FOOT.

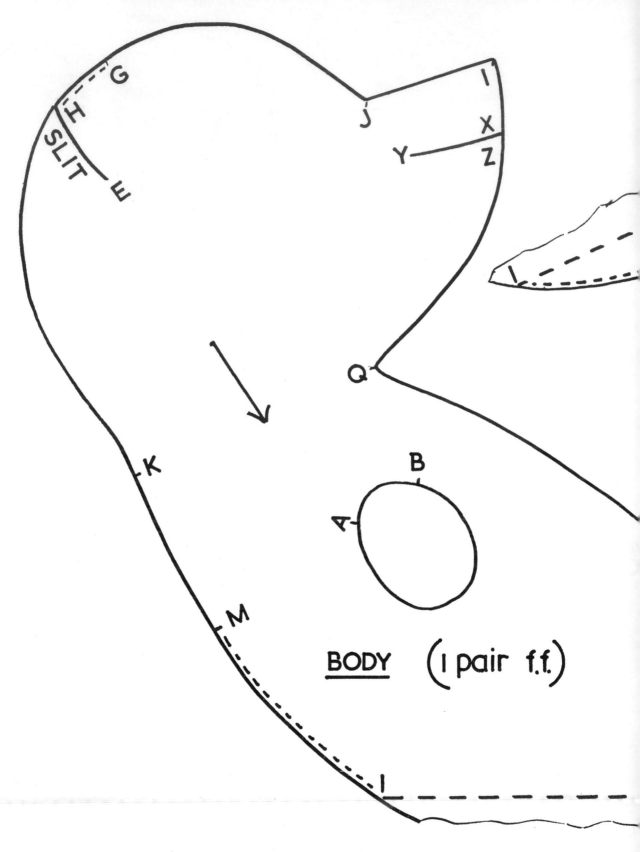

BODY (1 pair f.f.)

BEAR WITH A BEE

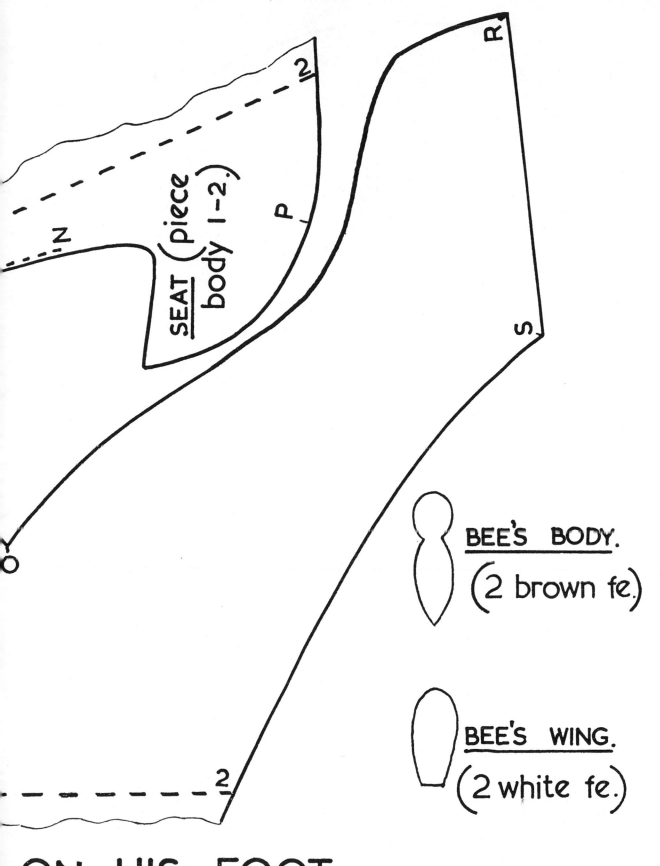

N

2

SEAT $\left(\text{piece} \atop \text{body } 1\text{-}2.\right)$

P

R

S

O

2

BEE'S BODY.
(2 brown fe.)

BEE'S WING.
(2 white fe.)

ON HIS FOOT.

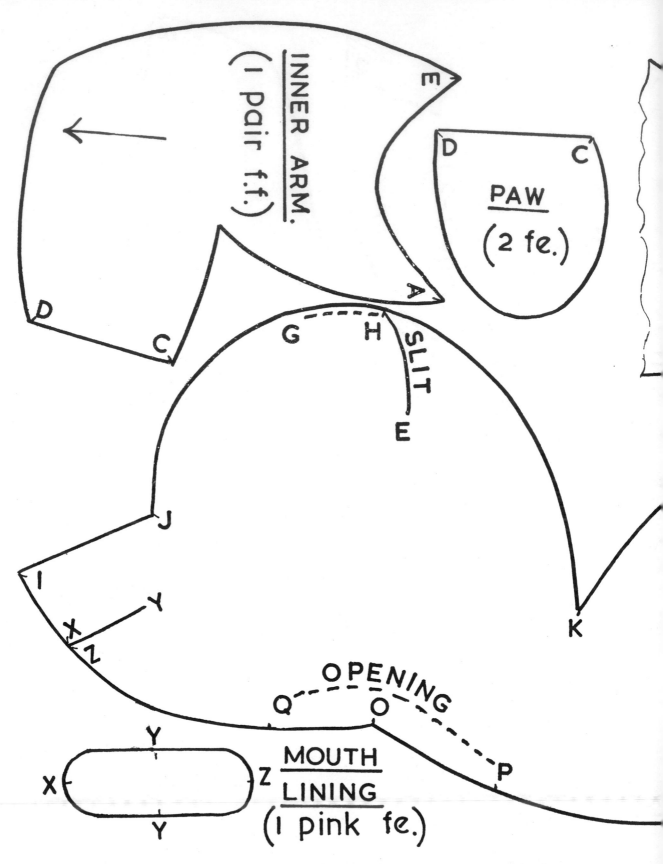

INNER ARM.
(1 pair f.f.)

E

D   C

PAW

(2 fe.)

D

C

A

G   H

SLIT

E

J

I

Y

X

Z

K

OPENING

Q   O

P

Y

X   Z

Y

MOUTH

LINING

(1 pink fe.)

THINKING BEAR LYING

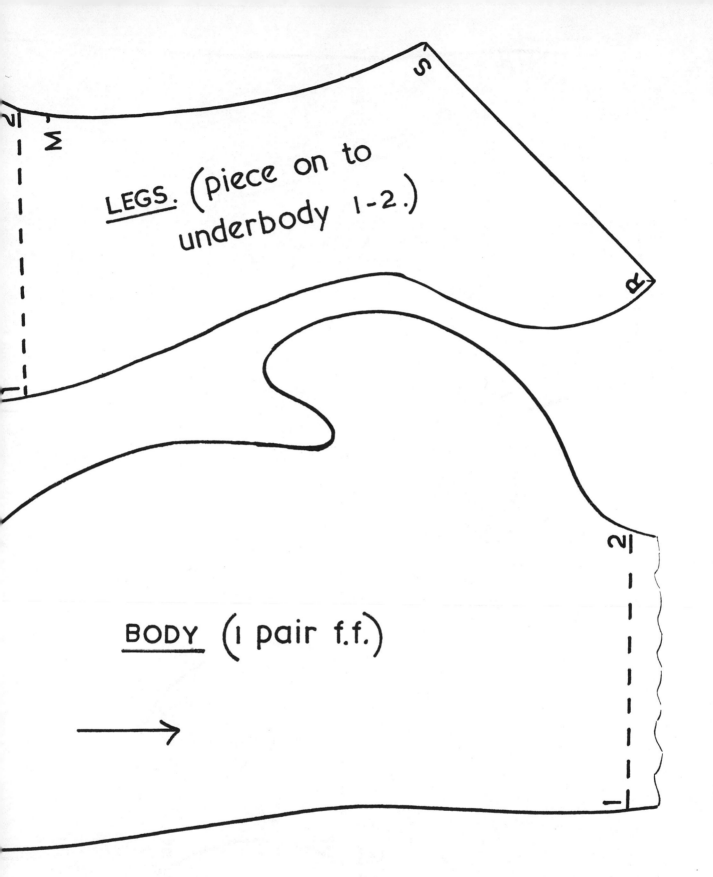

LEGS. (piece on to underbody 1-2.)

BODY (1 pair f.f.)

ON TUMMY.

219

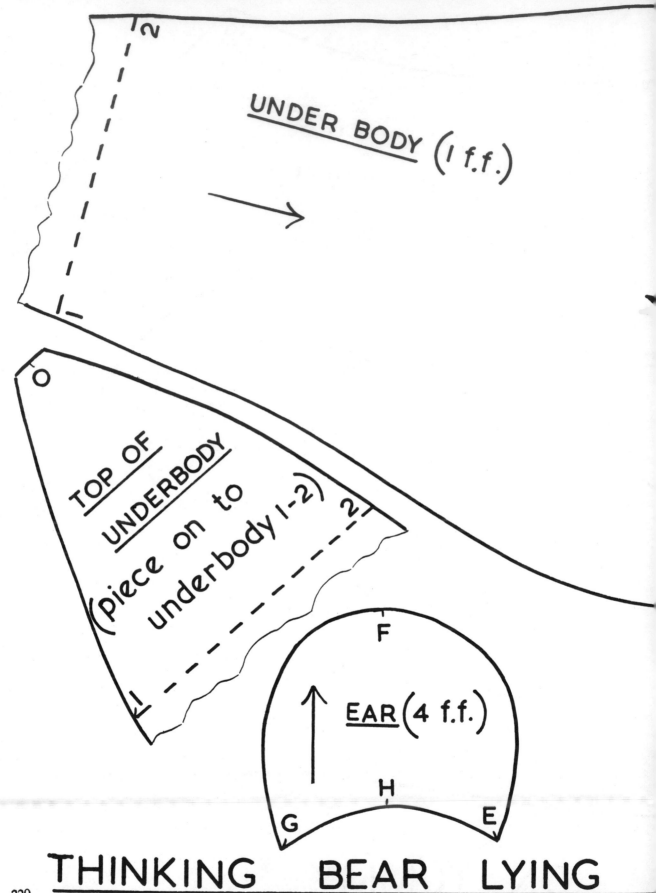

UNDER BODY (1 f.f.)

TOP OF UNDERBODY
(piece on to underbody 1-2)

EAR (4 f.f.)

THINKING BEAR LYING

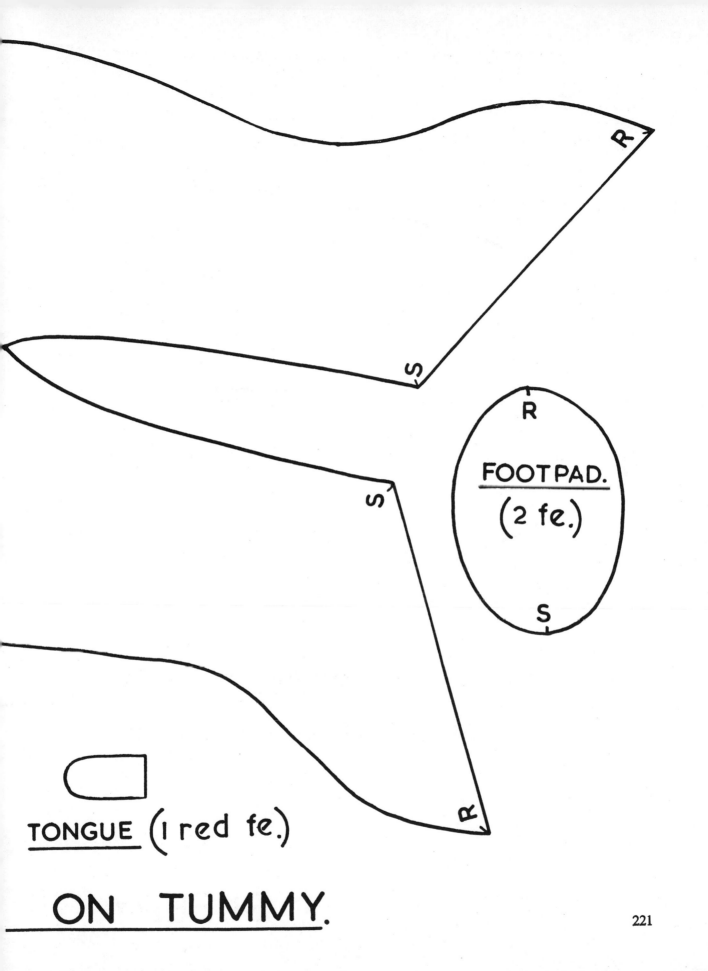

R

S

R
FOOTPAD.
(2 fe.)
S

TONGUE (1 red fe.)

ON TUMMY.

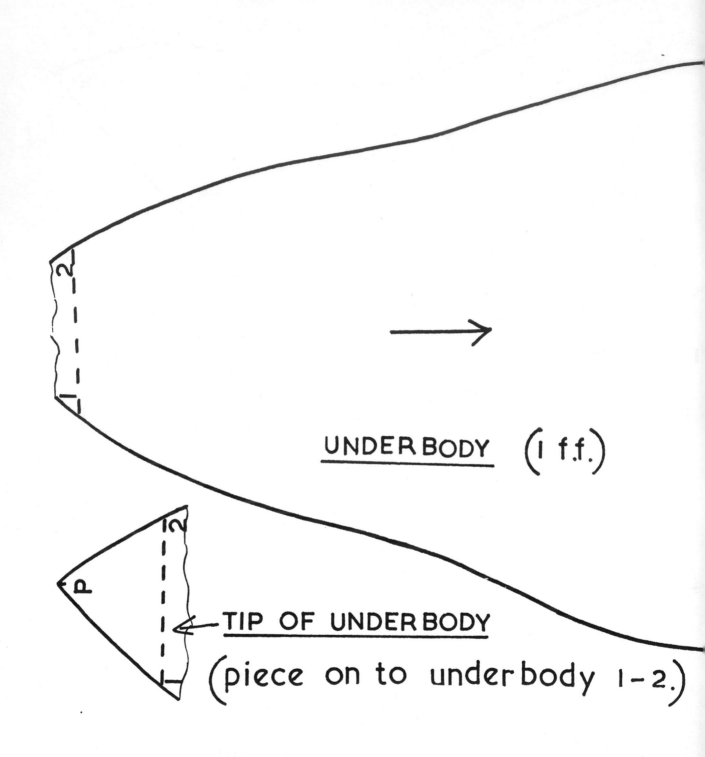

UNDER BODY (1 f.f.)

TIP OF UNDER BODY

(piece on to under body 1-2.)

SLEEPY

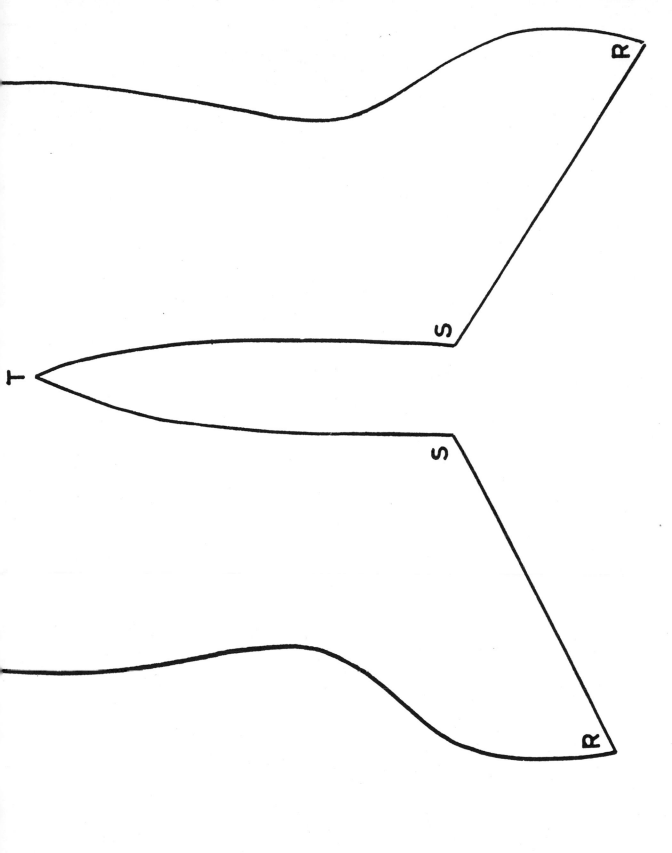

BEAR.

223

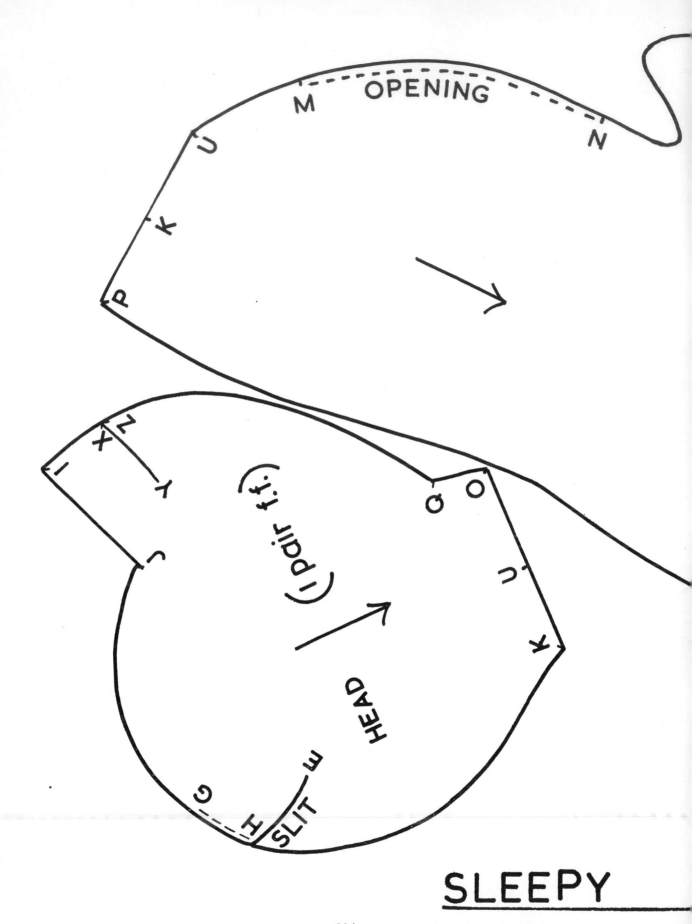

OPENING

M

N

U

K

P

Z

X

I

Y

J

(1 pair f.f.)

Q

O

L

K

HEAD

SLIT

M

G

H

SLEEPY

224

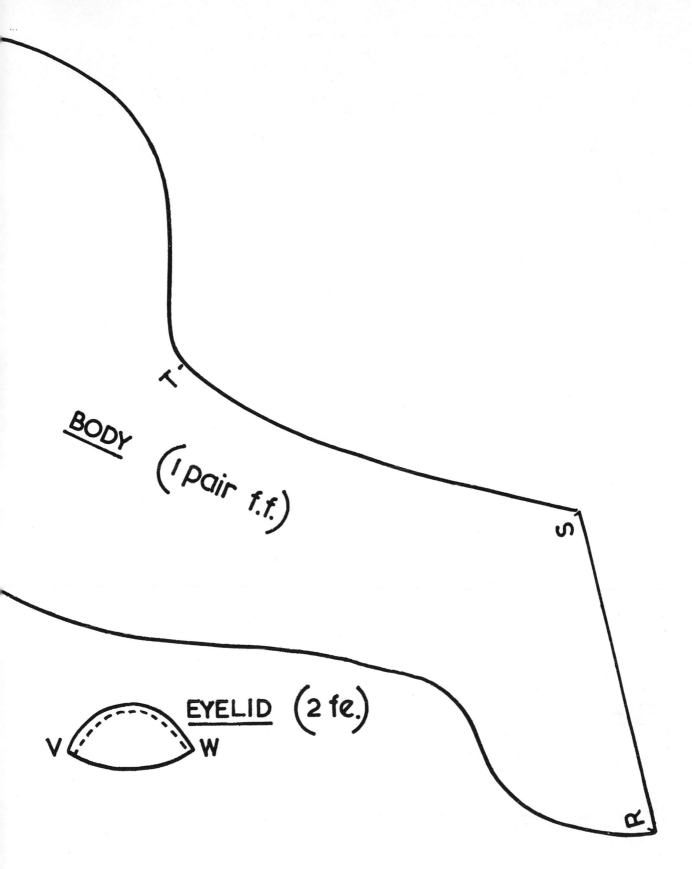

T

BODY *(1 pair f.f.)*

S

EYELID *(2 fe.)*

V W

R

BEAR.

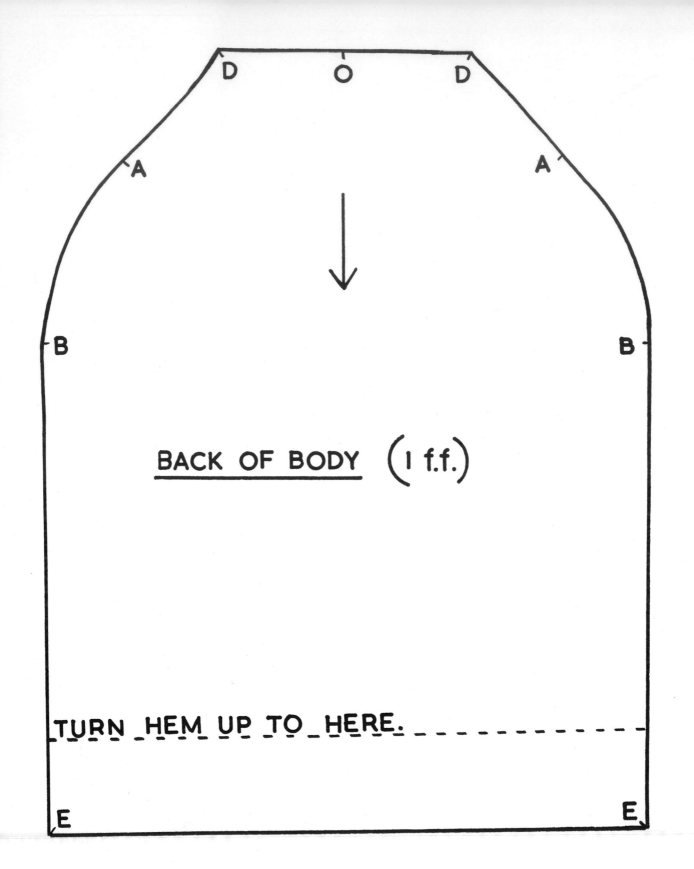

D   O   D

A   A

B   B

BACK OF BODY (1 f.f.)

TURN HEM UP TO HERE.

E   E

GLOVE

226

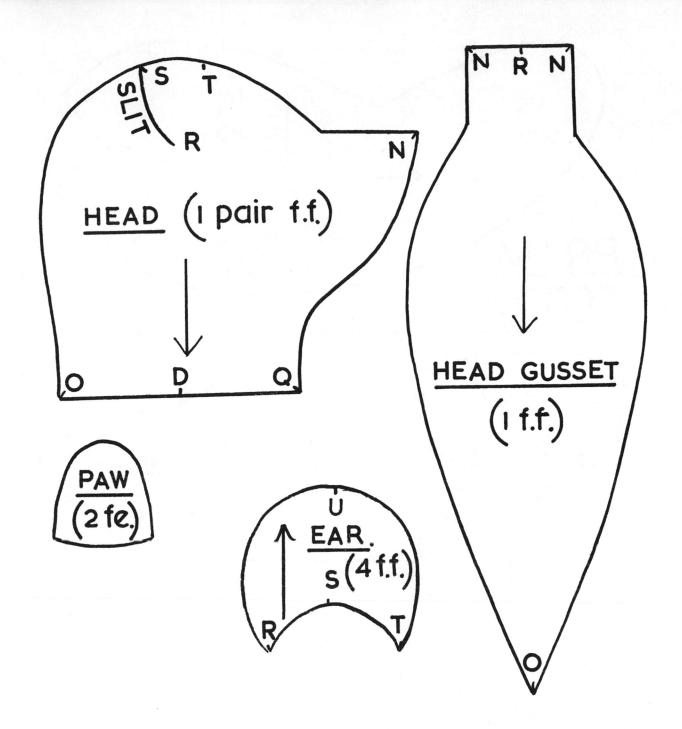

TEDDY.

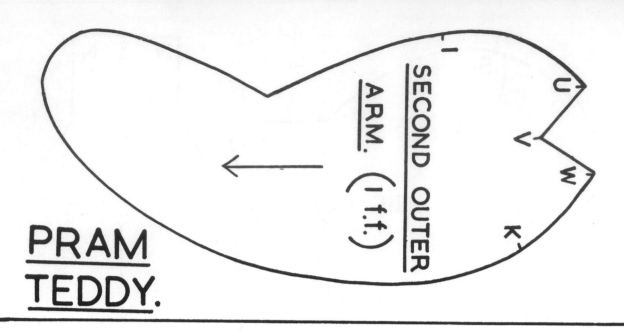

**PRAM
TEDDY.**

SECOND OUTER
ARM.
(1 f.f.)

U

W

K

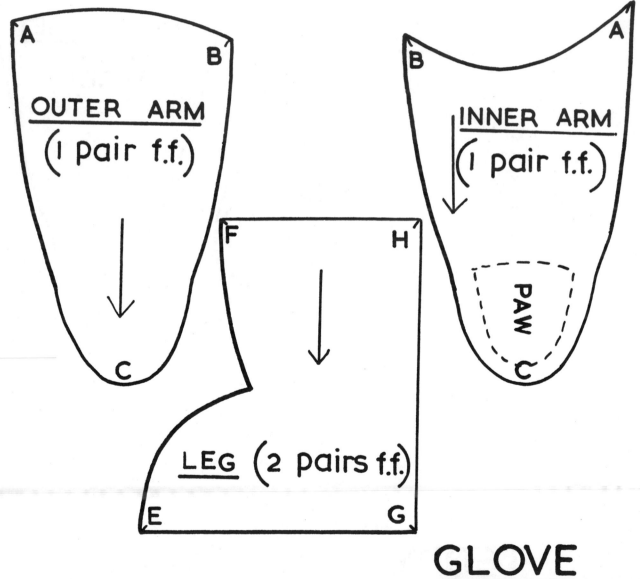

A   B

OUTER ARM
(1 pair f.f.)

C

B   A

INNER ARM
(1 pair f.f.)

PAW

C

F   H

LEG (2 pairs f.f.)

E   G

GLOVE

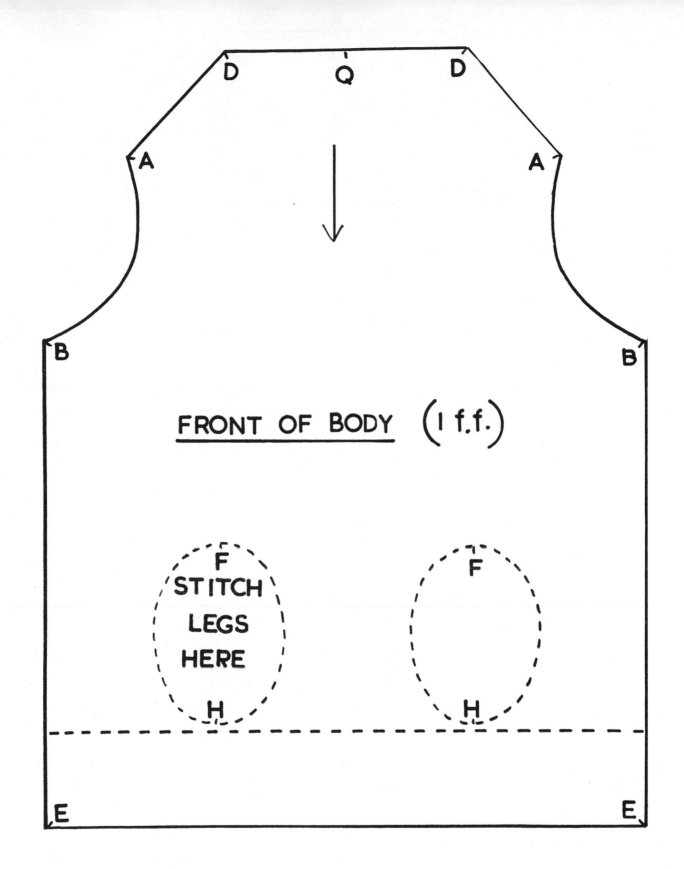

FRONT OF BODY (1 f.f.)

F
STITCH
LEGS
HERE
H

F
H

TEDDY.

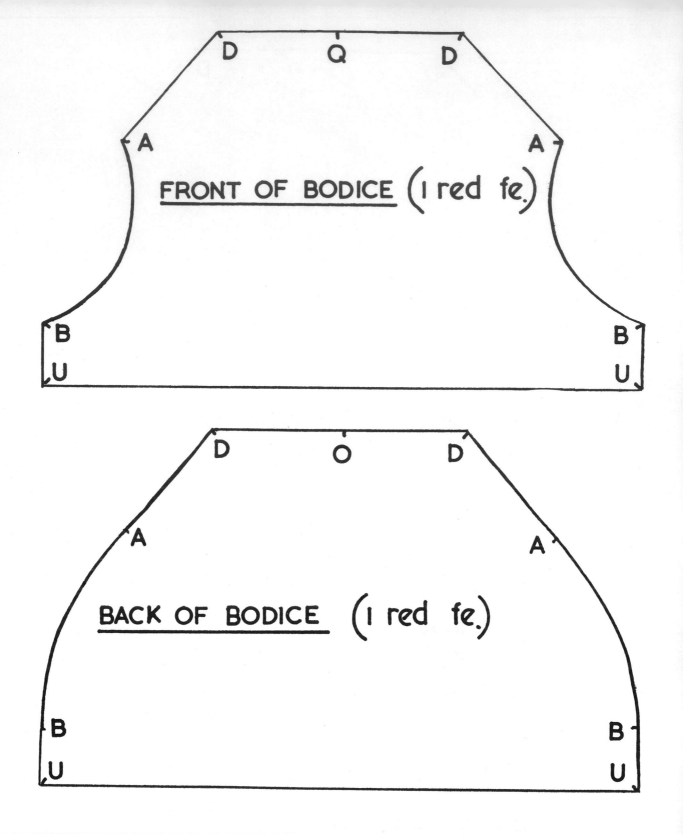

FRONT OF BODICE (1 red fe.)

BACK OF BODICE (1 red fe.)

TEDWINA.

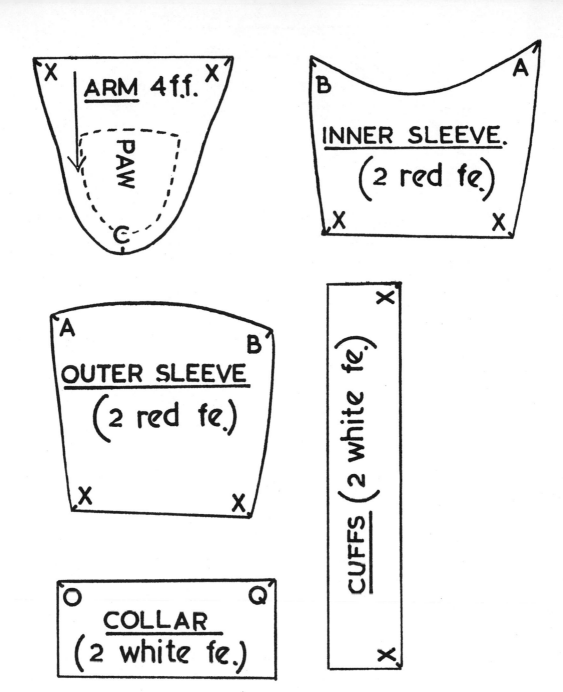

TEDWINA.

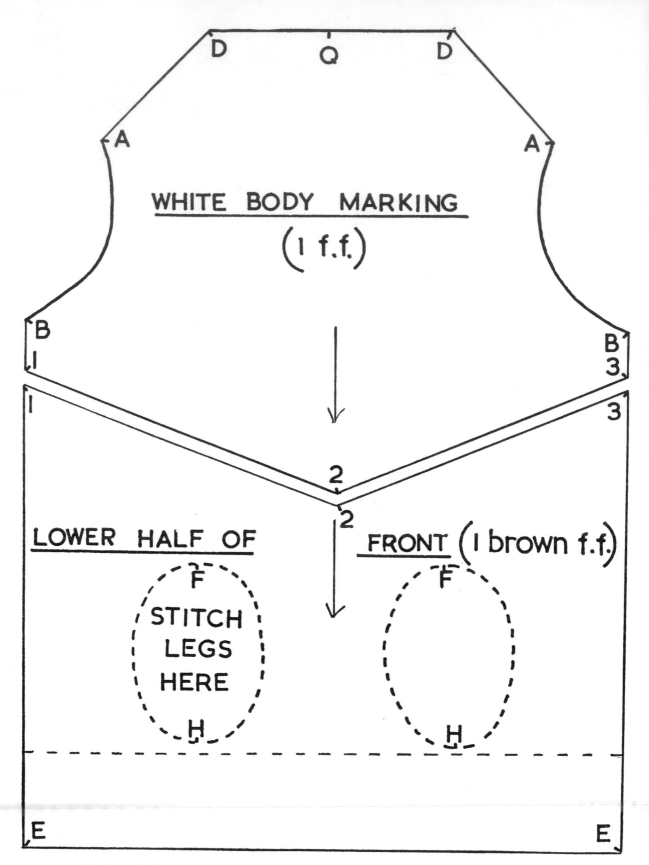

WHITE BODY MARKING

(1 f.f.)

LOWER HALF OF   FRONT (1 brown f.f.)

STITCH LEGS HERE

MISHKA.

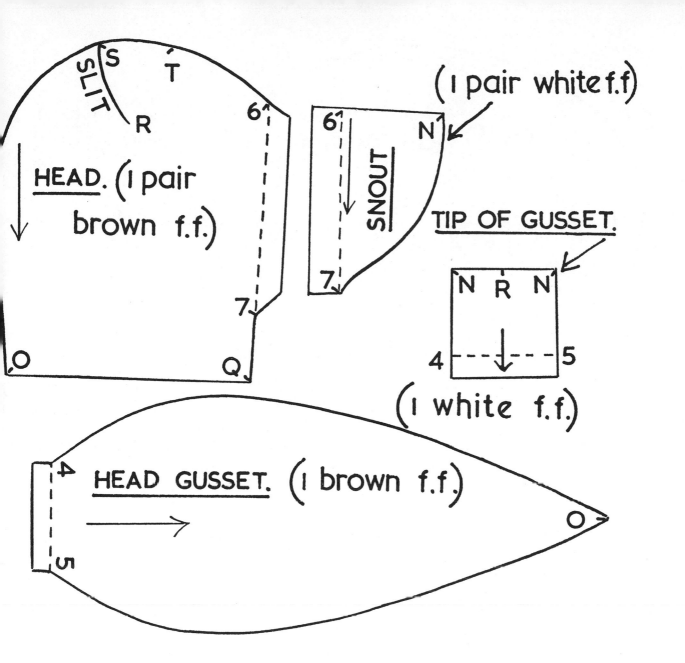

HEAD. (I pair brown f.f.)

SNOUT

(I pair white f.f)

TIP OF GUSSET.

(I white f.f.)

HEAD GUSSET. (I brown f.f.)

MISHKA.

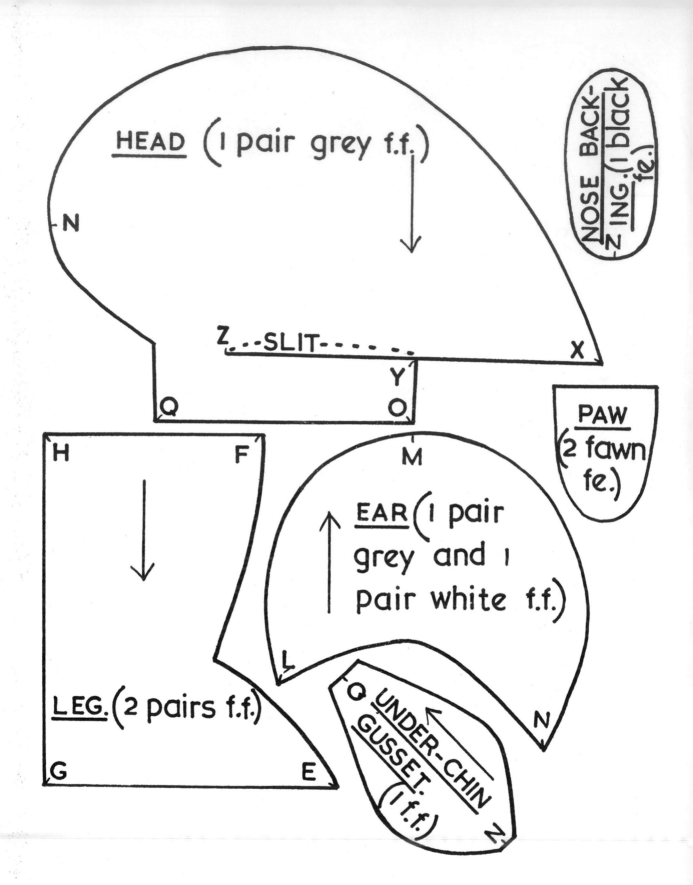

HEAD (1 pair grey f.f.)

NOSE BACK-ZING. (1 black fe.)

N

Z...-SLIT-.... X

Y

Q O

H F

PAW (2 fawn fe.)

M

EAR (1 pair grey and 1 pair white f.f.)

LEG. (2 pairs f.f.)

L

Q UNDER-CHIN GUSSET. (1 f.f.)

N

G E

Z

GLOVE KOALA.

234

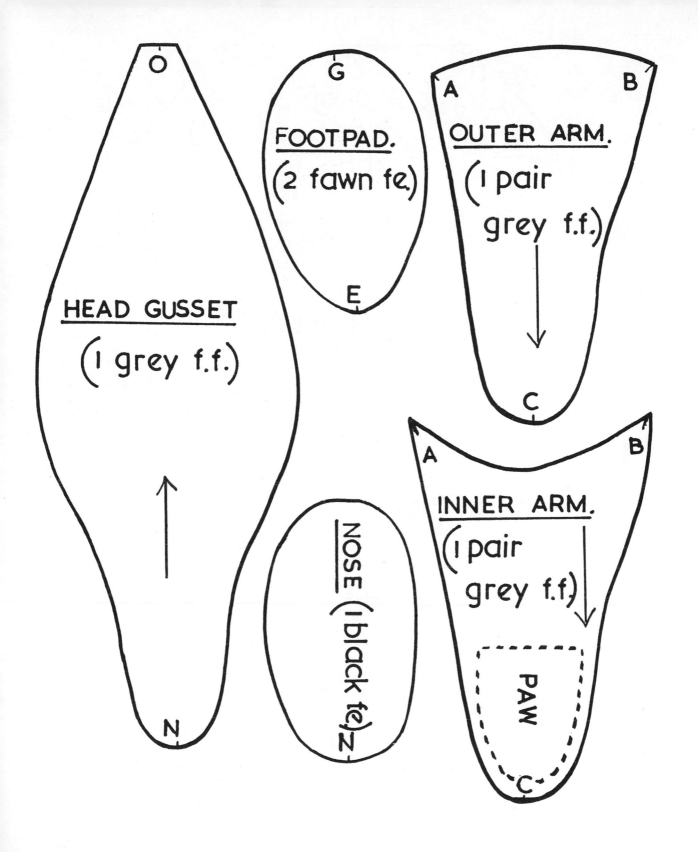

HEAD GUSSET

(1 grey f.f.)

O

N

FOOTPAD.

(2 fawn fe.)

G

E

NOSE (1 black fe.)

Z

OUTER ARM.

(1 pair

grey f.f.)

A

B

C

INNER ARM.

(1 pair

grey f.f)

A

B

PAW

C

GLOVE KOALA.

235

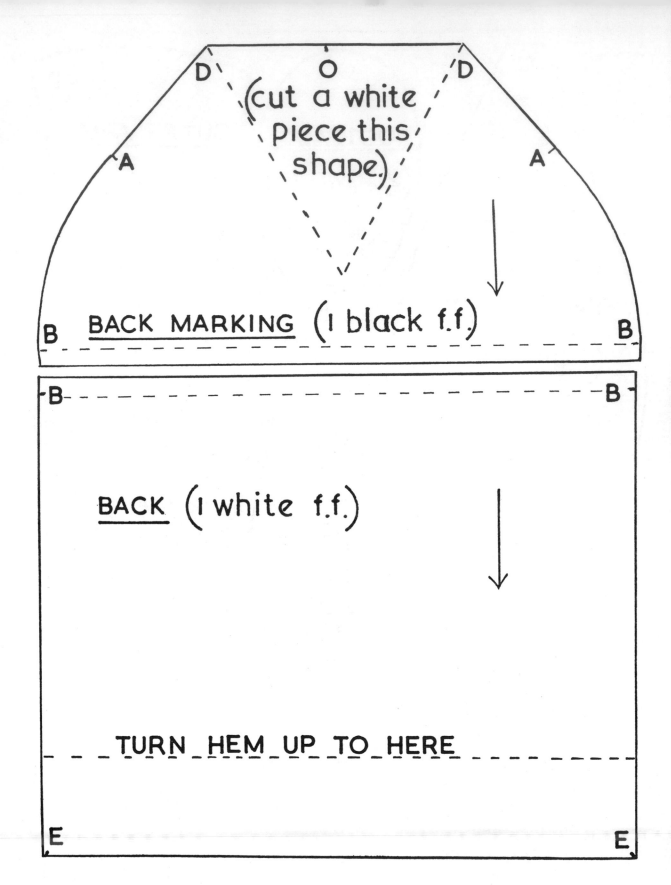

D O D
(cut a white piece this shape.)

A A

B **BACK MARKING** (1 black f.f.) B

B B

BACK (1 white f.f.)

TURN HEM UP TO HERE

E E

GLOVE

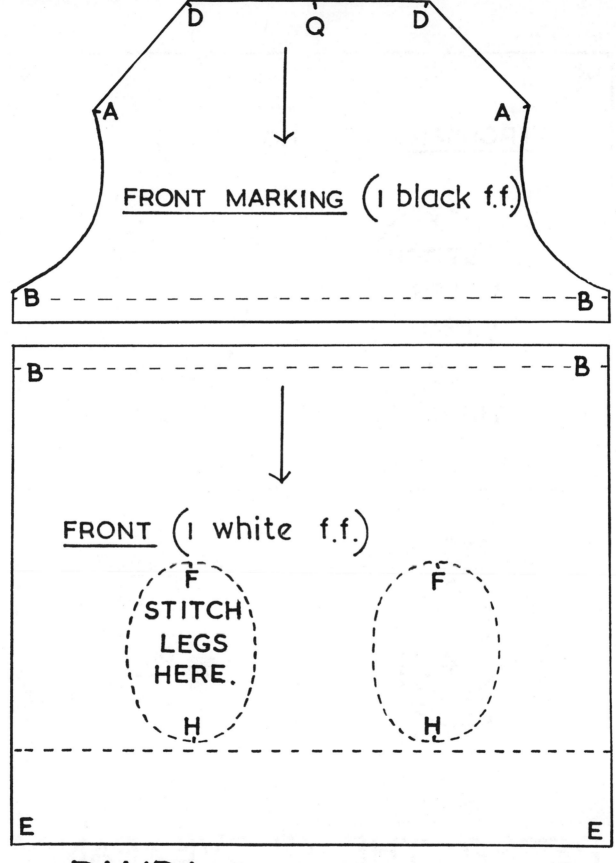

FRONT MARKING (1 black f.f.)

FRONT (1 white f.f.)

F
STITCH
LEGS
HERE.
H

F

H

PANDA.

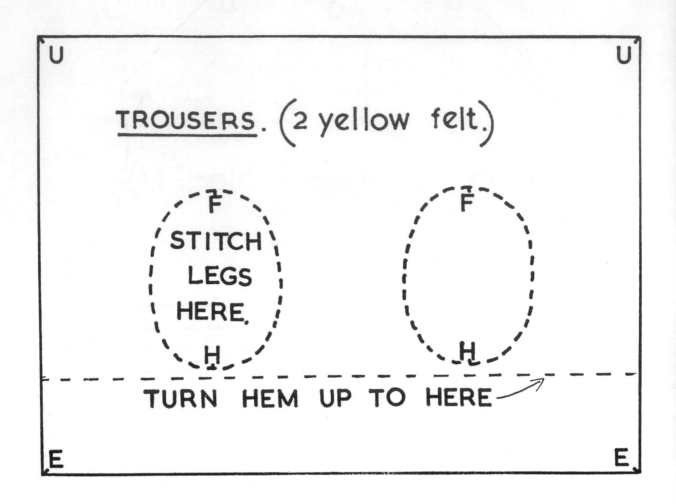

TROUSERS. (2 yellow felt.)

F

STITCH
LEGS
HERE.

H

F

H

TURN HEM UP TO HERE

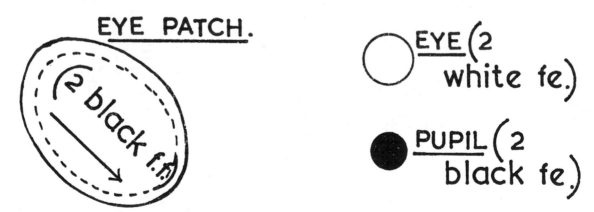

EYE PATCH.

(2 black fe.)

EYE (2 white fe.)

PUPIL (2 black fe.)

PETER THE GLOVE PANDA.

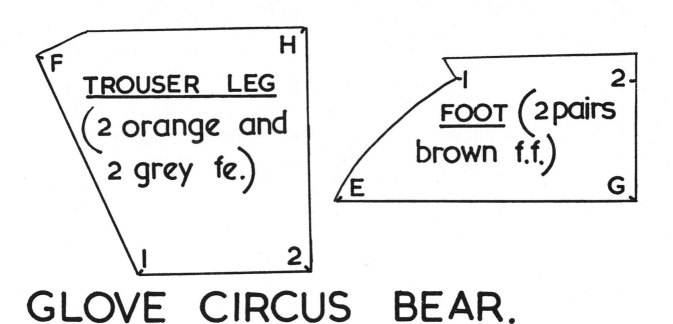

TROUSER LEG
(2 orange and
2 grey fe.)

FOOT (2 pairs
brown f.f.)

GLOVE CIRCUS BEAR.

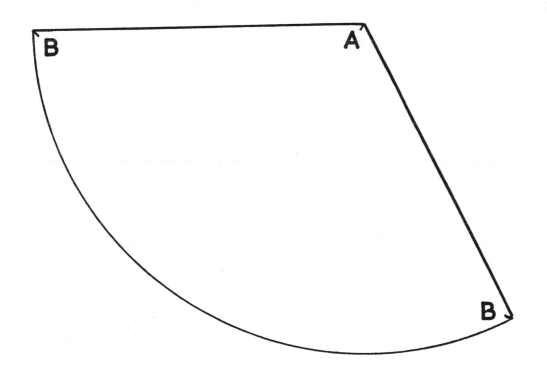

CLOWN'S HAT.

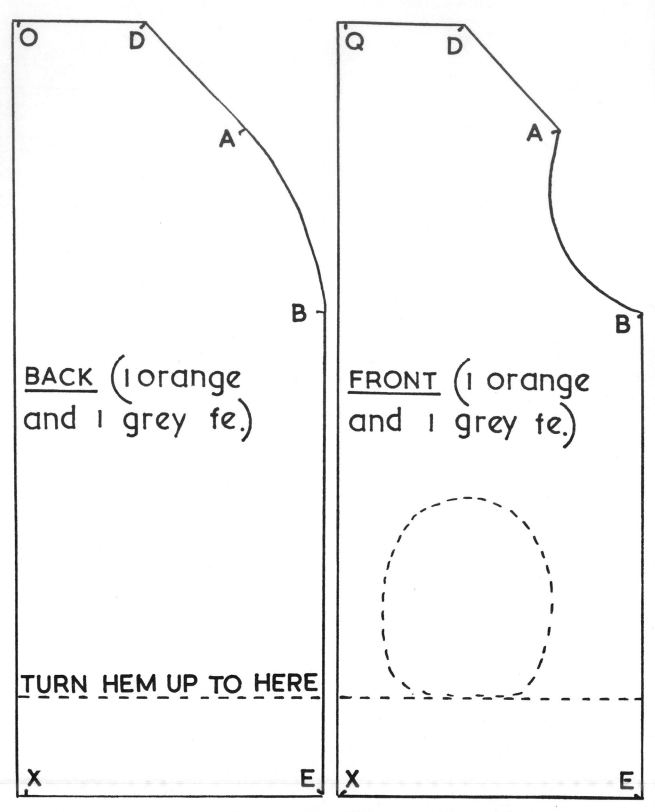

O D

A

B

BACK (1 orange
and 1 grey fe.)

TURN HEM UP TO HERE

X E

Q D

A

B

FRONT (1 orange
and 1 grey fe.)

X E

GLOVE CIRCUS BEAR.

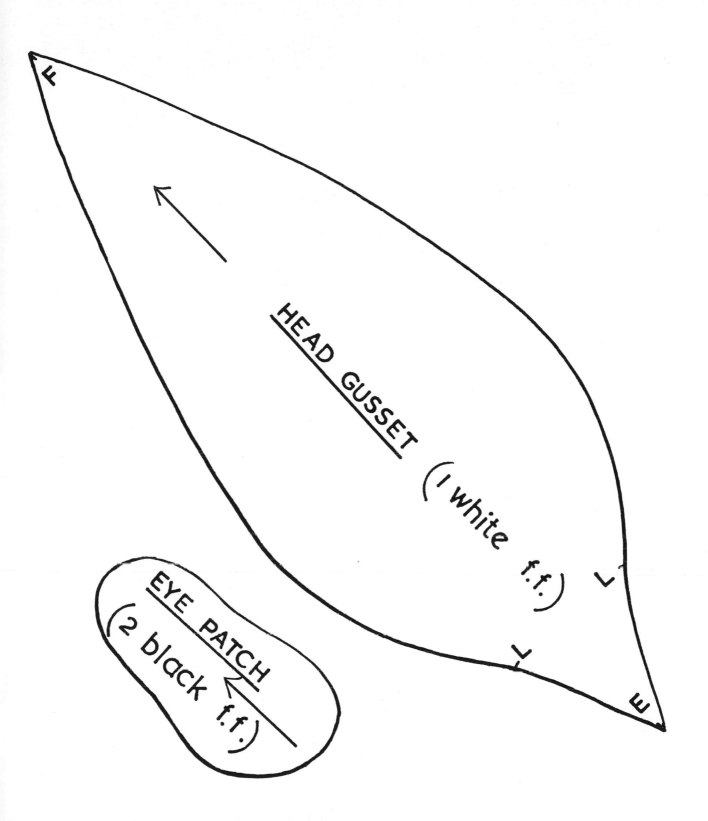

F

HEAD GUSSET (1 white f.f.)

E

EYE PATCH (2 black f.f.)

JOINTED PANDA

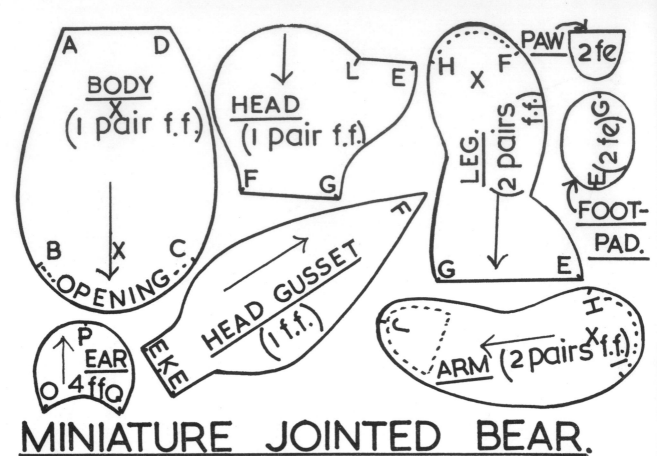

MINIATURE JOINTED BEAR.

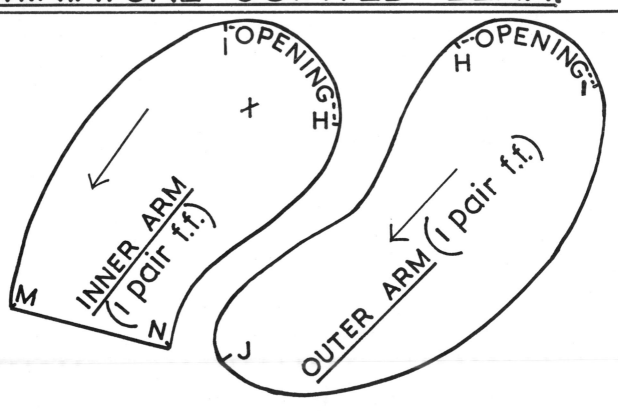

SMALL JOINTED BEAR.

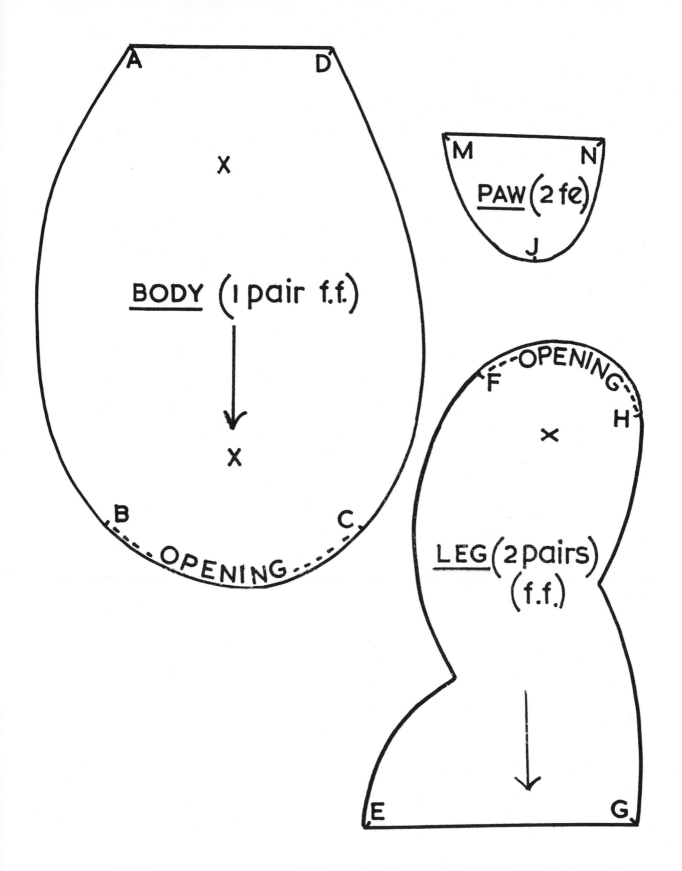

A   D

X

M   N

PAW (2 fe)

J

BODY (1 pair f.f.)

X

F   OPENING

H

X

B   C

OPENING

LEG (2 pairs) (f.f.)

E   G

SMALL JOINTED BEAR.

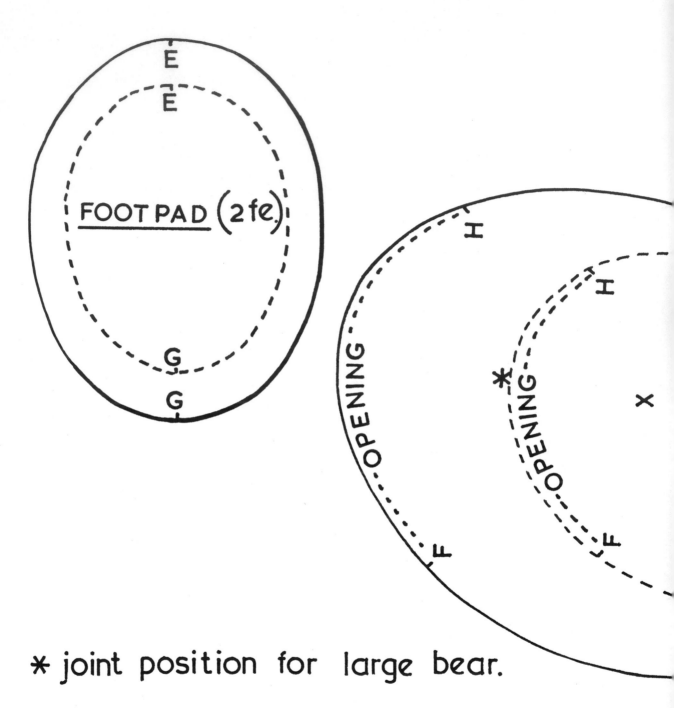

FOOT PAD (2 fe)

E
E

G
G

OPENING

OPENING

H

H

*

x

F

F

* joint position for large bear.

x for medium size bear.

JOINTED BEARS. LARGE SIZE

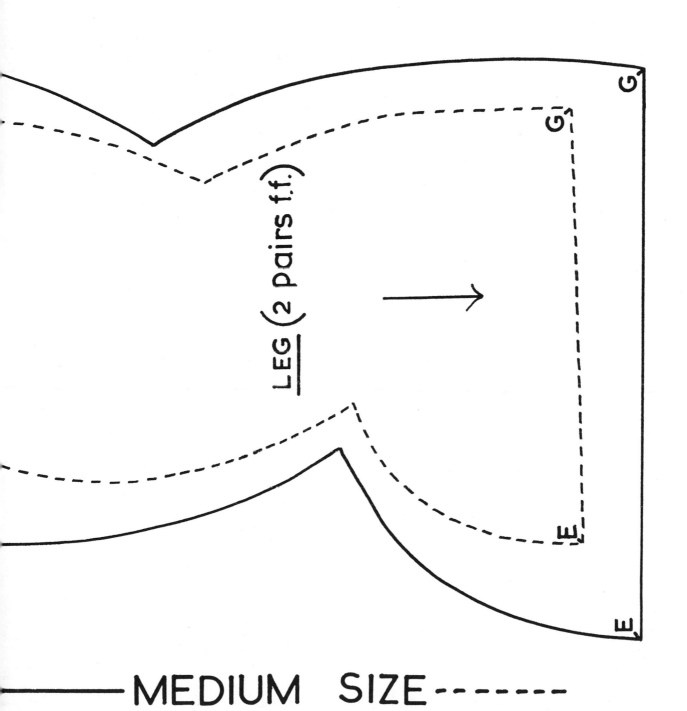

LEG (2 pairs f.f.)

G

G

E

E

MEDIUM SIZE --------

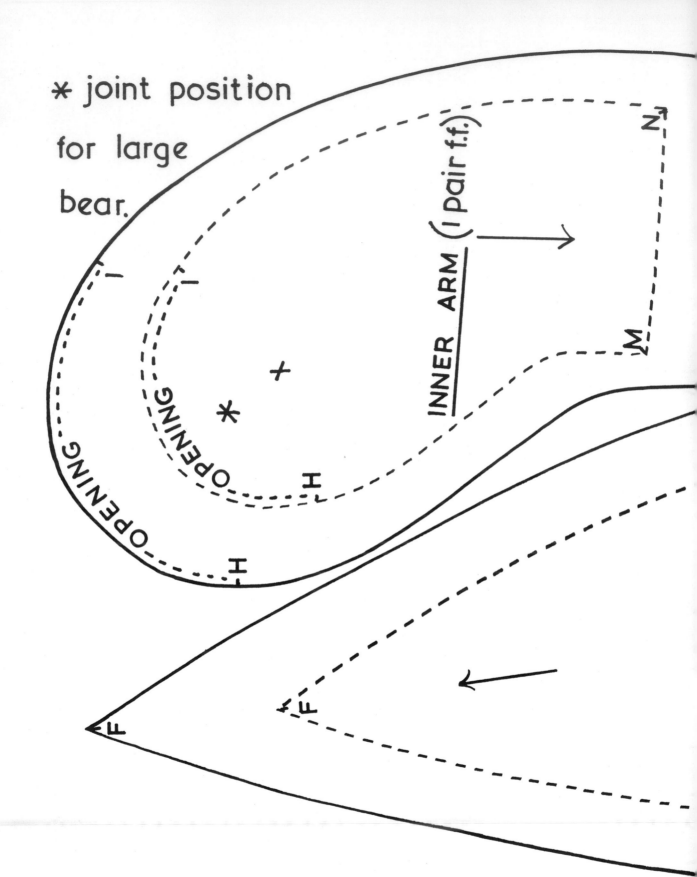

* joint position for large bear.

INNER ARM (1 Pair f.f.)

OPENING

OPENING

JOINTED BEARS.

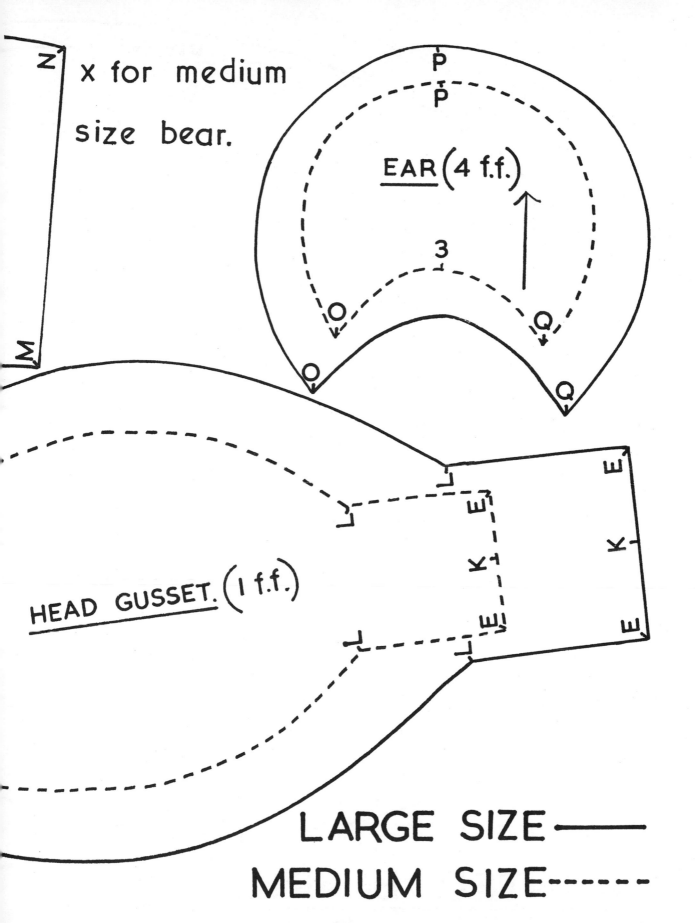

Z

x for medium
size bear.

M

EAR (4 f.f.)

P
P

3

O

Q

O

Q

L

L

E

E

K

K

HEAD GUSSET. (1 f.f.)

L

L

E

E

E

LARGE SIZE ——
MEDIUM SIZE------

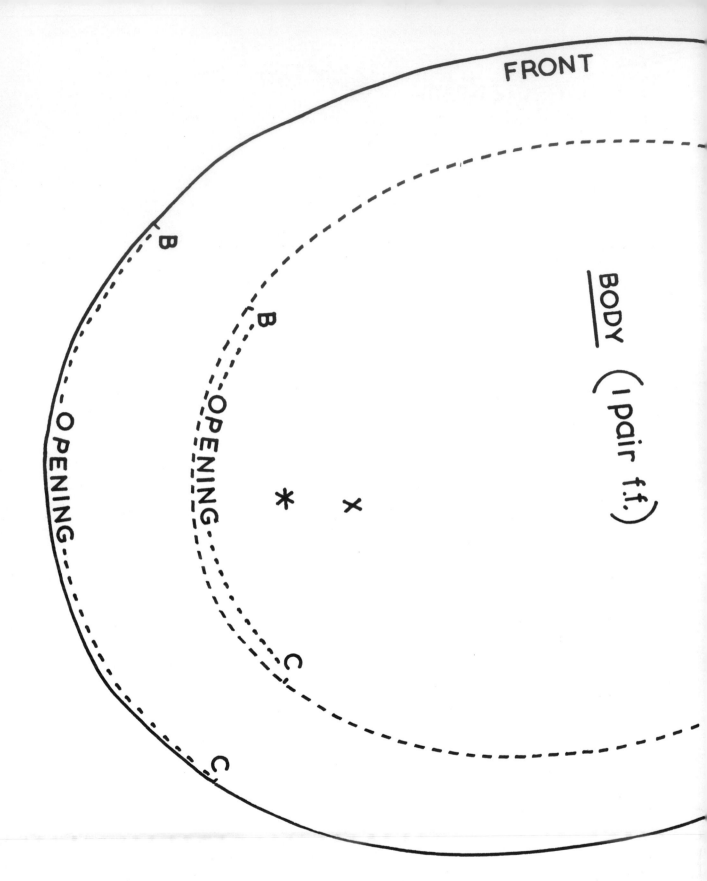

FRONT

BODY (1 pair f.f.)

OPENING

OPENING

B

B

C

C

*

×

JOINTED BEARS.

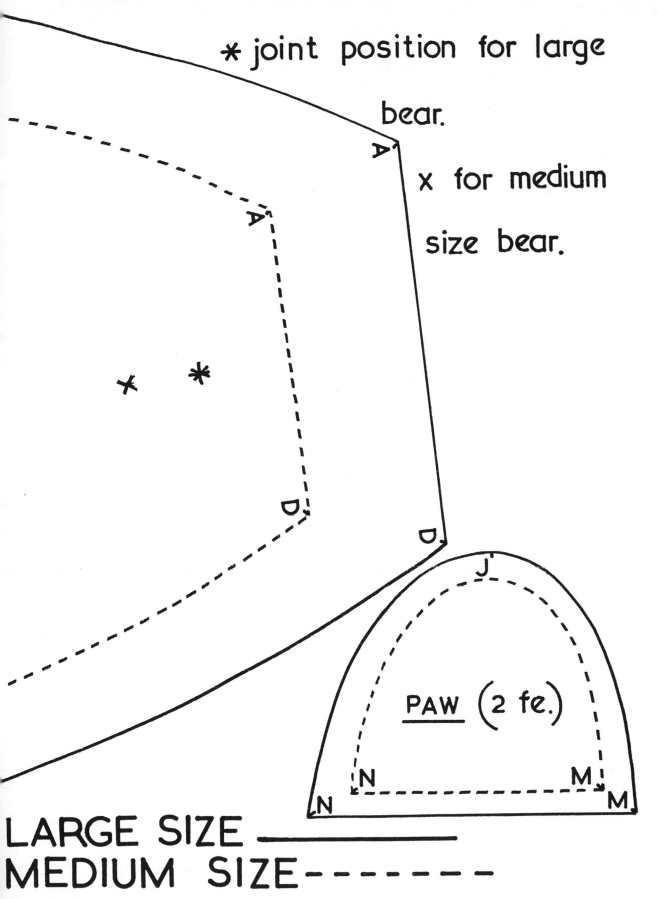

* joint position for large bear.

x for medium size bear.

A

A

D

D

J

PAW (2 fe.)

N

N

M

M

LARGE SIZE ——————
MEDIUM SIZE — — — — — —

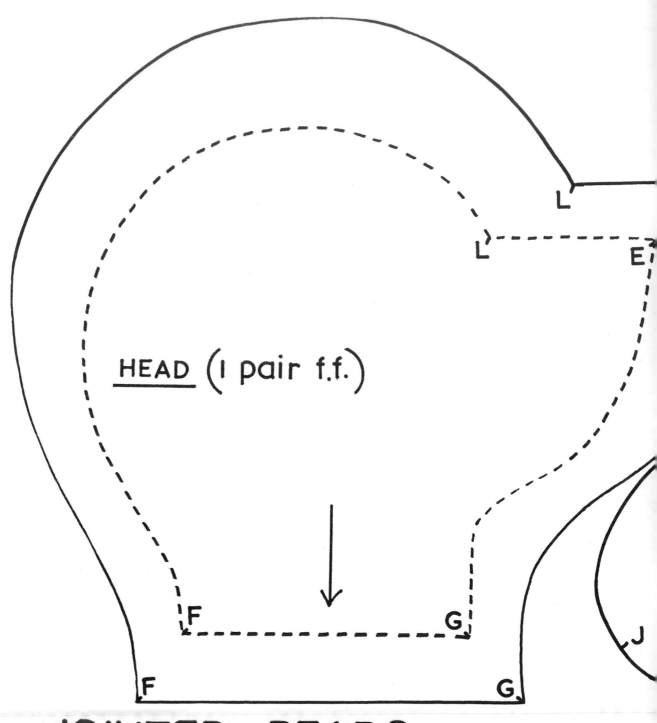

HEAD (1 pair f.f.)

JOINTED BEARS.

250

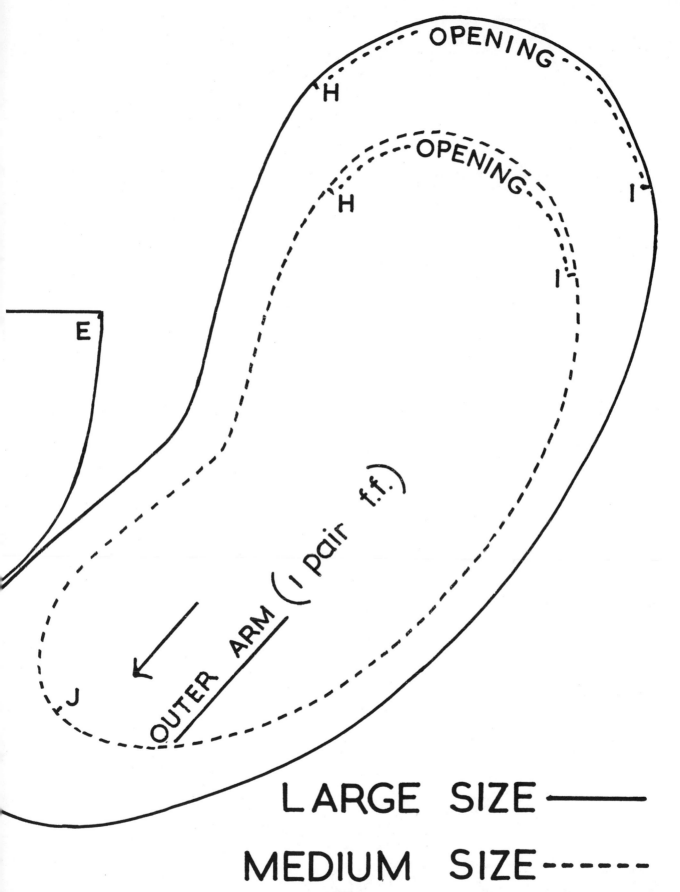

OPENING

H

H

OPENING

H

I

I

E

OUTER ARM (1 pair f.f.)

J

LARGE SIZE ———

MEDIUM SIZE ------

251

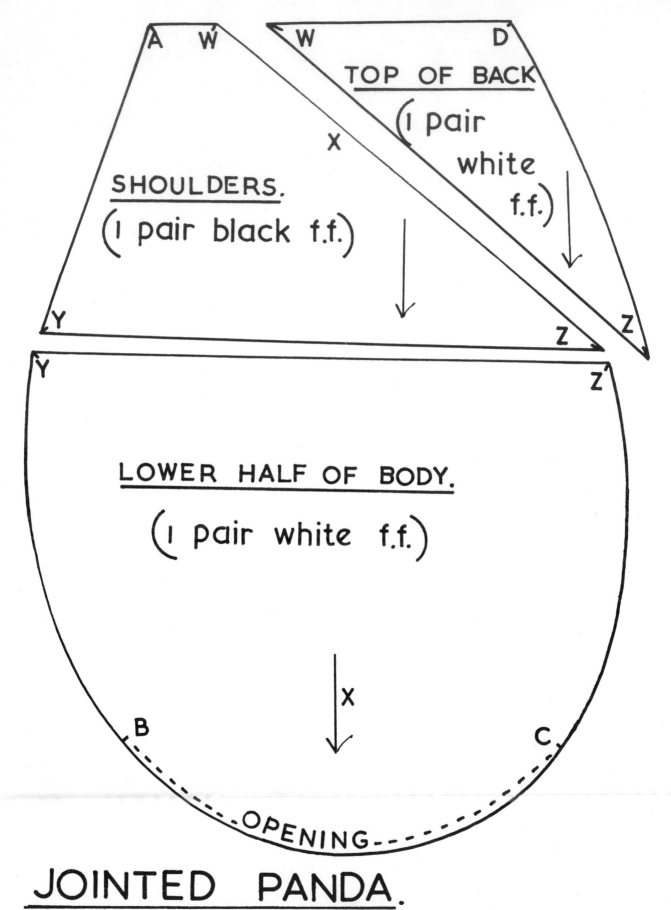

SHOULDERS.
(1 pair black f.f.)

TOP OF BACK
(1 pair white f.f.)

LOWER HALF OF BODY.
(1 pair white f.f.)

OPENING

JOINTED PANDA.

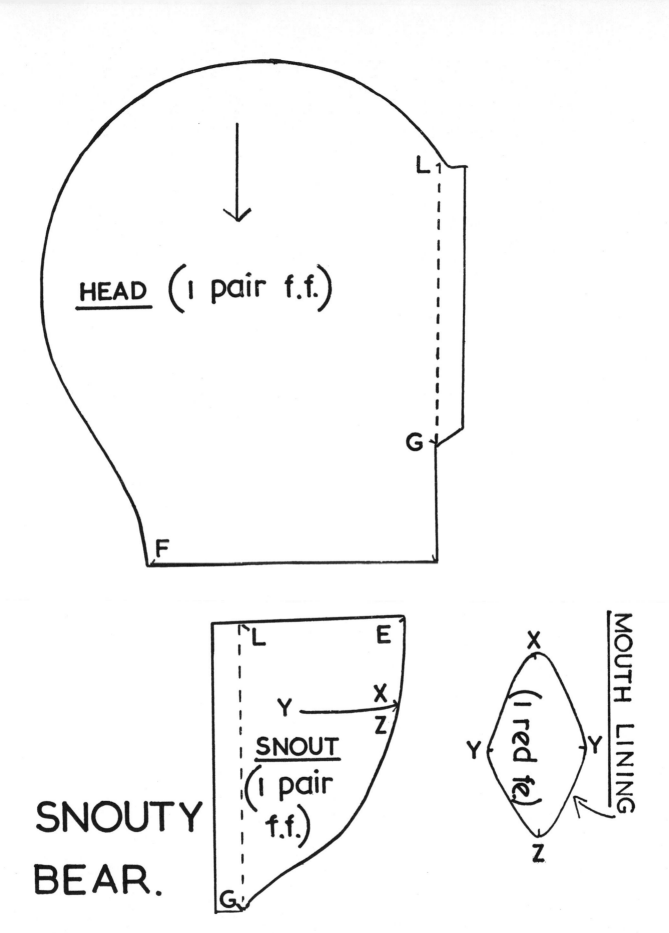

HEAD (1 pair f.f.)

L

G

F

SNOUTY
BEAR.

L   E

Y   X

Z

SNOUT
(1 pair
f.f.)

G

X

Y   Y

Z

(1 red fe.)

MOUTH LINING

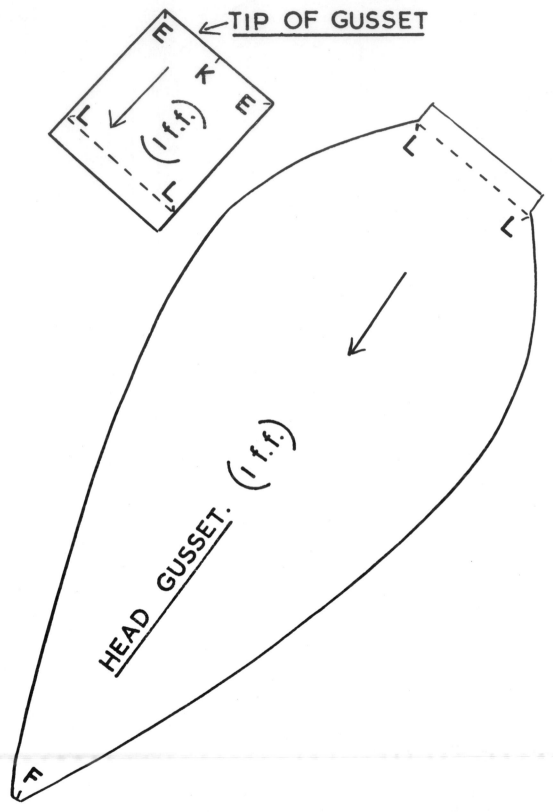

TIP OF GUSSET

(I.f.f.)

HEAD GUSSET. (I.f.f.)

SNOUTY BEAR.

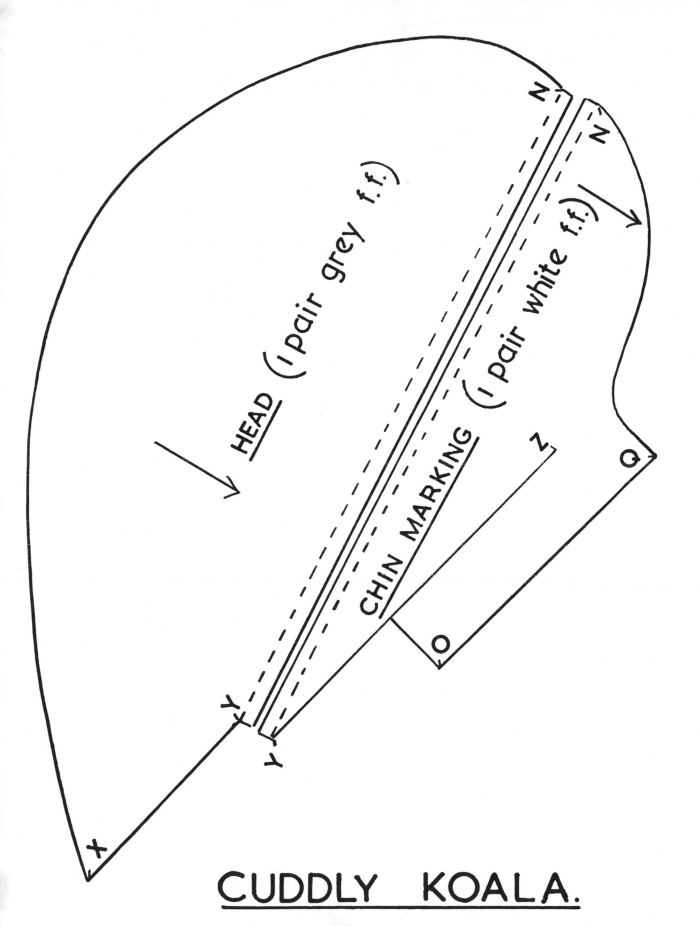

HEAD (1 pair grey f.f.)

CHIN MARKING (1 pair white f.f.)

CUDDLY KOALA.

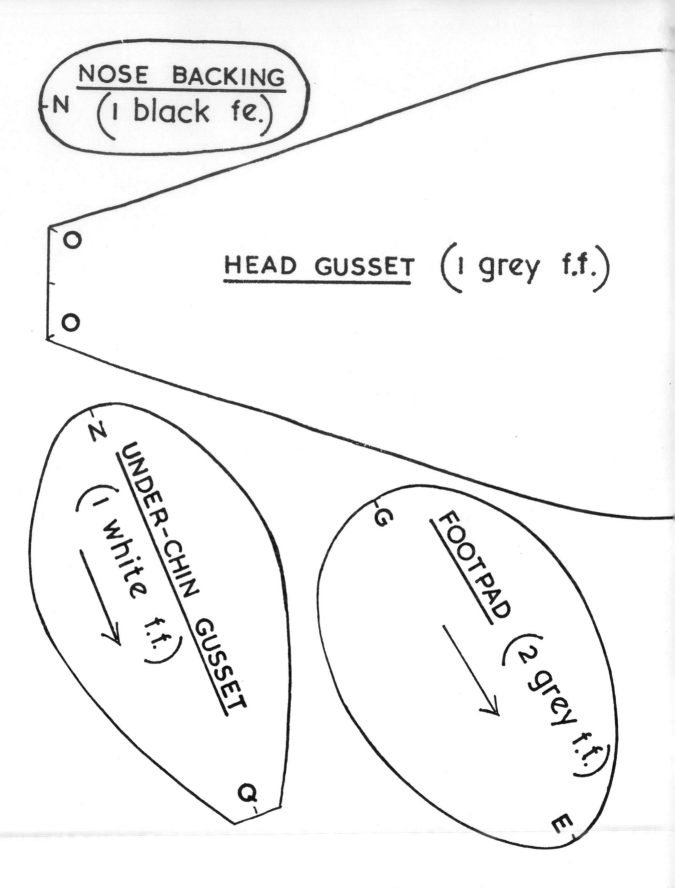

NOSE BACKING
(1 black fe.)
-N

O

HEAD GUSSET (1 grey f.f.)

O

N
UNDER-CHIN GUSSET
(1 white f.f.)
Q

G
FOOTPAD (2 grey f.f.)
E

CUDDLY

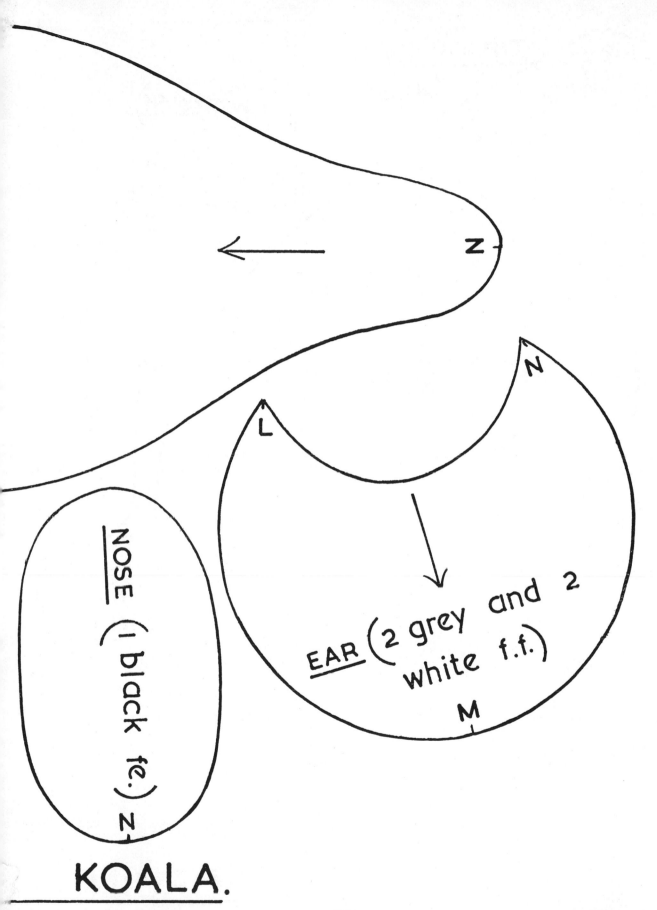

Z

N

L

NOSE (1 black fe.)

EAR (2 grey and 2 white f.f.)

M

KOALA.

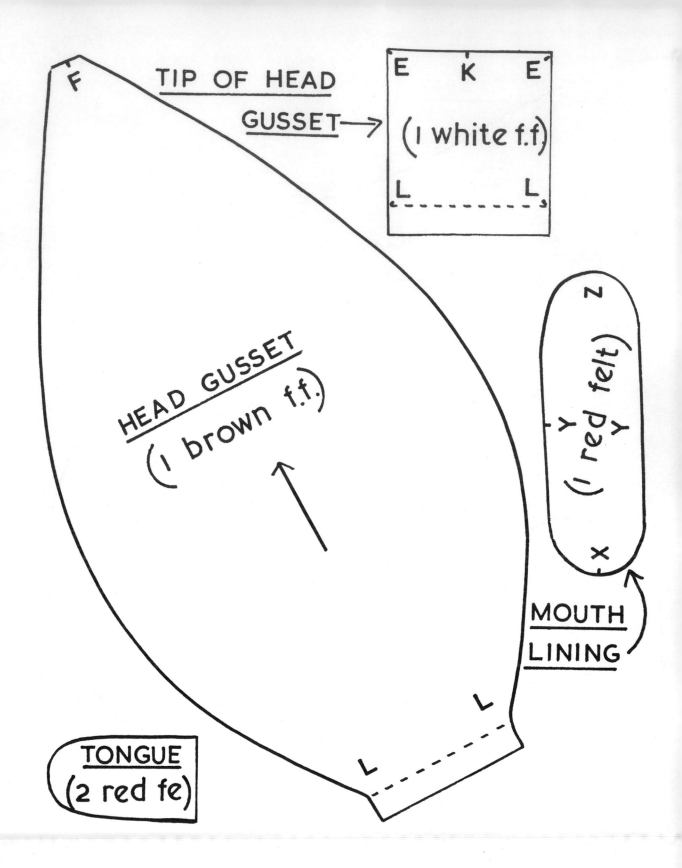

TIP OF HEAD
GUSSET →

E   K   E´

(1 white f.f)

L   L

HEAD GUSSET
(1 brown f.f.)

F

MOUTH
LINING

Z

(1 red felt)

Y
Y

X

L

L

TONGUE
(2 red fe)

258

BRUIN

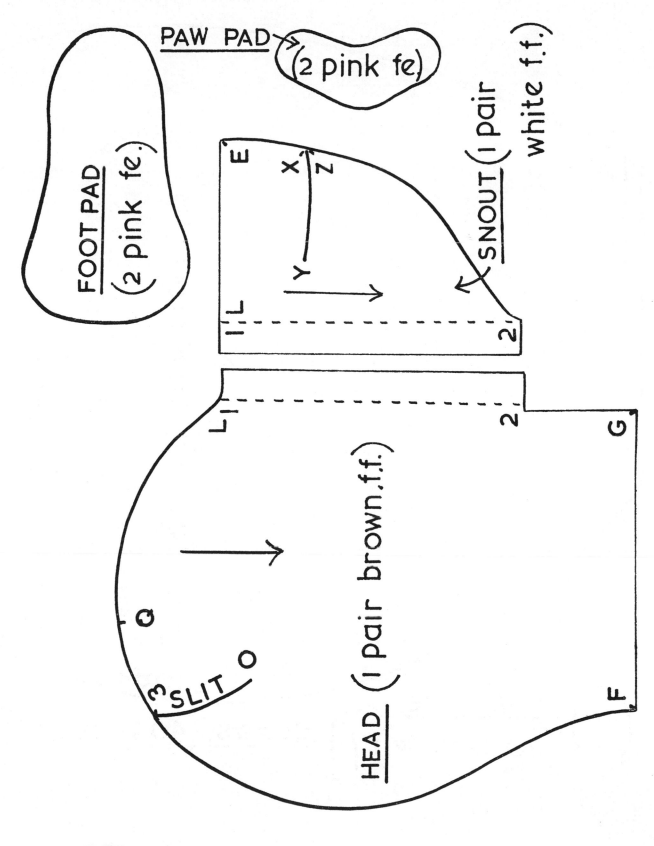

PAW PAD → (2 pink fe)

FOOT PAD (2 pink fe.)

E

X
Z
Y

SNOUT (1 pair white f.f.)

L 1

2

L 1

2

G

HEAD (1 pair brown.f.f.)

Q

O

3 SLIT

F

BEAR.

259

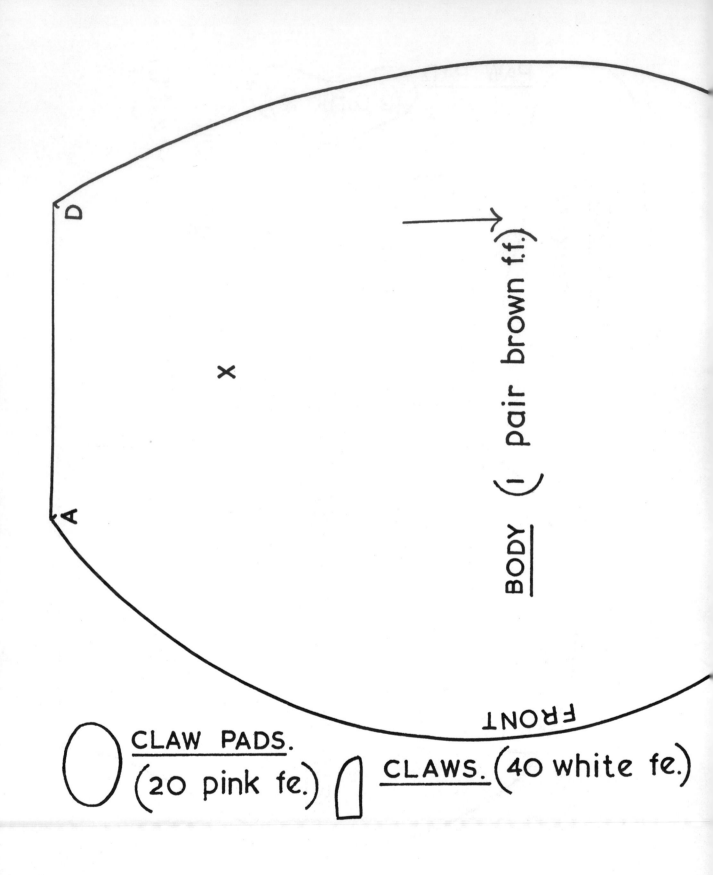

D

X

A

BODY (1 pair brown f.f.)

FRONT

CLAW PADS.
(20 pink fe.)

CLAWS. (40 white fe.)

BRUIN

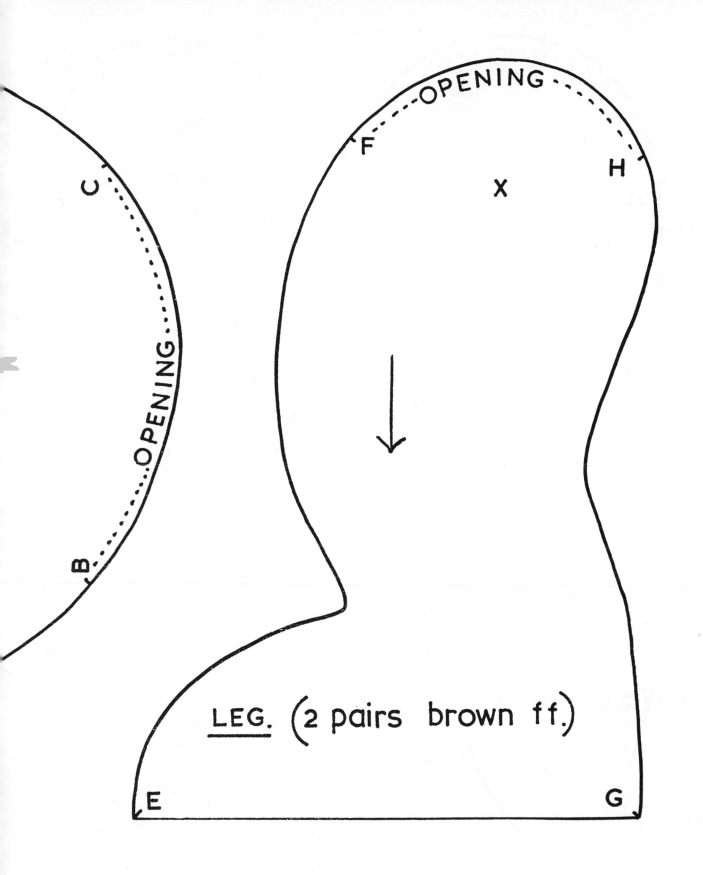

C

OPENING

B

F — OPENING

X

H

LEG. (2 pairs brown ff.)

E

G

BEAR.

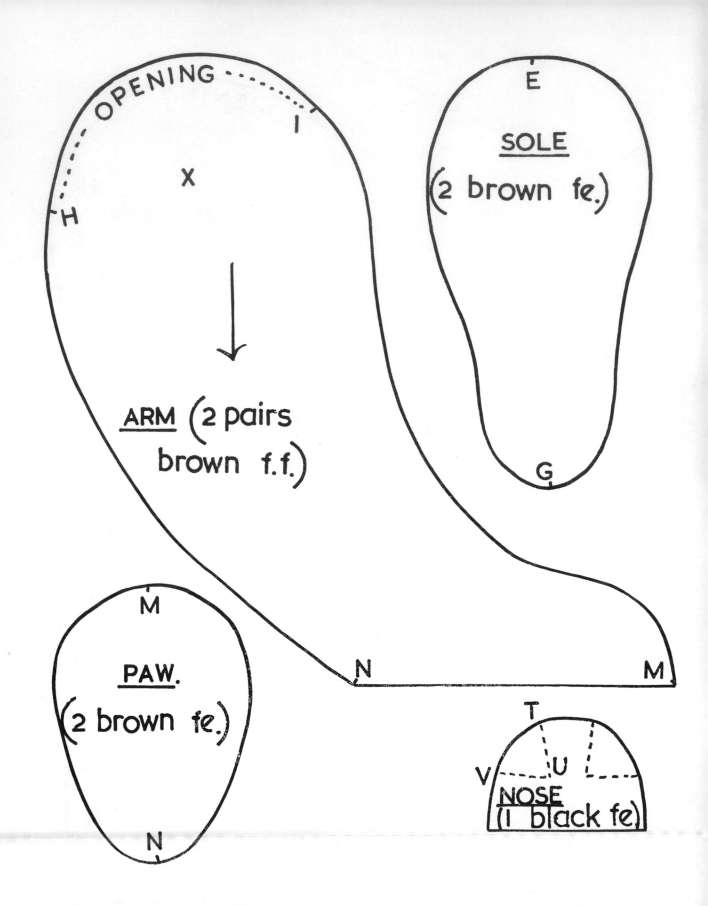

OPENING

H   I

X

<u>ARM</u> (2 pairs brown f.f.)

<u>SOLE</u>
(2 brown fe.)

E

G

M

<u>PAW.</u>
(2 brown fe.)

N

N   M

T

V   U

<u>NOSE</u>
(1 black fe)

<u>BRUIN BEAR.</u>

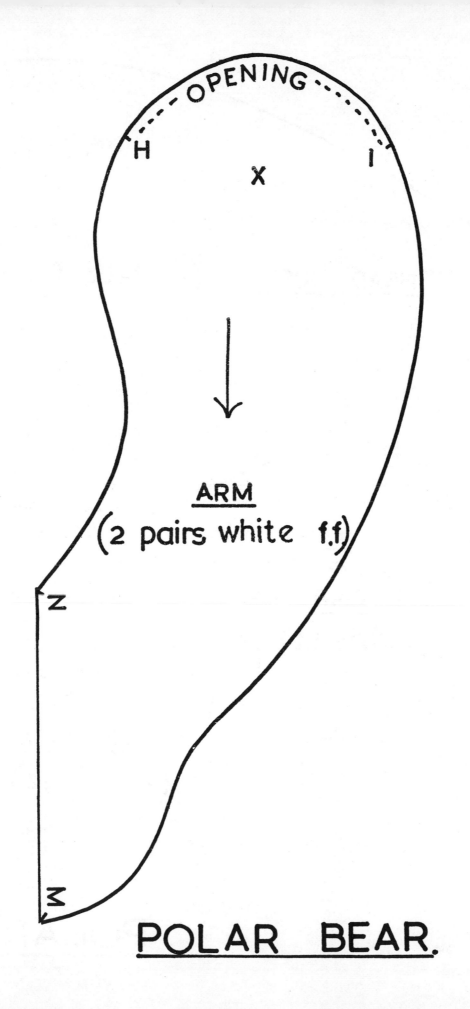

OPENING

H   I

X

ARM
(2 pairs white f.f)

N

M

POLAR BEAR.

263

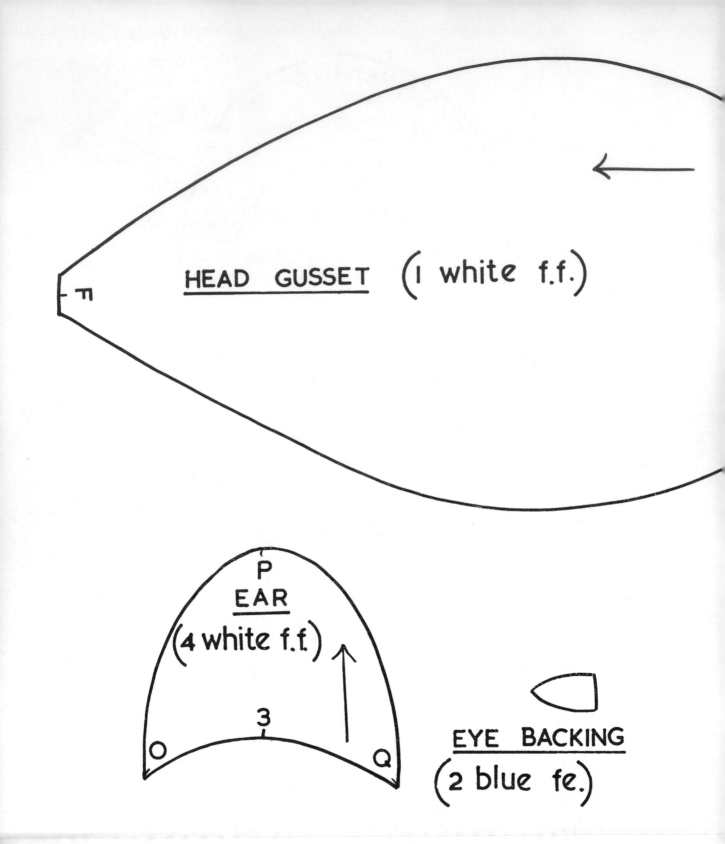

HEAD GUSSET (1 white f.f.)

F

EAR
P
(4 white f.f)
3
O   Q

EYE BACKING
(2 blue fe.)

POLAR

264

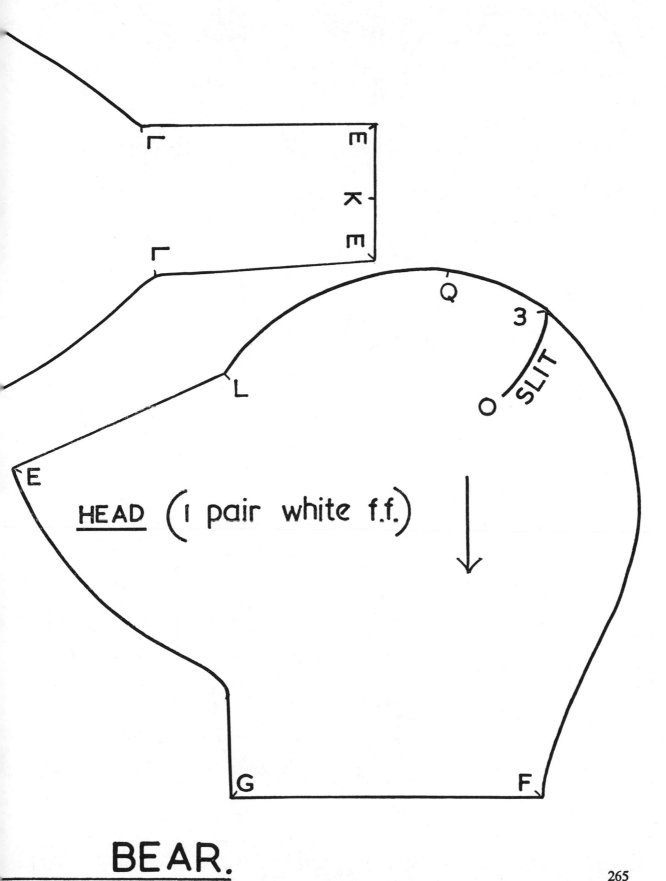

HEAD (1 pair white f.f.)

SLIT

BEAR.

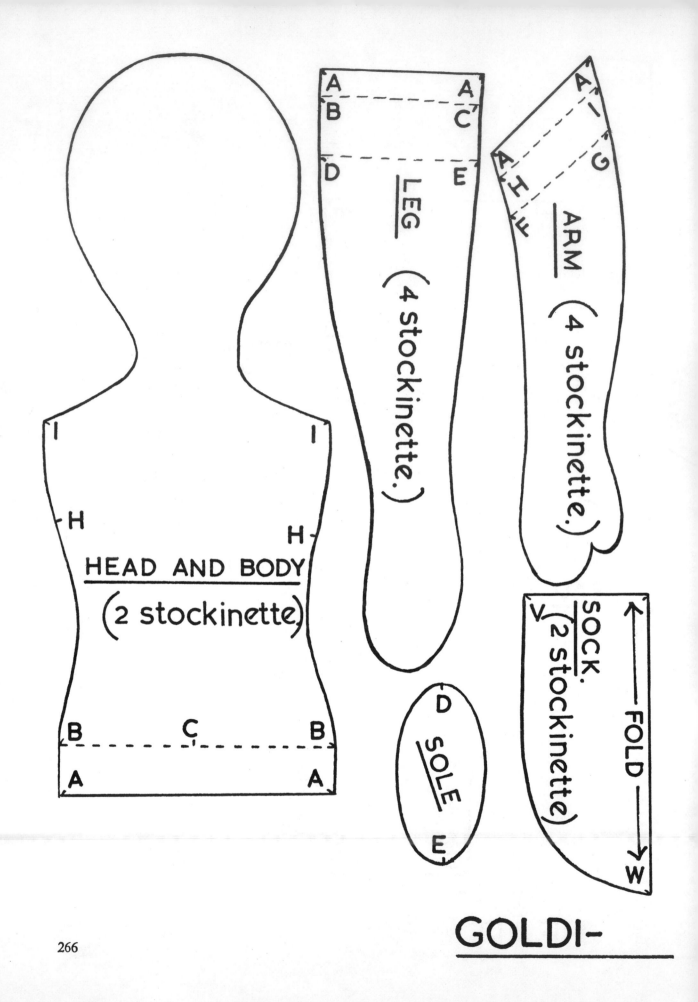

LEG (4 stockinette.)

ARM (4 stockinette.)

HEAD AND BODY
(2 stockinette)

SOCK.
(2 stockinette)

FOLD

SOLE

GOLDI-

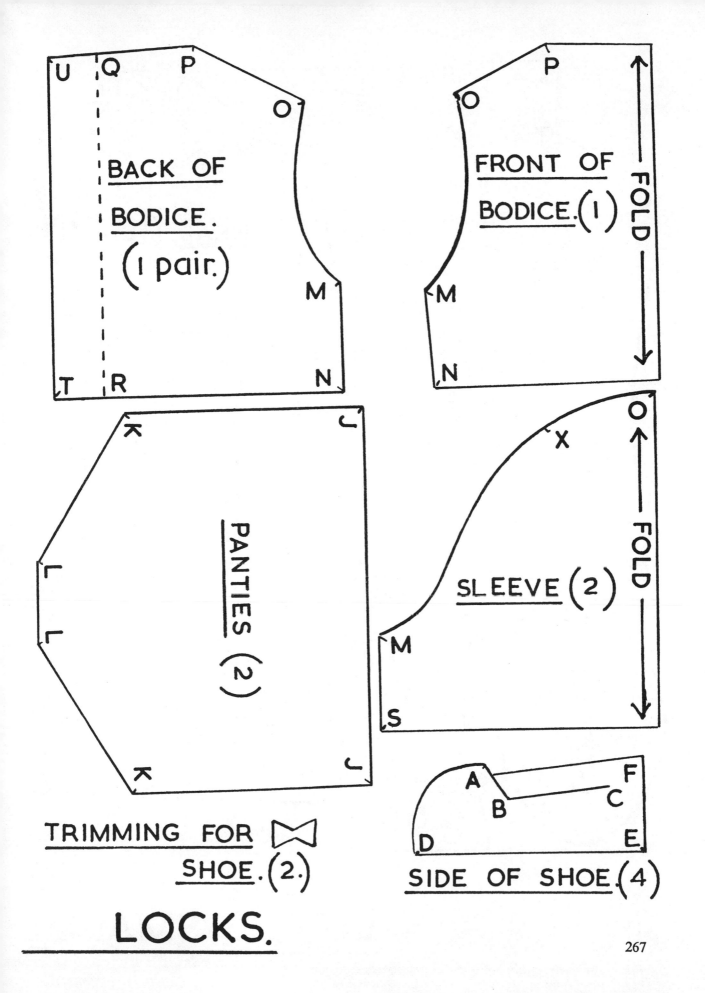

BACK OF BODICE. (1 pair.)

FRONT OF BODICE. (1)

FOLD

PANTIES (2)

SLEEVE (2)

FOLD

TRIMMING FOR SHOE. (2.)

SIDE OF SHOE. (4)

LOCKS.

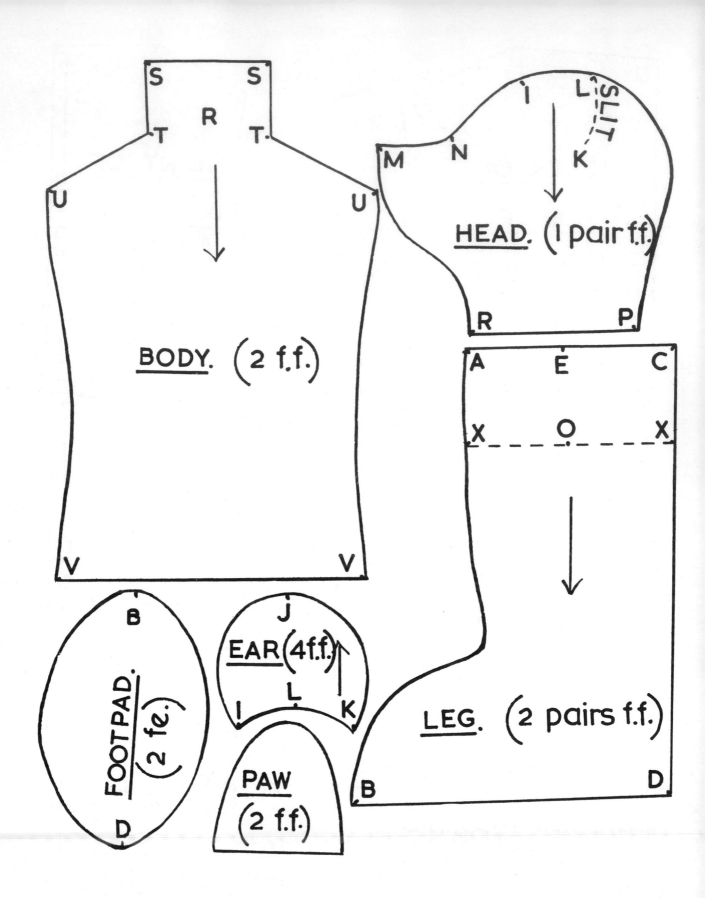

S S
T R T
U U

BODY. (2 f.f.)

V V

HEAD. (1 pair f.f.)

I L SLIT
M N K
R P

A E C
X O X

LEG. (2 pairs f.f.)

B

FOOTPAD. (2 fe.)

D

J

EAR (4 f.f.)

I L K

PAW (2 f.f.)

B D

LITTLE, SMALL,

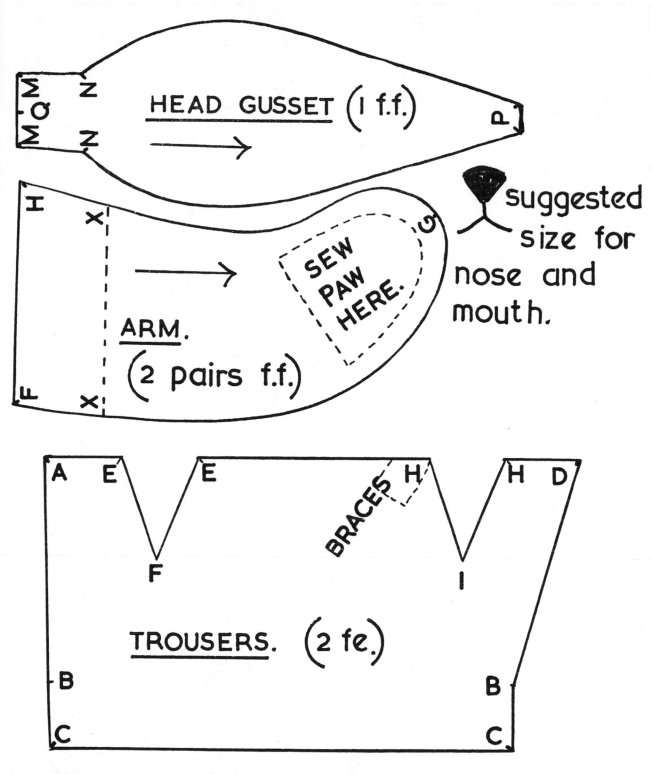

HEAD GUSSET (1 f.f.)

M Q M

N

N

P

H

X

F

X

ARM.

(2 pairs f.f.)

SEW PAW HERE.

G

suggested size for nose and mouth.

A E E H H D

BRACES

F

I

TROUSERS. (2 fe.)

B

B

C

C

◼ suggested size for eyes.

WEE BEAR.

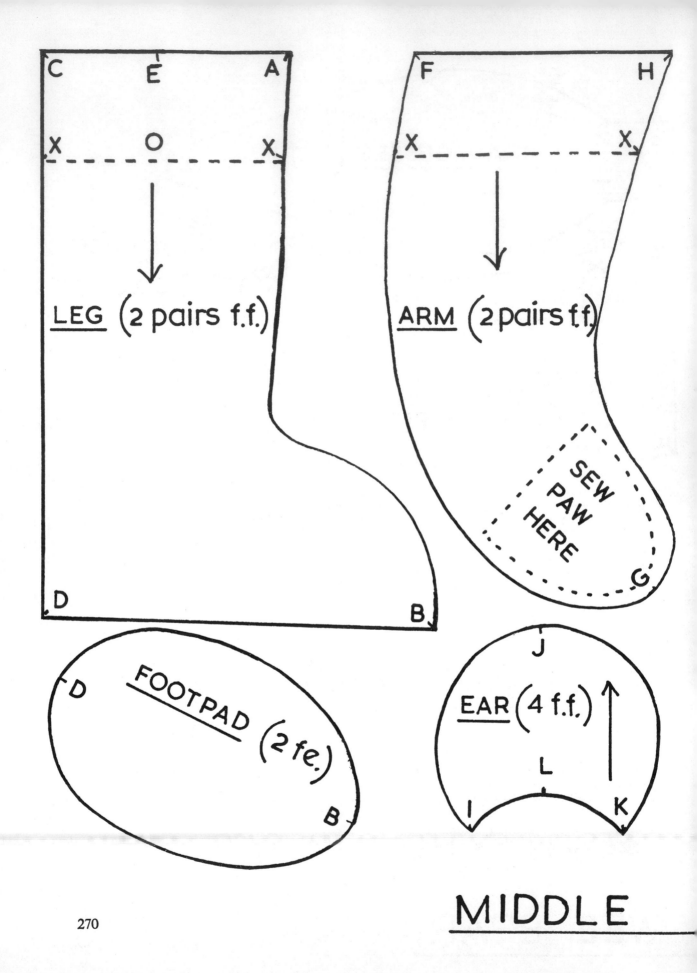

LEG (2 pairs f.f.)

ARM (2 pairs f.f.)

SEW PAW HERE

FOOTPAD (2 fe.)

EAR (4 f.f.)

MIDDLE

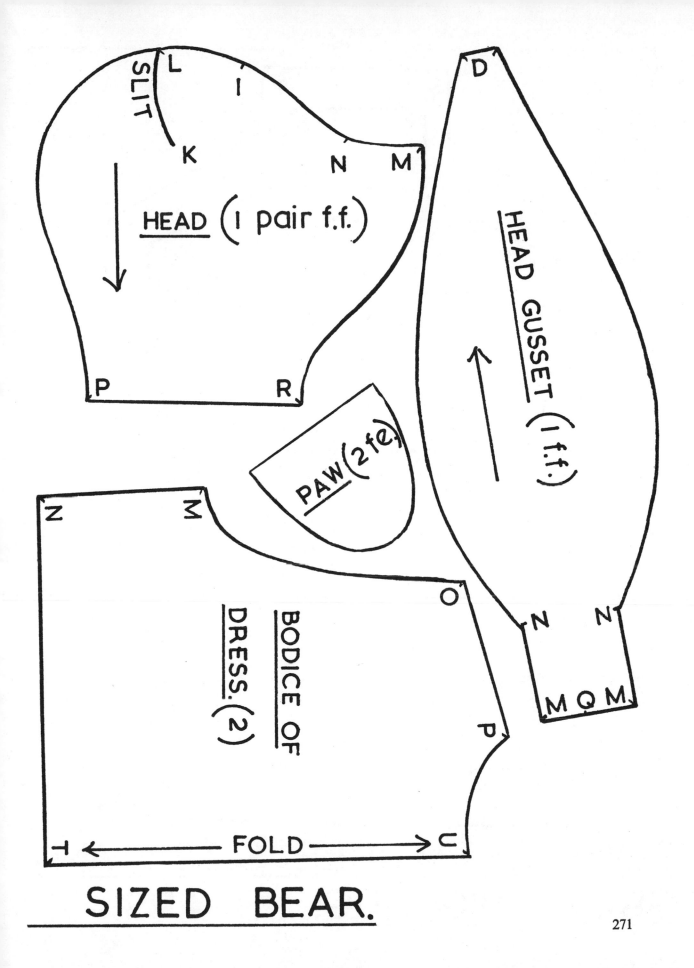

SIZED BEAR.

271

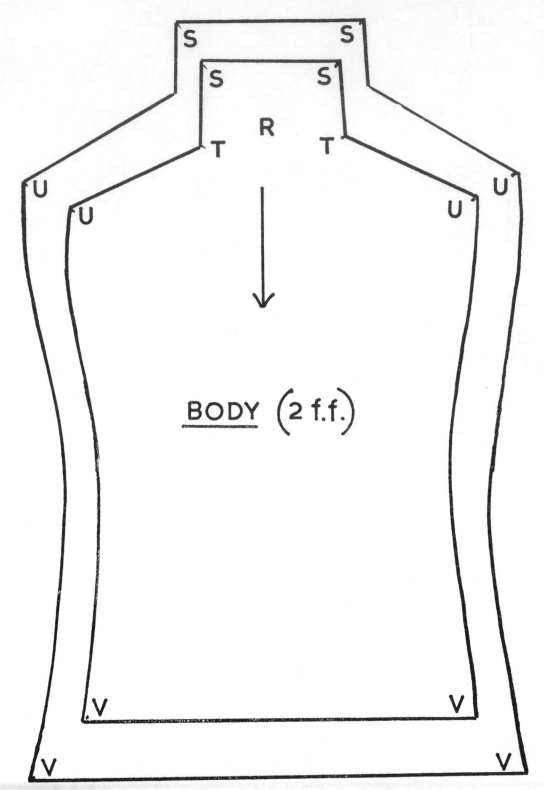

BODY (2 f.f.)

BODY OF MIDDLE SIZED AND GREAT BIG HUGE BEARS.

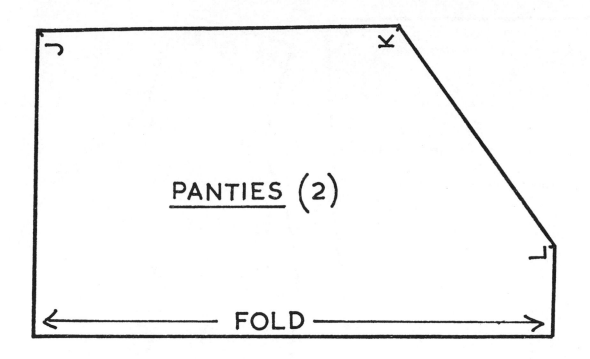

PANTIES (2)

FOLD

 suggested size for nose and mouth.

 suggested size for eyes.

MIDDLE SIZED BEAR.

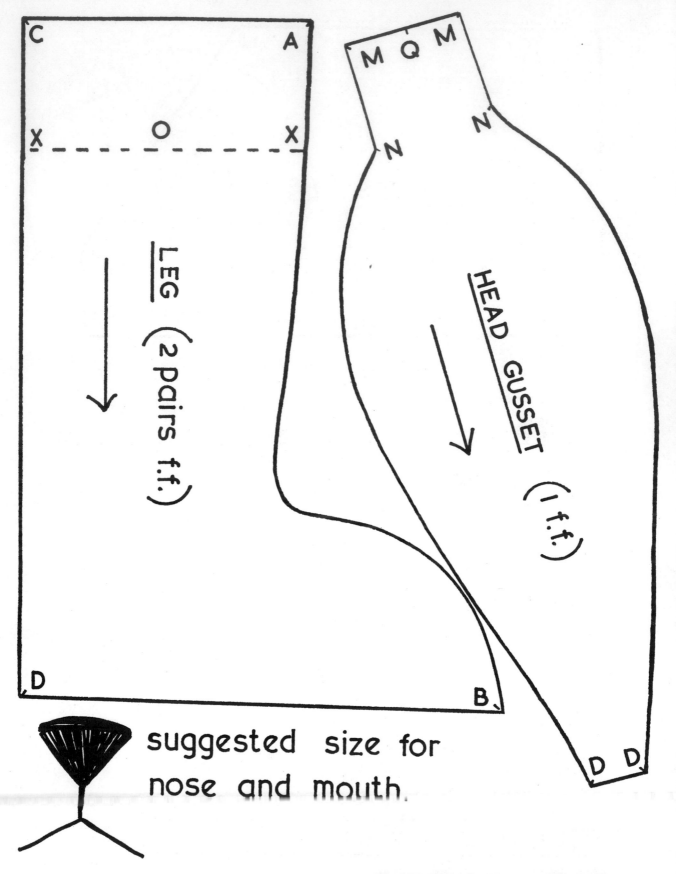

C · · · A

X · · O · · X

LEG (2 pairs f.f.)

M Q M

N · · · N

HEAD GUSSET (1 f.f.)

D · · · B

D D

suggested size for
nose and mouth.

GREAT. BIG.

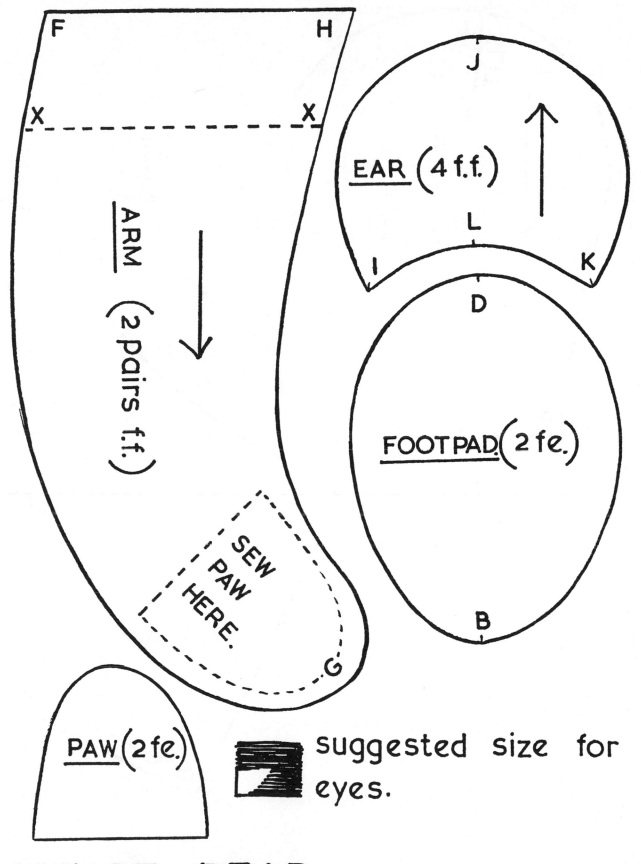

F

H

X   X

ARM (2 pairs f.f.)

J

EAR (4 f.f.)

I   L   K

D

FOOT PAD (2 fe.)

SEW PAW HERE.

G

B

PAW (2 fe.)

suggested size for eyes.

HUGE BEAR.

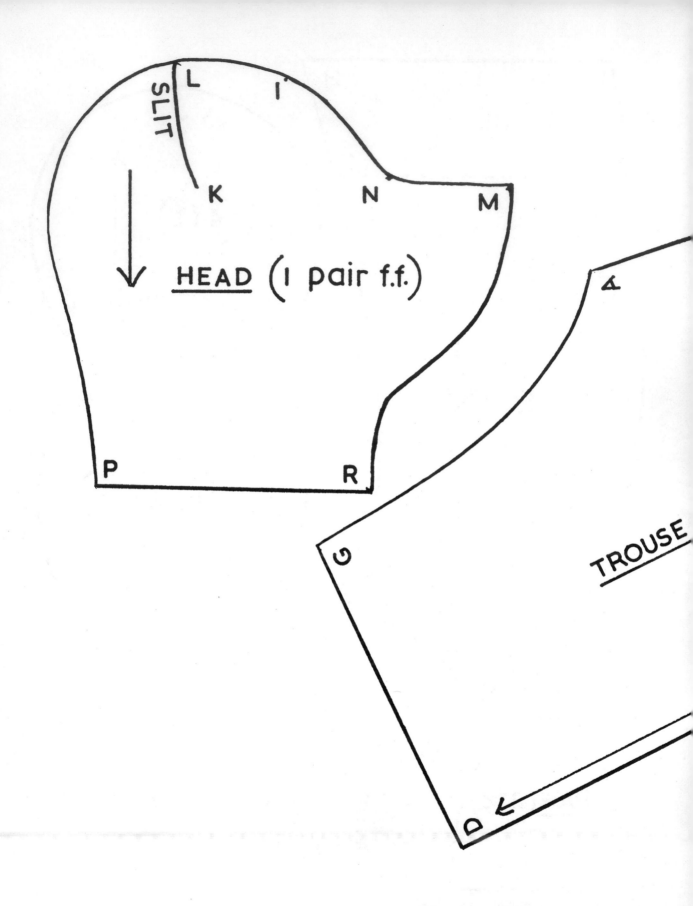

SLIT

L

I

K

N

M

HEAD (1 pair f.f.)

P

R

G

A

TROUSE

D

GREAT, BIG ,

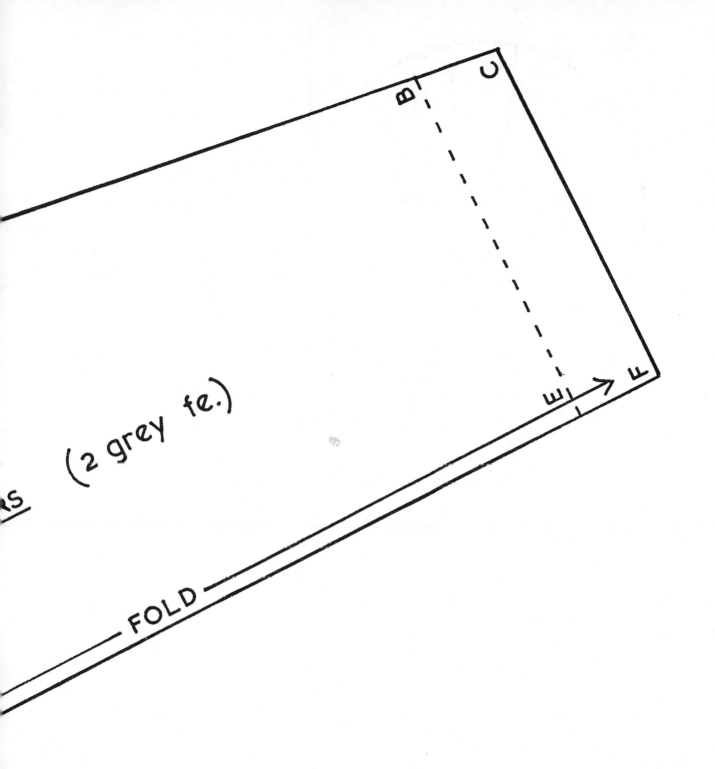

RS (2 grey fe.)

FOLD

HUGE BEAR.

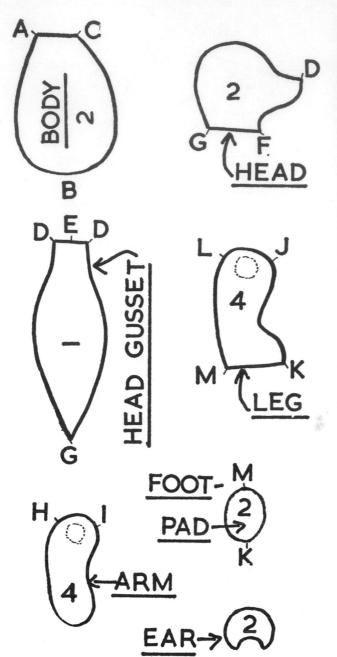

A <u>B</u>

BODY 2

<u>HEAD</u>

D E D

<u>HEAD GUSSET</u>

–

G

L J

4

M K

<u>LEG</u>

<u>FOOT</u> M

<u>PAD</u> 2

K

H I

4 <u>ARM</u>

<u>EAR</u> 2

<u>A TEDDY BEAR</u>
<u>FOR A TEDDY</u>
<u>BEAR</u>. (all pieces in felt.)

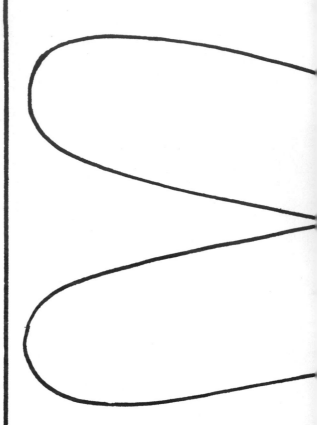

<u>BEAR FROM</u>

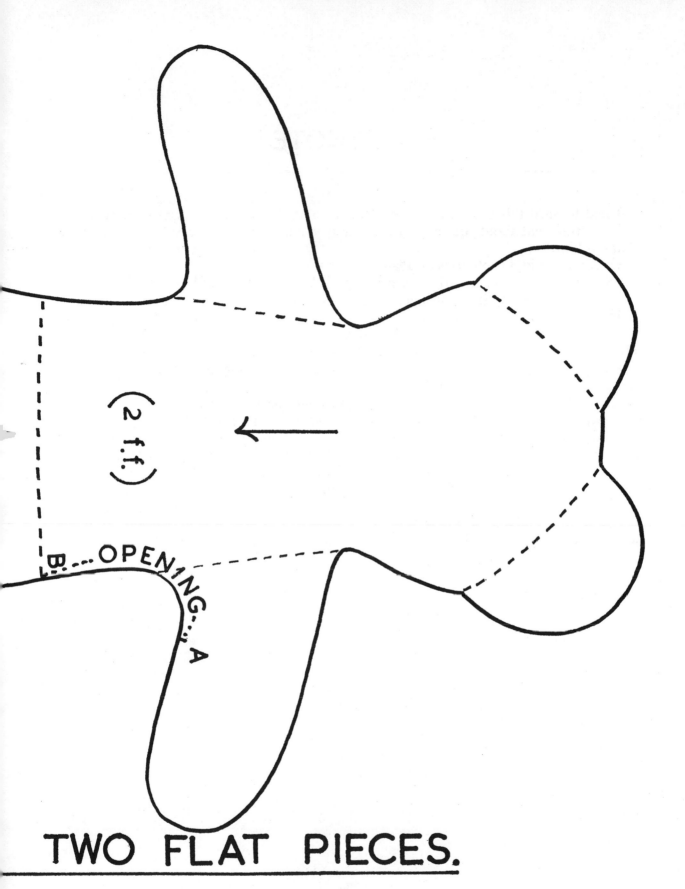

(2 f.f.)

B....OPENING....A

TWO FLAT PIECES.

FOOTNOTE

I had finished this book and a friend was reading the manuscript when she suddenly asked: "But what about your own bear? Surely you had one? The book is not complete without him!"

Of course I did, his photo is on Plate 7 and I still have him.

"Sir Edward Bear Esq.", who appears to be the twin of Winnie-the-Pooh, came to me on my fourth birthday sitting in a green wheelbarrow. About 2 ft. high, his coat is of light golden brown mohair and he has the typical humped back of the period. He has suffered many indignities! The day after I had my own appendix out he allowed me to anaesthetize him with a soap-dish sprinkled with Eau de Cologne and remove *his* (made of kapok and wood wool!) with a penknife. His wound, sutured with packing needle and string, healed more quickly than my own but less neatly.

His tonsillectomy was not a success, for although he was deeply anaesthetized (this time with the aid of a rubber hot-water bottle), it was impossible to open his mouth and the operation had to be abandoned. It was some consolation, however, for me to be able to eat the two red cherries which lay ready on a saucer to act as the removed organs instead of having to burn them, which is what I had been told had happened to my own tonsils, and Edward's throat was certainly less sore than my own.

This patient old friend has also suffered the administrations of my younger sister, and my own three children and their friends, and now lives in the spare bedroom awaiting joyfully each visit of my nieces, when he is once more the centre of attraction.

BIBLIOGRAPHY

ANDY PANDY'S TEDDY

Andy Pandy Books, by Maria Bird. Published by Brockhampton Press Ltd., Leicester—more than twenty titles always in print.
Andy Pandy's Annual and several other titles always in print. Published by Purnell and Sons, London.

ARCHIBALD ORMSBY-GORE

Summoned by Bells, by John Betjeman. Published by John Murray, London, England, and Houghton Mifflin Co., Boston, U.S.A.

BIG TEDDY AND LITTLE TEDDY

Josephine, John and the Puppy
Josephine Keeps House
Josephine Goes Travelling
Josephine Keeps School
Josephine's Christmas Party
Josephine's Pantomime

By Mrs. H. C. Cradock. Published by Blackie and Son Ltd., London, England.

RUPERT

The Rupert Annual. Published by Oldbourne Press.

SOOTY

Sooty's World Tour
Fun with Sooty and Sweep
Sooty Pop Up Book

Published by Purnell and Sons Ltd., London.

THE TEDDY BEARS' PICNIC

The Story of the Teddy Bears' Picnic, by Jimmy Kennedy. Published by B. Feldman and Co. Ltd., 125 Shaftesbury Avenue, London, W.C.2, and obtainable only from this address.

WINNIE-THE-POOH

Winnie-the-Pooh
The House at Pooh Corner
Now We are Six
The World of Pooh
The World of Christopher Robin
The Christopher Robin Story Book
Tales of Pooh
When We Were Very Young
Winnie Ille Pu
(Latin version of Winnie-the-Pooh)

Published by
Methuen and Co. Ltd., London,
and
Dutton and Co., New York, U.S.A.

Did you know that there is only one Giant Panda in the Western world today?—"Chi-Chi" (meaning naughty, mischievous little girl), who lives at the London Zoo. Her purchase price was never disclosed, but the Zoological Society value her at £12,000. Her diet consists of fresh bamboo (sent by train from Cornwall every few days) and a mash of chicken (roasted or boiled), rice, milk, eggs, carrots, apples, oranges, pears, bananas, vitamins, sugar and salt to taste!

Did you know that during 1963 a Teddy bear was responsible for jailing two men for receiving stolen cars?

"Sugar", a small blue nylon bear owned by four-year-old Amanda Blake of Billericay, was in her father's car when it was stolen. Two years later the bear was found among a pile of prams, books, car rugs and number plates in the corner of a garage in London. Investigating police, realizing that these articles had been cleared out of stolen cars, got in touch with everyone who had reported losing a car, giving a list of the things they had found, in the hope that someone would recognize something as having been in their vehicle. Amanda and her parents immediately identified Sugar and the garage owners were charged with receiving Mr. Blake's car from the thieves.

Throughout the trial at the Old Bailey, Sugar, with a card round his neck and labelled "exhibit No. 56", sat on a table and became a very important piece of evidence. When it was over, the Detective Sergeant in charge of the case himself brought the Teddy bear back to Amanda and watched while the excited little girl bathed him!

Did you know that "Alice" with whom Christopher Robin and Pooh often went down to the Palace, now lives happily with her husband in a pretty part of Sussex? Incidentally, she did not in fact marry one of the guards but a Royal Engineer!

Now Mrs. Alfred Brockwell, Olive, as her real name is, took over her famous charge at the age of two months and stayed with him until he was nine and went away to school. She still keeps in touch with the family of whom she grew so fond.

Mrs. Brockwell has many interesting tales to tell about their visits to the Palace to see the changing of the guard and to the Zoo to feed "Winnie" with condensed milk; of soaking bread to feed the swans at Polling (one of which was the first "Pooh") and of the famous dressing gowns in "Vespers"—her own it will be remembered being of not much interest to the little boy because although it was "a beautiful blue" it hadn't a hood!

Did you know that The Doll Club of Great Britain run a Home of Rest for Aged and Retired Teddies? Most of the inmates have had some exciting adventure or been of some great service to their owners, and are retired there together with a written account of their life story so that their identity may not be lost to future generations. Among the bears in the home is a collection of eight, each bought to commemorate a special flying occasion and named for the aviator concerned: Blériot, Graeme-White, Amy Johnson, etc.

Places have been booked for many bears who expect to retire in the fullness of time, but there is still room for more.

Did you know that an adult koala is roughly the size of a bulldog and lives for about fifteen years? That in order to help him cope with his bulky diet of about 2½ lbs. of gum leaves a day, he has a specially adapted digestive system, including an appendix which is 6–8 ft. long! That a baby koala is less than 1 in. long and is carried for about eight months in its mother's pouch, which unlike that of the kangaroo opens downwards? That "koala" is an aboriginal word meaning "no drink"? Koalas never seem to need water as other animals do, they get sufficient moisture from the gum leaves they chew and from the dew they find on them.

THE END